THE STAGES OF PROPERTY

Copyrighting Theatre in Spain

The manner in which a play is published often says as much about the culture that it comes from as the play itself. Using the example of nineteenth-century Spanish theatre, *The Stages of Property* argues that there is a great deal one can learn about a nation by examining its publication standards.

Lisa Surwillo discusses the ways in which notions of intellectual property transformed Spain's theatre – its agents, performance practices, and reception – over a period of fifty years, from 1830 to 1880. For three centuries, theatre had been the cultural arm of the monarchy. After the institution of copyright, however, it became the backbone of a new cultural industry controlled by a handful of publishers. In this atmosphere of private ownership, ideas of intellectual property and author's rights assumed a much greater immediacy than they had previously. The impact on theatrical practices was significant, resulting in the development of a homogenized national culture of shared theatre and reading experiences.

Through an integrative historicist approach to a wide range of literary texts and archival documents, *The Stages of Property* makes an important statement about the cultural, societal, and political roles of the theatre in Spain during the 1800s.

(Studies in Book and Print Culture)

LISA SURWILLO is an assistant professor in the Department of Spanish and Portuguese at Stanford University.

The Stages of Property

Copyrighting Theatre in Spain

LISA SURWILLO

UNIVERSITY OF TORONTO PRESS
Toronto Buffalo London

© University of Toronto Press 2007
Toronto Buffalo London
utorontopress.com

Reprinted in paperback 2022

ISBN 978-0-8020-9246-5 (cloth)
ISBN 978-1-4875-2629-0 (paper)

Library and Archives Canada Cataloguing in Publication

Title: The stages of property : copyrighting theatre in Spain / Lisa Surwillo.
Names: Surwillo, Lisa, author.
Series: Studies in book and print culture.
Description: Series statement: Studies in book and print culture | Paperback reprint. Originally published 2007. | Includes bibliographical references and index. | Includes some text in Spanish.
Identifiers: Canadiana 20220165130 | ISBN 9781487526290 (softcover)
Subjects: LCSH: Copyright – Drama – Spain – History – 19th century. | LCSH: Intellectual property – Spain – History – 19th century. | LCSH: Theater – Law and legislation – Spain – History – 19th century.
Classification: LCC KKT1186 .S87 2022 | DDC 346.4604/8209034–dc23

We wish to acknowledge the land on which the University of Toronto Press operates. This land is the traditional territory of the Wendat, the Anishnaabeg, the Haudenosaunee, the Métis, and the Mississaugas of the Credit First Nation.

University of Toronto Press acknowledges the financial support of the Government of Canada, the Canada Council for the Arts, and the Ontario Arts Council, an agency of the Government of Ontario, for its publishing activities.

 Canada Council for the Arts / Conseil des Arts du Canada

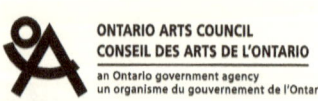 Ontario Arts Council / Conseil des Arts de l'Ontario
an Ontario government agency
un organisme du gouvernement de l'Ontario

Funded by the Government of Canada / Financé par le gouvernement du Canada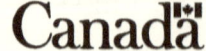

Contents

Preface vii

Introduction: Law, Theatre, and the Republic of Letters 3

Stage I: Literary Property and Modern Spain 21

1 Cultivating Property: *Desamortización* and the Culture of Authors' Rights 25
2 Performative Appeal: From *El trovador* to the Royal Decree 41

Stage II: Poets and Publishers 63

3 Authors between Stage and Page 67
4 *Editores* and Owners 83

Stage III: National Literary Galleries 107

5 Textual Museums 111
6 Paratextual Performances in the 'Galerías dramáticas' 124

Conclusion 147

Appendix 151
Notes 161
Sources Cited and Consulted 193
Illustration Credits 207
Index 209

Illustrations follow p. 86

Preface

Literary scholars rarely have the opportunity to study books from the viewpoint of the collection or the archive. This book is the result of an unusual and fortuitous cross-pollination of literary criticism and librarianship. My academic training in Romance languages and literatures provided me with the tools of textual analysis and a strong background in literary history. Three years in the rare books division of the Bancroft Library at the University of California, Berkeley, gave me first-hand knowledge of the ways in which the particulars of the physical format of books and the perseverance of Romantic ideas on authorship affect the accessibility of nineteenth-century literature for scholars today. When I began to survey and catalogue what is one of the largest collections of Spanish theatre in North America, I optimistically imagined that I might have the opportunity to *read* the five thousand plays owned by Bancroft. Theatre is society's mask, a representation that conceals and reveals a given culture's preoccupations. Because the Spanish stage was where nearly every issue important to nineteenth-century Spanish culture and society was presented, debated, represented, and, sometimes, resolved, I was certain that my work with the collection would provide me with unique insight into the relationship between Spanish theatre and culture at mid-century. I was surprised to find answers to my questions about nineteenth-century Spanish culture in the format, rather than in the content, of the plays.

Although I did manage to read a significant number of plays, my assigned task was to transpose – or *translate* – information on the book's title page regarding the author, title, place of publication, date, and genre into a catalogue format prescribed by the U.S. Library of Congress. I quickly became frustrated that these uniform items were grounded in a presentism that did not allow for a literary reality in which authorship was unclear, nineteenth-century genres were untranslatable into contemporary American terms, and the heavy hand of the *editor* (publisher) was as important as that of the 'author.' It was out of this gap between the triumph of Romantic theories of authorship and present expectations of book production, at one extreme, and the realities of nineteenth-century Spanish dramatic literature, at the other, that our academic assumptions about dramatic authorship became patently unsatisfactory.

The process of cataloguing requires substantial analysis of the introductory pages that most scholars of literature hastily – and erroneously – bypass in an attempt to arrive immediately at the 'real' text. Each time I opened these modest paperbacks (most were octavo in format with thirty-two pages) and noted the author, title and publication information, I also considered the way that these plays were presented to me, the reader, as property. Elaborate copyright declarations that became more complex and stringent in each decade (often including entire reprintings of the current law) separated the reader from the verses of the play. These were not simply obscure © symbols in the corner of a page, but rather prominently displayed declarations of ownership and elaborate directions regarding the reader's responsibilities with respect to the text in his or her hands. As I read nineteenth-century editions, I was obliged to behave like a nineteenth-century reader and receive these plays first as property and secondly as literature. Because these copyright statements constituted a significant part of the introductory pages, I reconsidered how copyright came to have such prominence in these play editions. Did intellectual property for dramatic literature develop in a different way than it had for lyric poetry or novels? Did it change? And how did copyright affect the later performances of these plays? Stepping back into my role as literary scholar, I decided to ask exactly when Spanish dramatists began to be treated as authors (as the Library of Congress cataloguing rules required) and how copyrighted authorship changed the way that plays were received by the public (as either readers or members of an audience).

Equally important, as I catalogued the theatre collection, I encountered hundreds of authors' names and thousands of titles, but only a handful of names of *editores*. They were the agents who served as 'contractors' in the creation of Spanish play editions: similar to today's publishers, *editores* owned the copyright of a piece and brought together the various agents (printers, dramatists, booksellers) necessary to create a printed copy. Very early in the cataloguing project, it became possible to recognize the *editor* of a given play and then anticipate the theatre in which the play had been premiered, the quality of the typeface, and the name of the printer. The publisher, not the author, began to be the unifying element in the huge corpus of nineteenth-century theatre. Yet the overwhelming textual presence of the *editor* stood in stark contrast to his absence in literary histories. Certainly, Cotarelo y Mori, Cervera, Botrel, Simón Palmer, and Martínez Martín, among others, had noted the publisher's role in nineteenth-century literature. However, given that fewer than ten families owned and controlled nearly every play published in nineteenth-century Spain, it was surprising that most scholars of Spanish literature had largely overlooked their impact on theatre.

Studies of literary ownership and authorship have tended to focus on narrative works from the Anglo-American tradition. The aim of this book is to broaden the ongoing discussion in terms of both genre and geography. In the most recent phase of this project, I have considered the question of authorship in light of modern treatments of Spain's supposed marginality to European trends (or, as the Fascist dictator Francisco Franco put it, of the view that 'España es diferente'). But theatre is certainly different. Theatre is a temporary composition of the textual and the spectacular, with aspects such as staging, costume, and actors' skill of equal if not greater importance than the literary quality of the text. This, in turn, is necessarily unstable, dependent upon actors' memory or prompters' aptitude. In this book, I argue that a thorough understanding of the relationship between literature and copyright requires an examination of the impact of property on theatre. The dual nature (page and stage) of dramatic literature demonstrates the complexities of authorship and reception more than does the printed word alone. Moreover, Spanish concepts and practices of authorship and copyright varied from those of their European neighbours. For example, not only were Spanish dramatists surprisingly ambivalent about the 'birth' of authorship, but also the legal and economic value of author's copyright rested upon its definition as an 'alienable right' to be bought and sold an infinite number of times. As a result, nineteenth-century Spain produced a variety of plural and simultaneous authorships. Although the possibility for multiple authorships of a work written by one person disappeared in the twentieth century, the contemporary definition of authorship was not the only, or necessarily the best, model to emerge from the modern era. Moreover, because of Spain's important theatre tradition dating from the seventeenth century, political policies during the modern period (including an internal colonizing project upon the loss of the majority of its overseas provinces), and the rather late, and rapid, promulgation of copyright laws in the 1830s and '40s, the context for the development of Spanish dramatic authorship and copyright was very different from that of its northern neighbours. Today, copyright crosses international boundaries every day, for both digital formats and the colophon. Less than two hundred years ago, it was intimately tied to the cultural identity and policies of economic health for Spain. These reasons for its development have long disappeared, but they continue to condition the way that dramatic literature is printed, read, and performed today.

This is a book about books, written in libraries and archives throughout the United States and Spain. Through their inspired guidance, Tony Bliss and Patrick Russell taught me to see these institutions in a new light, and I am deeply indebted to them both. I am particularly grateful to Professor Dru Dougherty, who first recognized that what I needed for my career was the opportunity to lose myself in the stacks. He and the other members of my graduate committee, Michael Iarocci and Carla Hesse, made me think harder about the culture of books and how to write about literature. This project was improved by their challenges to my ideas and rigorous reviews of my writing. My thanks, as well, to two anonymous readers for University of Toronto Press, whose careful and measured criticisms have made this a better book.

Numerous colleagues in Spain, California, and Pennsylvania inspired and motivated me through conversations on libraries, literature, theatre, and the art of writing books. The insights of Hester Blum, Charles Faulhaber, María del Mar Fernández Vega, David Gies, Kathryn Hume, Christine Lim, Ruth MacKay, Sophia McClennan, Ralph Rodriguez, and Sherry Roush are greatly appreciated. I would also like to thank Barbara Surwillo, the bibliographer extraordinaire who managed the paper trail of my archival meanderings. Finally, Alex Zepka merits special thanks for his limitless patience as an astrophysicist and engineer subjected to hundreds of hours of monologue about copyright, publishers, and the pleasures of the archive. I thank him for his unwavering support of this book.

In somewhat different form, sections of chapters 1 have appeared in 'Mendizábal and the Poetics of Spanish Land Reform,' *Arizona Journal of Hispanic Cultural Studies* 6 (2002): 43–56.

THE STAGES OF PROPERTY:
COPYRIGHTING THEATRE IN SPAIN

Introduction:
Law, Theatre, and the Republic of Letters

During the late twentieth and early twenty-first centuries, 'intellectual property' has become a household term that, for most people, is about the legality and ease of peer-to-peer sharing of movies and music via Internet file-sharing tools. The concept of intellectual property is now widely known, although its genesis and early development during the nineteenth century, which continue to guide its contemporary applications, are not. Most histories (academic or otherwise) relate the history of literary copyright in Western Europe and the Americas around the case of novels or lyric poetry. While this is certainly an integral part of the story, surprisingly, the distinct process of copyright legislation for theatre has been overlooked. In many ways, the popular entertainment industry of theatre in Spain in the nineteenth century is closer to some of the realities of the relationship between intellectual property and culture today. My objective in this book is not to compare nineteenth-century Spain to the United States of the twenty-first century, but rather to expand the academic treatment of intellectual property beyond the study of novels and poetry in the Anglo-American tradition. Scholars of contemporary global culture may be surprised to find precedents in Spanish theatre of the nineteenth century.

Although carrying out a sustained and in-depth study of the early stages of intellectual property and its development has given me a unique perspective on the role of copyright in contemporary society, in this book I am neither a champion nor a critic of literary property. Rather, I propose, in order to expand the discussion of copyright in modern Western societies, to ask *why* dramatists wanted copyright and *why* the Spanish monarchy ultimately promoted it.

A study of Spanish theatre enriches our understanding of the impact of copyright on modern literature because through most of its history, unlike the case for lyric poetry and prose, plays were intended primarily for performance, not publication. Theatre was a collective product and infinitely adaptable to both the abilities of the acting company and the tastes of the public. Moreover, in contrast to the 'novelist as genius' model, in Spanish theatre the monarchy traditionally had a very involved, authoritative role, and the poet who wrote the verses a lesser one. Although several dramatists of Spain's Golden Age were famously celebrated (such as Lope de Vega and Pedro Calderón de la Barca, among others), dramatic poets only became central to both spectacle and book productions in the nineteenth century.[1]

Theatre became an arm of Spanish cultural policy during the seventeenth century, and many of the greatest pieces in the Spanish repertoire date from this period. Presented and manipulated as the monarchy's proprietary images, theatre pieces were inseparable from the person of the Ancien Régime. As a cultural tool of the monarchy, the theatre served two essential propagandistic functions. First, the opulence of the spectacle and the literary quality of the verse were understood to manifest the power and magnificence of the King to foreign powers, while the plots often held a strong ideological message for Spanish subjects. Second, the institution itself was a testament to royal beneficence. Beginning in the sixteenth century, the monarchy granted performance privileges exclusively to royally appointed directors at theatres funded by the Crown, and their receipts went to hospitals and orphanages. The result of the Spanish monarchy's active involvement through the 1820s (everything from printing privileges to actors' salaries and stage props were decided by royal decree) was a regularization of theatre practices far beyond that of neighbouring countries.[2]

It is precisely Golden Age theatre, by writers such as Tirso de Molina, Lope de Vega, and even Miguel de Cervantes (the novelist), that is best known by scholars outside of the field of Spanish literature. This book pays significant attention to that period, but only in terms of how its rich legacy influenced Spanish theatre performance and publication through the nineteenth century. Likewise, there is a wealth of studies on Golden Age authorship, but it is an issue that I consider only as it impinges on the nineteenth-century definition of authorship as a capitalist and liberal enterprise. I highlight the Golden Age antecedents to the nineteenth century in order to note how the moderns recycled previous practices and reinvented them as new after intellectual property initiated a 'copyrite' of passage from traditional to modern theatre. While dramatic copyright did not usher in an entirely new system, it did profoundly modify existing laws and traditions to redefine theatre as a text-based art. While modern theatre still continues to build upon traditions from the Golden Age, as Aguilera Sastre has argued, the greatest transformation of Spanish theatre to date resulted from the commercialization and industrialization of theatre through the privatization of acting companies and presses as part of the implementation of economic liberalism in nineteenth-century Spain.[3]

Because this book is about copyright for theatre, my readings of specific plays are situated within the larger analysis of royal documents, copyright deeds and mortgages, anecdotes, canonical and non-canonical literature, and paratexts, in order to analyse the competing ideologies of modern authorships, the interplay between intellectual property and state power, and the cultural and political roles of theatre in Spanish society. My reassessment of the cultural history of theatre books reintroduces the publisher and the culture industry as integral elements of Spanish drama. This approach recontextualizes the well-known plays of the Spanish canon through a reconsideration of the entire corpus of modern theatre and the cultural and historical environments in which it was written.

In this study, I also address essays by important nineteenth-century Spanish prose writers ('costumbristas') and short, sometimes anonymous, articles in local newspapers from contemporary Madrid, alongside documents from government archives and copies of the original play editions. I do not offer a 'history of Spanish theatre' or a reassessment of the twenty or so 'greatest hits' in the academic canon of nineteenth-century Spanish theatre. My perspective in this book is rather both more detailed and more general in its examination of how theatre evolved in Spain from an ancient institution grounded in the practices of spectacle to a readerly art. To that end, I pay a significant amount of attention to the history of Spanish theatre as books.

Because I am writing about Spain, a country whose theatrical and literary history may be unfamiliar to some readers, a few words regarding terminology are in order. Firstly, through most of the 1800s, Spanish theatre pieces were written in verse. I have chosen to follow nineteenth-century usage and refer to writers for the stage as 'poetas dramáticos' [dramatic poets] or, more simply, as 'poets,' rather than employ the more modern term 'dramaturgo' [dramatist]. Although the term eventually fell into disuse at the end of the century, the early-twentieth-century dramatist Federico García Lorca insisted he was a 'poeta dramático' to emphasize the poetic aspect of his craft. When I discuss the *poetas* as 'authors,' I am specifically referring to their status as copyright owners after 1837. Similarly, the Spanish term 'autor' cannot be translated easily into English. (See chapter 3 for a full discussion of the term *autor de comedias*.) Defined in its strictest sense, the word means 'author'; however, in nineteenth-century Spain, the term referred equally to creators of any kind (such as God), a poet, and – as concerns us here – the legal owner of a copyright, whether or not he wrote the literary work in question. The title of 'autor,' as relates to ownership of a copyright, could be bought and sold, and it is precisely this multiple authorship that this book attempts to address. In addition, I am writing, largely, about male writers. While there certainly were women writing for the stage during the 1800s, they were not part of the campaign for intellectual property.[4] Therefore I use masculine pronouns throughout – not as a default neuter, but rather to consciously describe male authors.

Throughout this book, I use the word 'copyright' to refer to the ownership rights conferred upon poets who wrote plays in Spain after 1837. Nevertheless, the use of this word, while useful for a readership versed in the Anglo-American tradition, is not the most precise translation of the term for ownership of the immaterial literary property in Spain. Whereas 'copyright' developed out of the ownership over a copy and the rights to reproduce that copy, in Spain (as in most of Europe), the emphasis was not on the text, but on the personality of the poet. Accordingly, the term used in Spain is 'derecho de autor' or, literally, 'author's right.' In general, I have tried to avoid using this clumsy term, but it is important to note the differences in terminology and the focus on the figure of the 'autor' in the Spanish tradition. In addition, at times I refer to 'intellectual property' more generally when discussing the modern concept of ownership of any immaterial property tied to a product of the mind (such as all literary property or a patent for 'useful works').

Finally, my discussion of *modern* Spain, as relates to political economy (not philosophy or culture), points to 1837 as the turning point in the liberal cultural revolution of the nineteenth century. The turbulence of the preceding three decades introduced new ideas and especially intensified debate around the questions of sovereignty, ownership, and the role of literature in society. In 1808, Napoleon Bonaparte entered

Spain, deposed the Bourbon King, and placed his own brother on the throne as José I. Spaniards of all political stripes and classes were divided over Spain's future. However, apart from a minority known as *afrancesados*, most fiercely resisted the Bonaparte King and the French occupiers, as memorialized in Goya's *The Second of May*. The southern port city of Cadiz was the centre of resistance; here, the liberals opposed to Napoleon debated and drafted a modern constitution (Constitution of 1812 or Constitution of Cadiz) that would be rejected, resurrected, and remodelled throughout the century. In 1814, following Napoleon's defeat, Fernando VII, the Bourbon heir to the throne, returned to Spain and promptly imposed a harsh return to Ancien Régime policy. Liberalism was entangled in the questions of national identity and French interventions in Spain.

Politically and culturally, the death of Fernando VII in September 1833 and the regency of his wife, María Cristina, heralded the end of absolutism in Spain and the initial attempts at a government based on property and individualism. This new government was conservative but set into motion a series of radical changes. Among the most important events were the return of liberals exiled by Fernando VII, a new constitution in 1836, the 'success' of modern economic and political policies beginning in 1837, and, in terms of culture, the first royal order decreeing *derecho de autor* for dramatic works. While the Ancien Régime was a legacy only slowly relinquished and its passing contested and arrested by a series of civil wars (culminating in the Civil War of 1936–9), copyright law – likewise born out of both Enlightenment and liberalism – marked the beginning of a new era.

When discussing liberalism or the liberal project of intellectual property, I am referring specifically to an economic and political philosophy, not to social attitudes or to a widening of cultural ideas, although these were related, to varying degrees. The Spanish liberals were politicians and critics (and, in some cases, also poets) who advocated economic individualism, ownership, and a free market, as well as a uniform government throughout the nation, national sovereignty, civic equality, and semi-direct representation in the Spanish *Cortes* [Parliament]. They first came to prominence by writing the liberal Constitution of 1812 (Constitution of Cadiz). However, upon the return of King Fernando VII to Spain, they continued their education in the new schools of political economy in exile. After his death, Fernando VII's young wife, María Cristina, regent for her infant daughter Isabel II, negotiated the liberals' return to Spain. An absolutist at heart, she was nevertheless obliged to ally herself and her daughter with them in order to protect Isabel's claim to the throne. Fernando's brother Carlos, the pretender to the throne, based his claims on Bourbon Salic Law and allied with the traditional sectors of Spanish society. María Cristina's calculated embrace of the liberals guaranteed her daughter's hold on the monarchy and inaugurated a series of cultural and economic innovations that mark the beginning of Spain's modern period.

It is also important to remember that the 1820s and 1830s were a turning point in Spanish history because they witnessed the definitive demise of Spain's global empire. While the imperial project continued to be important in the nineteenth century in terms of international policy and the domestic economy, geographically, it was greatly diminished after the loss of most of the American territories. As a result, and in combination with new interpretations of Enlightenment concepts of culture and nation, Spain's colonizing gaze turned inward. Theatre, along with a wide variety of government policies, was treated in a more uniform, national manner and there was an attempt to nationalize, or regularize, culture on many levels. As concerns theatre, whose strength as a cultural tool is discussed above, this was carried out in part by the owners of theatre copyrights whose financial interests enforced strict adherence to the 'authorized' piece emanating from Madrid.

These particularities of Spanish history lead to a final comment on perspective. Several cities had vibrant theatres: a unique example is the Liceu in Barcelona, which departed from the Madrid-centred model. But, given the centralized nature of government, cultural policy, and theatre practices during the nineteenth century, I focus my discussions on the poets, publishers, and theatre companies working in Madrid. Not only was Madrid the political capital of Spain (and its empire) in the nineteenth century, but also most dramatic works were premiered and published there. In addition, because most dramatic *editores* resided in Madrid, the notarial archives that documented their financial arrangements are found there. The majority of small periodical papers (such as *El entreacto* [*The intermission*]) dedicated exclusively to serious theatre criticism and gossip regarding popular actors and poets were written in Madrid. Finally, the plays performed in Madrid set the standard for the stages throughout the rest of the nation: I refer here to what I will explain as an economically and culturally colonialist attempt to establish a text in Madrid and control its 'identical' repetition (as a tool of cultural homogeneity) in provincial cities.

A Pre-history of Spanish Literary Property

The modern concept of literary property was first legislated in Spain by the parliament of the Cadiz Regency that ruled in King Fernando's name during the Napoleonic occupation. However, these laws were never put into effect. The concept of an author with a natural right to create and own property was associated with the issue of popular sovereignty and re-legislated at moments of strong political challenges to Fernando's ancien régime government (particularly, the Liberal Triennium, 1820–3). These laws proposed that writers could make themselves into authors through (perceived) solitary creation, and thus hold authority over their own minds, thoughts, and intellectual possessions. Mark Rose has argued that, generally, 'the figure of the proprietary author depends on a conception of the individual as essentially independent and creative, a notion incompatible with the ideology of the absolutist state.'[5] In the most radical departure from royal absolutism, individual rights come before those of the government,[6] and intellectual property and authorship are primary among these rights. The Spanish Monarch's two repressions of literary property, following his return to Spain in 1814 and in 1823 (after three years of a liberal interlude in his absolute power), and his refusal to consider it at any other moment during his reign, illustrate his perception of its potentially subversive effect on his rule. Before there could be stable literary property for dramatic works, these would first have to be recast as literary creations that could be appreciated independently from the stage, but also the author's voice in the text would have to supersede the authority derived traditionally from the use of plays as royally regulated spectacles.

The Cadiz Regency declared a free press on 10 November 1810, allowing anyone to write, print, or publish his or her ideas. On 10 June 1813, it established limited authors' rights, declaring authors the owners of their written works. This decree also appropriated the exclusive right to authorize publication of a text from the Monarch and placed it in the hands of its author. Through the reorganization of the relationship of control by individual writers over their literature as one of authorship by right, rather than by privilege, *authority* was thus diffused from a theocratic centre to a 'natural' one, based on the merit and intellectual faculties of each writer. The possibility for authorship was nascent in every citizen with the talent to utilize it.

Upon his restitution to the Spanish throne in May 1814, Fernando VII annulled the political measures passed by the Cadiz Regency, including the Constitution and the decree of literary property.[7] The question of intellectual property for lyric poetry arose again during the Liberal Triennium (1820–3) and was passed by the *Cortes* in July 1823.[8] This law was only in effect briefly but is noteworthy because it married the issue of natural rights with the modern, liberal aspect of authors' rights by equating literary property with all other property. Article 1 stated: 'Los autores, traductores, comentadores ó anotadores de cualquier escrito, y los geógrafos, músicos, pendolistas y dibujantes, son propietarios de las producciones de su ingenio, y pueden disponer de ellas del mismo modo que de los demás bienes' [Authors, translators, commentators or annotators of any work, and geographers, musicians, calligraphers, and pictorial artists are the owners of the products of their mind, and they may dispose of them in the same way as all other goods]. Unlike the 1813 decree, as well as the laws in neighbouring European countries and all subsequent Spanish literary property laws, there were no temporal limitations to the Spanish *derecho de autor* in 1823, and it, like all other possessions (such as a parcel of land), could indefinitely remain under private, exclusive control, or be transferred an infinite number of times to anyone (heirs or others). These authors' rights (*derechos de autor*) were also based upon the idea that the source of individuals' rights lay outside of the person of the Monarch. As in 1814, Fernando annulled this law in 1823, at the end of the Liberal Triennium, in the *Decreto-manifiesto en el Puerto de Santa Maria*, which marked his return to monarchical authoritarianism.

Although he twice suppressed literary property, Fernando VII did recognize creative genius, and in 1826 he promulgated a decree to protect it for 'obras útiles' [useful works] ('Decreto de 26 de marzo de 1826 sobre propiedad industrial') [Decree of 26 March 1826 concerning industrial property].[9] Works of literature with a perceived practical use (e.g., Mesonero Romanos's *Manual de Madrid*) and mechanical ideas (e.g., blueprints for a new machine) were protected if considered beneficial to the general public and to the improvement of Spanish society. As Martha Woodmansee and Peter Jaszi have explained, there are two fundamental models for copyright protection: the natural law model, seen in the laws discussed above, and an 'economic' model. The second 'justifies protection only insofar as it promotes social welfare by providing an incentive to create and/or distribute new works.'[10] This model formed the philosophy behind the 1826 decree, which was intended to spur intellectual creation in Spain and encourage inventors to share their ideas. Fernando VII and his ministers were keenly aware of the need for industrial reform for the economic health of Spain, and this measure was part of a larger plan to implement it. In contrast, the Cadiz laws regarding artistic and literary works were not informed by a desire for literature to foster social and industrial development, but instead by an ideological protection of 'natural law' rights.

Copyright for novels developed on this model in a much more straightforward manner than for dramatic works. When the collaboration with actors, directors, and stage craftsmen that is always intrinsic to performance was absent, and when the venue in which the work was introduced to the public was clearly a private entity, *derecho de autor* was similar to its development in other European countries. For novels, the source of an 'original' work was the individual writer, and the locus of textual authority was seldom in question. In contrast to dramatic literature, copyright for narrative was not impacted by debates over the nature of its art as collective versus private or performative versus textual. Novels were still subject to strict censorship at various times throughout the nineteenth century but were legally classified as 'obras literarias' [literary works] and afforded the same protection as writers of non-fiction books; dramatic texts were classified altogether differently.

Works for the theatre were not included in authors' rights before 1837. During the reign of Fernando VII, Mariano José de Larra (1809–37), the foremost social critic of the 1830s, was among the few who called for such an inclusion, but only in terms of how it would help the institution of the theatre and, by extension, the state (considering it more as *utile* than as *dulce*). For example, in his article from 1832, 'Reflexiones acerca del modo de hacer resucitar el teatro español' [Reflections on how to resuscitate Spanish theatre], Larra emphasized the place of theatre in improving the nation through its certain influence upon Fernando's subjects in attendance. Although he also discusses theatre as an art form in that essay, he defines the institution of the theatre as, fundamentally, 'una diversión indispensable; una diversión que dirige la opinión pública de las masas que la frecuentan; un instrumento del mismo gobernante' [an indispensable diversion; a diversion that directs the public opinion of the masses who frequent it; an instrument of the ruler himself].[11] After arguing the political necessity of better theatre productions, and in spite of the refusals by the Monarch to permit literary property, Larra states with his characteristic irony that 'nuestro ilustrado Gobierno, que siempre ha manifestado en esta parte los mejores deseos ... conoció que el talento es una propiedad como otra cualquiera, y de mejor ley; propiedad que debe producir a su dueño en relación de su mérito' [our enlightened Government, which has always manifested the best wishes on this issue ... saw that talent is a property like any other, and subject to a greater law; a property that ought to produce a return for its owner based upon its merit].[12] Larra is referring here to a measure by the city government of Madrid in 1807 (*Reglamento de teatros*) to create a royalty system for dramatic works, in which impresarios were to pay poets according to a play's success. The local rule had no real effect, even in the capital, and was not re-promulgated during Fernando's reign. Nevertheless, Larra's commitment to the issue was unceasing: he was to remain one of the most vociferous advocates in the campaign throughout the rest of his life, and his voice was to echo afterwards, in the final articulation of the law in 1837.

Modern literary property for drama was a further impossibility under the reign of Fernando VII because it would have shattered the relationship between theatre and state that had been solidified during the seventeenth century. John Elliott has studied the deployment of art, architecture, and theatre by the Spanish monarchy of this period as an attempt to persuasively articulate its political legitimacy. He explains that 'the application of the arts of the theatre to political life, and especially to the projection of kingship,' was part of the judicious use of spectacle as propaganda, to illustrate and confirm claims of authority.[13] Under the Hapsburg dynasty, court life and drama had fused fiction and truth into a hybrid image projected in a perpetual spectacle: for the court and the public alike, the portrayal of the King on Madrid stages supposedly reflected his actions and virtue.[14] More specifically, these *comedias* actively dramatized the effectiveness of the King and, as Maravall has argued, were stronger articulations of the divine rights of Spanish kings than any to be found in contemporary treatises on political theory.[15]

In terms of international relations, the theatrical projection of the grandeur of the Hapsburg and Bourbon monarchs, through the seventeenth and eighteenth centuries, had served as a gauge by which Spain's European neighbours judged its degree of power and civilization. However, as Elliott suggests, the magnitude of the visual proclamations of monarchical authority was inversely proportional to the actual degree of the King's supremacy: when uncontested, a spectacle of splendour was unnecessary.[16] Although the function of the theatre as a tool of the state changed in the early nineteenth century, the perception of its cultural importance did not. The determination of nineteenth-century liberals to transform the political organization of the nature of theatre in Spain through the legislation of dramatic property was part of their project to legitimize the new political system of popular sovereignty.

One example of the political function of stage spectacle in international relations was its employment by the Count-Duke Olivares at the marriage of the daughter of King Philip IV of Spain, Infanta María Teresa, to Louis XIV of France in 1660.[17] Each royal dynasty deployed theatrical spectacle at the nuptial celebrations to exhibit its magnificence and pomp and to impress its cultural and political significance upon the other. Although the marriage of the heirs to the Spanish and French thrones (and the peace treaty that it sealed) was an especially momentous occasion, the political function of theatre should be seen as typical for the period. This was the Golden Age of Spanish theatre: the age that served as a model to both the Spanish Romantics and the Queen Regent, María Cristina, as they attempted to reinvent the modern nation artistically and politically. The flourishing of dramatic poetry during the reign of Philip IV exemplifies the sort of effects that Larra argued would result from literary property for dramatic works in his century: the skilful use of the theatre as a representation of state power would lead to new modern works of a quality equivalent to those by Calderón, Lope, or Tirso de Molina.

The question of dramatic literary property during the reign of Fernando VII was essentially a struggle over the ownership of the spectacle of national sovereignty, and consequently, of the nature of that sovereignty. Fundamentally, the issue of dramatic literary property was a question of representation, pitting a popular sovereignty that represented a nation of propertied citizens against a King who personally embodied Spain, for dramatic copyright recognized the right of individuals (authors or anyone who held the deed to the literary property) to own the image of the nation portrayed in the theatre. A privately owned representation of the state could only occur in a nation with popular sovereignty – with an image of the people (not a Monarch) presented on the stage. Under the rule of Fernando VII, the population was one of subjects, who were represented neither by the state nor by the stage spectacle of the nation, and who were forbidden the right to claim ownership of that spectacle. But Spain after 1837 inverted the currents of authority of the nation, and sovereignty was subsequently understood as rising from the people who legitimated the Queen's position as head of state.[18] The modern Spanish nation governed itself in the *Cortes* (albeit in a limited fashion), which functioned theatrically: propertied citizens elected an actor/politician to represent the line of discourse (theoretically) scripted, authored, or at least approved by them. The Monarch-centred arrangement of the theatrical representation of Spain on its stages gave way, like sovereignty itself, to an understanding of the theatre as a representation of Spain as a nation of citizens.

After the death of the King in 1833, the Romantics claimed a grand status for the national stage, alleging that its characterization as a space of more or less facile entertainment by and for Fernando VII – a condition confirmed by recent scholarship – was merely a temporary interruption of the grandeur of both Spain and its theatre.[19] Early nineteenth-century debates over the need to reform Spanish theatre articulated the new political role of the stage in a new nation of propertied individuals as much as artistic and literary concerns. More generally, there was no clear distinction between discussions of the nature of art and of contemporary politics. As Susan Kirkpatrick has argued, 'Romanticism was central to the cultural agenda of the liberal movement of the 1830s, for the artistic cult of individual subjectivity supplied imaginative and emotional meanings for the new structures that the liberals sought to constitute in Spanish society.'[20] Recalling Elliott's observation that the spectacle of royal authority was wielded in the seventeenth century in times of political debility, the Romantics' urgency for a 'new' literature (in all genres) likewise reflected the 'relative insecurity of bourgeois cultural premises in Spain' in the 1830s.[21]

Nevertheless, the first author to petition the Queen Regent formally for dramatic literary property (in September 1834), Pedro José de Contreras, saw intellectual property as a means to sustain Ancien Régime morals by and for the 'juventud' [youth] of Spain, both literally and figuratively. Following the logic of an economic model for authors' rights, Contreras argued that social mores of the nation's youth, 'la clase mas numerosa y significante del estado' [the largest and most important class in the state], were being compromised by a lack of *derechos de autor* for dramatic poets that would, if promulgated, encourage the composition of morally edifying plays and thus improve the nation.[22] The members of Spain's future society were, according to Contreras, being corrupted by the substandard (Romantic?) plays produced on its stages. Of course, 'youth' refers, in a general sense, to the future of Spain itself:

if the new (young) nation was to remain morally sound and ideologically uncorrupted, it required a theatre founded upon the political and aesthetic principles of absolutism. In Contreras's view, a law of dramatic literary property was vital, lest the Queen and traditional society be lost to Romantic and liberal principles (precisely the philosophies which had engendered the idea of literary property in Spain).

In order to prevent social chaos, Contreras requested the Queen Regent to decree *derecho de autor* as a form of literary criticism and censorship, and, by encouraging works in 'puro castellano' [pure Castilian], forbid exaggerated Romantic plays and foreign opera and orchestras. In this arrangement, literary property would glorify the native elements of Spanish culture by restricting outside (and provincial) influences and encouraging original pieces by young Spanish poets based on neoclassical precepts.

Contreras urged that new voices be encouraged to articulate and represent their image of Spain in a conservative brand of nationalism. Taken to its logical conclusion, his argument implied that if directed to express themselves within the frame of eighteenth-century rules of dramatic discourse, the nation's youth would be more likely to conform to eighteenth-century conservative social ideology. Liberal literary property would then be inverted, and the threat of literary Romanticism thwarted.

María Cristina apparently remained unconvinced by this request, since she did not publish a royal order until 1837 (and then, in response to a very different petition and political circumstances). However, Contreras's petition illustrates the perceived utility of a dramatic literary property law by a critic opposed to the literary innovations of Romanticism – with which natural law, creative genius, and the articulation of selfhood were tightly associated. Although in its final articulation, dramatic literary property principally responded to liberal economic measures, this was not a law desired only by *Progresistas* and dramatic writers with a self-conscious creative genius: many members of society were keenly aware of its potential to harness the legal control of discourses for their own ideological programs.

The royal order decreeing theatre copyright created a very different generation of writers than that proposed by Contreras. Literary property treated individual authors as owners, and in the 1830s it was considered to hold the potential to expand political franchise through the creation of new property and a corresponding increase in the number of *propietarios* in Spain (for only property holders could vote). If enough poets successfully rewrote themselves as political participants through the composition of propertied literary works (and attained the requisite level of income to vote), the system could even lead to a liberal 'republic of letters' – no longer a space of shared knowledge, but a voice in the government, earned through the creation of parcels of private intellectual property. Thus, dramatic literary property was understood to bring together the old and new barometers for social health – the artistic and the economic – in a novel way. The legal process of the textualization of theatre according to liberal ideologies of property, owned and controlled by one individual who excluded all others from using it, was definitively initiated in 1837. The first royal order was to be re-promulgated in 1839, formulated into law in 1847, and reiterated in several later orders and laws.[23]

The chapters that follow analyse what I call the three stages of copyright for theatre. The first stage addresses the campaign for copyright law in the public sphere and the process that led to the first law. The campaign for literary property for dramatic literature that developed upon the death of Fernando VII later intensified as an economic repartitioning of the shared patrimony of the national image. Chapter 1 takes an oft-repeated, though never explained, anecdote of Spanish theatre as a point of departure to analyse how dramatic copyright was convincingly argued before the Spanish public at large. According to theatre lore, on 5 March 1836 the public at the premiere of *El trovador* at Madrid's Príncipe Theatre was spontaneously inspired by the magnificent play they had just seen to call for the play's unnamed author to appear on stage and receive their applause. This was the first time that such recognition of authorship had ever occurred in Spain, and subsequently, as if by means of a capricious *deus ex machina*, all dramatic poets in Spain were ever after unequivocally recognized as authors and rewarded for their literary skill and intellectual labour.

Since 1836, versions of this anecdote have appeared in nearly every literary history of Spanish theatre; but, in spite of its repetition, the meaning of the story has never been analysed. Why exactly did *this* play (unarguably a good one, but certainly not the best play ever staged in the history of the Spanish theatre – including the impressive works of the rich Early Modern period) elicit a call for the 'author'? How did the general public learn to apply the word 'autor' (which, until then, had a very different meaning) to a dramatic poet? Why did they do so on 5 March 1836? And who penned and circulated this anecdote? In chapter 1, I propose answers to these questions, employing a historicist approach and reading this event alongside the economic, social, and imperial events of the weeks and days leading up to this performance. I argue that the premiere of *El trovador* was a strategically choreographed event that successfully propelled the campaign for dramatic copyright into the public sphere and presented it as a means of extending the new economic logic of land reform to Spain's important theatre tradition.

Chapter 2 brings together a wide variety of documents and artifacts (petitions to the Queen, newspaper articles, and ministerial memos) from the months between the premiere of *El trovador* and the initial 1837 copyright decree. I carry out a close reading of these texts, in which ideas and even specific phrases that later appeared in the official decree were first expressed, in order to examine the competing ideologies of authorship, ownership, public domain, and national culture at work in the drafting of the law. Among the documents I analyse here are the manuscript drafts of the decree, replete with marginal notes, deletions, and rewrites in a number of hands (including that of the Queen Regent). Each projected a different ideology, and the official decree is a chorus of these various, sometimes contradictory, voices. Chapter 2 argues that the 1837 decree was clearly written in response to *El trovador* and the specific political, economic, and cultural concerns of the 1830s. Nevertheless, this decree has remained the basis of theatre copyright in all subsequent Spanish laws, and its wording has undergone only minor modifications. While legal historians have studied the judicial precedents for intellectual property, I propose an alternate story of dramatic copyright's genesis through an investigation of the context in which it came about and consultation of the manuscripts 'behind the scenes.'

The second stage of my study of copyright for dramatic literature examines the accompanying changes to authorship and the evolving roles of poets and publishers in the new literary marketplace. Chapter 3 examines the emergence of a new type of propertied dramatic author and explains the practical and philosophical similarities and differences between the traditional *autor* and the copyrighted dramatist. In this chapter, I argue that the 1837 copyright decree did not so much establish authorship in the theatre as transform it from royal responsibility and control over the *stage* to ownership and commerce of a single poet's words and ideas as printed on the protected *page*. As the text became the legally recognized source of artistic authority, stage practices changed too, and theatre evolved from a spectacle-based event to a textually grounded one. By addressing the historical nature of dramatic authorship and its legal and practical transformation following copyright, this chapter considers the changes to the art of theatre and performance practices that took place in Spain during the nineteenth century.

Throughout history, a host of mediators have negotiated between poets and readers or playwrights and public, including censors, printers, booksellers, and other artisans. However, the *editor* was, like his counterpart, the propertied dramatist, born after 1837 and was a product of the particulars of modern Spanish copyright. Chapter 4 focuses on how and why this figure emerged in the 1830s, assesses his initial impact on the development of theatre in the nineteenth century, and reincorporates him into the definition of modern authorships. The importance of the multifaceted relationship between dramatic poets and *editores* to the history of Spanish letters has been traditionally dismissed in terms of a crudely articulated labour-management dispute, with *editores* depicted as rapaciously exploiting victimized poets. Indeed, a handful of *editores* did acquire complete ownership of all Spanish theatre after the 1830s. However, without offering an apology for *editores*, I argue that a reappraisal of their unarguably significant role is crucial to enriching our understanding of the complexities of copyright and the history of Spanish theatre.

In the 1830s and 1840s, poets enthusiastically turned to *editores* to publicly avoid the economic and legal aspects of authorship that were redefining what had long been deemed a leisurely pastime. More than simply a publisher or literary agent, *editores* in this period functioned as shadow authors, with the right to concede to or deny performance of the plays they owned, and the responsibility of attending a performance, script in hand, to verify that the verses declaimed on stage matched the printed versions that they owned. Their aggressive enforcement of copyright law contributed to the development of the text-based approach to theatre.

In stage three of this book, I turn to the new formats developed in the early nineteenth century to print and market theatre pieces as literature after copyright for drama was decreed. While only the bourgeoisie or the wealthily connected attended stage performances in the early and mid-nineteenth century, all classes purchased inexpensive and widely available printed versions of the plays on the boards for private reading at home.[24] Presenting themselves as self-styled curators, the dramatic *editores* published these works in collections called 'galerías dramáticas' [dramatic galleries]. A wholly nineteenth-century phenomenon, the *galerías* were met with immediate acclaim in literary and theatre circles, not only for their aesthetically pleasing print, but also because they successfully attracted readers.

Chapter 5 examines the rise of the editorial *galerías* and their role in attracting new readers and popularizing national art in the post-absolutist age. In particular, I read the novel development of *galerías dramáticas* in the 1830s as a print phenomenon in conjunction with the contemporary opening of the Prado Museum to the middle class. In this chapter, I analyse publishers' attempts to market dramatic literature as a textual museum: a means for the general populace to access Spain's celebrated theatre and new national art gallery by proxy. There were sporadic efforts as early as 1810 to stimulate performance through publication (and publication through performance) of classical Spanish plays. What was novel about the textual museums of the 1830s was the systemic nature of the enterprise. Among the artifacts I examine are the cover pages of the *galería* editions, all of which were illustrated with pillars and ornate picture frames. With the text standing in for a canvas, the potential reader was encouraged to purchase and display the various titles available in the *galería* as a private, domestic reproduction of the celebrated national theatre. Art, literature, and the visual experience of drama combined in a new publishing format designed to engage with the excitement around a new popularization of high culture.

Chapter 6 examines the implications of the new *galerías*. First, this chapter offers an exhaustive reading of the individual elements of the material format of the *galería* editions; second, it examines how copyright impinged upon readers' and performers' interaction with plays; and third, it analyses the interplay between intellectual property and state power in order to address the twin processes of Spain's internal colonization and the formation of a national culture through theatre. Every aspect of the paratext functioned to direct or restrict reception. In addition to long, poetic copyright declarations that prefaced theatre books, stage directions first began to be included in *galería* editions – a novelty that changed the way that the verses were not only read as literature but also staged, if the author chose to write lengthy didascalia.[25] (Because they were part of the author's original copyrighted words, directions on lighting and costume, and other 'stage languages,' were subjected to the supremacy of the text.) Reversing the ancient tradition of actors' improvisation and response to audience reaction, copyright fixed the performance, just as it had fixed the text, and imposed a nationally uniform theatrical experience, independent of local tastes. The theatre again served the state as its colonizing gaze turned inward and it began to regularize policies within the various regions of Iberia. In this chapter, I argue that, in conjunction with direct legislation, the Crown outsourced the execution of its nationalizing project to the *editores*, whose attempts to enforce copyright law carried out cultural policy for the modern nation.

STAGE ONE

Literary Property and Modern Spain

Dramatic literature was excluded from the legal protection afforded to 'useful' works of literature by Fernando VII in 1826 and to lyric poetry by María Cristina in 1834. This section examines the separate process by which literary property was applied specifically to works of theatre. The poets who successfully campaigned for the new literary property emphasized copyright's utility as a political and economic policy for the state, rather than its potential to reform the stage artistically. Many social and cultural factors were related to the political changes that conditioned the passage of literary property for theatre; this section addresses three economic, performative, and legal aspects. First, the laissez-faire policies of land reform under Spain's first *Progresista* liberal minister, Juan de Dios Álvarez Mendizábal, and the immediate appropriation are shown to have been reformulated to argue for intellectual property. Second, this section addresses the role performed by a young dramatic poet whose Romantic plays glorified outsiders and exalted commoners as heroes. Antonio García Gutiérrez was cast as the protagonist of the contemporary drama for individual success in an obsolete legal world of privilege: a solitary hero graced with intelligence and talent attempting to attain self-reliance in a hostile world. The third point in this section is an analysis of the immediate outcome of this dramatic campaign: the unusual royal decree that reinscribed the principles of labour, individualism, and service to the state in terms of this new type of property. To that end, this section brings to light a series of archival documents authored by several of Spain's most eminent Romantic poets who argued this case before the young Queen Regent, María Cristina, and follows the textual evolution of the decree from an early essay by Mariano José de Larra to its proclamation in 1837.

1 Cultivating Property: *Desamortización* and the Culture of Authors' Rights

At the 1836 premiere of *El trovador* [*The troubadour*], Antonio García Gutiérrez became the first dramatic author to be hailed by the audience in Spain. The story of his appearance is one of the most oft-repeated anecdotes of nineteenth-century Spanish literary and theatrical histories. Nevertheless, this incident is a prism that draws together contemporary concerns regarding Romantic authorship, labour, and the relationship between property and citizenship in nineteenth-century Spain, and its political and aesthetic implications merit our attention. A young and successful dramatic poet, but a poor outsider in Madrid's political circles, Gutiérrez personalized and protagonized the campaign for dramatic literary property.

Political Economy and Poetry

The Spanish variety of liberalism that guided the government administration at the beginning of the campaign for dramatic literary property, in February 1836, was grounded in 'the priority of the individual and the sanctity of property.'[1] These stemmed from a Lockean conception of the individual, whereby every person is his or her own property, and the product of the labour executed by the body (or mind) is the natural property of the same person. As Mark Rose has explained in his discussion of authorship in England, individual liberty and the right to control private possessions are indivisible according to classical liberal discourse, and 'the freedom of the individual to employ his efforts to create property and the freedom to dispose of that property as he saw fit ... were the principles inscribed by reason in the very order of nature.' This was the ideology codified as 'sagrada' [holy] private property, in the *Tabla de derechos*.[2] This most fundamental of individual rights, in a nation built not of estates but of classes and individuals, was also explored in the parallel glorification of the self in Spanish Romantic literature. Political economy and poetry intersected in literary property, according to which the individual writer's texts were recognized as an extension of his person and a creation of his talents, a condition that allowed them an independent, extra-literary value in society as 'property.'

These ideas of political economy were elaborated upon in terms of labour in Spain by, among others, Álvaro Flórez Estrada. His appeal for society's reorganization corresponded to the ideas of the *Progresista* political party and reflected the general sentiment of optimism for real change after the death of Fernando VII. Flórez Estrada presented his influential ideas on property in *Curso de economía política*, reprinted four times in the 1830s.[3] This text recognizes 'propiedad' ['property' or 'possessions'] as the 'justa recompensa del trabajo' [just recompense for work]. Both of these terms are historically coded and subject to the assumptions and expectations of a given society.[4] The compensation for work in the form of property (instead of some other reward) is specific to a capitalist society in which only property holders are accorded the right to participate in the governing of the nation.

Spanish liberals sought to carry out the destruction of what they deemed a non-productive heritage of leisure and sloth, and to construct a nation of property founded on labour and individualism. Flórez Estrada is an example of the tendency, recently explained by Michael Iarocci, of Spanish liberals to internalize Northern European views of Spaniards as lazy and then to attempt to reject the myths of Spain's past in a radical embrace of modernity.[5] Flórez Estrada argued that under the traditional system of property, work was penalized and the individual strangled: The Ancien Régime

> [c]reó y premió la ociosidad; dió existencia á unas leyes que; so color de proteger el derecho de propiedad, le destruian de raiz, arrancando al trabajador parte del fruto de su sudor y entregándola al *propietario* ocioso; á leyes que, justificando la usurpacion mas criminal, hacian depender el precepto del Criador de la voluntad de la criatura: en una palabra, destruyó las bases de la sociedad humana, *la obligación de trabajar, y la facultad de disponer del producto del trabajo*, sin cuyas bases el sistema quedó falseado, y la lucha del género humano se hizo interminable. (Original emphasis)[6]

[created and rewarded leisure, fostered the existence of laws which, while seeming to protect the right of property, destroyed it to its roots, tearing away from the worker part of the fruits of his sweat and delivering it to the leisurely *proprietor*, laws which, justifying the most criminal usurpation, made the precept of the Creator depend upon the will of the creature: in a word, they destroyed the bases of human society, *the obligation to work, and the possibility to dispose of the product of labour*; without this foundation, the system was delegitimized, and the battle of humankind was rendered interminable.]

Flórez Estrada clearly articulates the modern concern for property (possessions) as tied to the labour of each person: all have not only the obligation to work, but also the right to make use of the product of their labour. He furthers his denunciation of the previous misappropriation of property by declaring that a wholescale reorganization of society, from one that privileged leisure to one that privileges work, is imperative for national progress. 'No nos hagamos ilusion; no es posible mejora alguna positiva en la sociedad humana, sean las instituciones políticas las que fueren, mientras ... la obligacion de trabajar no sea realmente estensiva á todos los asociados, mientras la facultad de gozar del producto entero del trabajo no sea una verdad' [Let's not fool ourselves; no positive improvement in human society is possible, whatever the political institutions may be, while the obligation to work is not truly extended to all members, while the possibility to enjoy the entire product of one's labours is not a reality].[7]

The call for a reform of the system of compensation was part of a call for a complete cultural renovation that was at the heart of the radical branch of liberalism that chose to see no continuity with institutions and practices in Spain's own past. As we will see in chapter 2, the specific arguments for intellectual property for theatre did draw on historical models. Indeed, even in terms of theatre, many of the specific goals had precedents in earlier periods of Spanish theatre, but the moderns wanted to emphasize what was new, different, and revolutionary. Flórez Estrada cast the eighteenth century as a culture of privilege and leisure that had destroyed society. By eradicating the rewards of leisure and replacing them with a Lockean understanding of the rights of property and exploitation, he intended to rearrange the (working) individual's relationship to both the state and society. Property, thus, was both created by the individual and, in turn, validated and inscribed him into the post-absolutist community of individuals: membership in this new ideal society required labour.

With the bourgeois cultural (and necessarily economic) revolution in Spain, old privileges and societal values were challenged, and members of the leisure class began to assume activities that would mark them as bourgeois.[8] Poetry had long been a tenant of the demesne of leisure and seen as a result of the contemplation and meditation associated with *otium*. But in the nineteenth century, the appreciation of the folk, uncultivated literature, and marginalized voices by Romanticism intersected with an economic perspective that perceived the world through the lenses of labour and property. This trend converted poetry from an activity of 'ocio' [leisure] to one of 'negocio' [business].

Art and poetry continued to be a means for social ascension. Two young Romantic poets were the most visible parvenus to Madrid's elite literary circles in the mid-1830s: Antonio García Gutiérrez and Juan Eugenio Hartzenbusch. The identity of Hartzenbusch and García Gutiérrez as poor labourers did not change, even after they were placed in the royal bureaucracy; it was poetry that had become popular.[9] Thus, in the paradigm dramatized by García Gutiérrez at his theatrical presentation to the Madrid public (addressed at length below), the poet was first introduced, not as an aristocrat, but as one of the dispossessed – the intellectual kinsman of the agricultural peasantry in Flórez Estrada's narrative – and his play was re-evaluated as labour. Literary property law inscribed the poet, and by extension Poetry, into the world of work and property. This distinction between working poets, for whom new laws were destined and who were to determine Spain's literary future, and 'altas notabilidades literarias' [high literary notables] would be echoed by the Queen's ministers in their suggestion that she be advised on *derecho de autor* by poets who would benefit from the introduction of property law.

Mendizábal and the Ascent of Spanish Liberalism

The law of literary property for dramatic works was developed within the political and ideological framework of the *Progresista* Mendizábal ministry (14 September 1835 – 15 May 1836). It was argued around a liberal appreciation of individualism, manifested as self-expression, originality, and private property. If poets expended effort and employed their own property (minds and bodies) in creating their verses, then copyright was their due, as property was liberal society's just reward for labour and production. This philosophy of property intersected with the ideas of literary Romanticism in their common protagonist: the solitary creative genius, whose work was, ideally, to be protected by *derecho de autor*.

As minister of *Hacienda* [Treasury] and *Estado* [State] and as president, Mendizábal was inspired by laissez-faire economics and classical liberalism.[10] He exhibited Spain's anxiety to become a modern European state through a blind faith in the invisible hand of the market and economic development. His interpretation of democracy entailed the protection of the interests of male property holders and was much more inclusive in theory than in practice.[11] Although Mendizábal's liberalism did find national sovereignty exclusively in 'el pueblo' rather than in a Monarch, it did not intend to establish a republic.[12] His clearly articulated goal was to increase and enfranchise landowners in Spain, but not to extend the rights of national representation to everyone. Isabel Burdiel has explained that the *Progresistas* intended to reformulate political franchise according to talent and economic success:

> This would occur through the free play of the market and legislation designed to increase the opportunity for political participation. Thus, the revolution was a process open to the most characteristic social basis of progressivism: 'those enlightened and noble classes which are the ornament of nations in which ingenuity and talent, which are acquired through work, make up for the titles of birth and chance.' It was a narrow social constituency made up largely of members of the liberal professions who had acquired a political prominence far superior to their sociological strength.[13]

Inclusion in the ruling class was unambiguously selective: the new regime was founded on the idea that a nation's lawmakers were to be elected by 'those capable of owning property and getting an education within the context of legal equality and the free market.'[14] According to the *Ley electoral* of 12 July 1837, 'Para ser elector ... Se necesitaba ser mayor de 25 años y pagar un mínimo de 200 reales de contribución, o tener una renta anual mayor de 1.500 reales, o pagar un alquiler de 1.000 a 2.500 reales, según la población' [To be an elector ... One had to be over 25 years old and pay a minimum of 200 *reales* in contribution, or have an annual income of more than 1,500 *reales*, or pay rent of at least 1,000 to 2,500 *reales*, according to the place of residence].[15] In contrast, property had been unrelated to the right to participate in government under the Constitution of Cadiz in 1812: 'Para ser nombrado elector parroquial se requiere ser ciudadano, mayor de veinticinco años, vecino y residente en la parroquia' (Capitulo III, Art. 45) [To be named a parish elector one must be a citizen, at least 25 years old, inhabitant and resident of the parish]. The requirements were similar for *electores de partido* (Cap. IV, Art. 75).[16]

The result of liberalism's property-based suffrage, when put into practice by Mendizábal, was an enormous decrease in the number of people allowed to vote: from essentially all adult male citizens under the Cadiz Constitution to only 4.5 to 5.5 per cent of the population in 1837.[17] While many of the same families remained in power after the new system of political participation, it did advance significant social, political, and economic innovations, including literary property.[18] Burdiel has suggested that the most fundamental contributions of this liberal ministry were 'a new political arrangement of the mechanisms of social and economic power, and of the sources of cultural legitimacy.'[19] As concerns this study, cultural legitimacy was of primary importance. The representation of the nation on Spanish stages was commodified and transformed into a private possession, as outlined in the Introduction. The outcome of the categorization of verse as property was an effective *embourgeoisement*, if not complete popularization, of dramatic poets.

Mendizábal promoted the ideals of property in one measure that forever changed the face of Spain: the public auction of ecclesiastic and municipal lands. *Desamortización* was an economic policy begun in the late eighteenth century; however, according to Antonio Moliner Prada, there were three ideological and financial objectives of Mendizábal's *desamortización*: 'hacer que los compradores de estos bienes defendieran el régimen liberal ...; transferir las propiedades eclesiásticas a manos de gentes con mentalidad capitalista ...; y obtener fondos para enjugar el déficit de la Hacienda' [to ensure that the purchasers of these goods defended the liberal regime; to transfer ecclesiastic property into the hands of people with a capitalist mentality; and to obtain funds to eliminate the Treasury deficit].[20] That is, *desamortización* was a specific measure intended to actualize liberalism in Spain by opening government participation to propertied individuals, countering the economic prowess of Carlism's stronghold in the Church, and resolving Spain's insolvency through a belief in private money as the organizing principle in society.

In January 1836, Mendizábal had received full powers to begin *desamortización* through a vote of confidence in the *Cortes*. His intent to seize municipal and Church lands and reclassify them as 'national goods' for partition among private owners was extremely well publicized and argued at length in the newspapers and salons of Madrid. Álvaro Flórez Estrada, although equally committed to a property-based society and political economy, was one of the most vocal challengers to Mendizábal's plan, claiming (correctly) that the majority of Spaniards would be excluded from its benefits.[21] In a flurry of pamphlets and articles, the benefits and risks of the repartition of land (and by whom the individual ownership of Spain was to be decided) were vehemently debated almost daily in the press during the months of February and March 1836.[22] The 'politics of the individual' debated in the *Cortes* by day were to be carried out in the theatre that members of the bourgeoisie attended by night.

The reorganization of land into the hands of liberal capitalists was written by Mendizábal and decreed by the Regent, María Cristina, on 19 February 1836; the protocol regarding the execution of the sale was decreed on 1 March 1836. García Gutiérrez's play *El trovador* was premiered on that same day, in the midst of one of the most revolutionary moments of the liberal administrations of the early nineteenth century. Yet, the especially momentous historical context in which this play was staged has not been addressed.[23] Antonio García Gutiérrez revealed the limitations of *desamortización* as originally conceived, but also its greater potential when applied to the wealth of culture and the terrain of talent.

The Premiere of *El trovador*

The premiere of *El trovador* at the Teatro del Príncipe on 1 March 1836 is usually remembered because the audience, inspired by the ingenuity of the play just completed, called its unnamed author onto the stage in order both to discover the source of this piece of theatrical perfection and to honour him with applause. This anecdote, retold innumerable times (in nearly every edition of García Gutiérrez's works), has served for almost two hundred years to convincingly explain the origin of a supposedly just recognition of authorial genius in dramatic works in Spain. First composed at the time of the premiere of *El trovador* (by Larra), this semi-fictional account has entered into the annals of Spanish literary history as fact (principally through the version written by Antonio Ferrer del Río in 1846). The story that it tells is not untrue, yet it is more allegorical than factual. As theatre critic Cayetano Rosell, writing in 1881, declared: the 1836 premiere of *El trovador* 'n[o] dejará nunca de marcar una época divisoria en los anales de nuestra literatura' [will never cease to mark a division between eras in the annals of our literature].[24] However, the epochs of art and authorship that it divided remain to be clearly defined.

The standard interpretation of the premiere of *El trovador* tends to analogize it obliquely with the Parisian premiere of Victor Hugo's *Hernani*, as the ardent approbation of a new artistic school; however, they were two very different events, alike only in the fact that some of the audience reacted passionately. Although *El trovador* cannot be defined as the first Romantic play to be performed in Spain, as it was preceded by many others (both French and Spanish), its *audience* has been described as the first to have enacted a Romantic response: swooning with emotion at its conclusion. This account of the premiere foregrounds the degree of artistic Romanticism in the piece that affected the members of the audience, but it does not query why the call for the author first happened on 1 March 1836. Gutiérrez's play was unarguably popular: Ferrer del Río relates that printed copies flew off booksellers' shelves, and its verses were heard in the streets immediately.[25] In subsequent years, the play was staged frequently in the principal theatres of Spain, and later rewritten into an opera by Verdi and parodied by countless Spanish contemporaries. That is, the play was an undeniable artistic and theatrical success. However, recognition of the play's resounding success does not explain why the audience (made up of mostly middle- and upper-class *madrileños*) would call for the author to appear upon its conclusion, when this was not an established practice (whereas many other reactions of approval to a well-performed play were common). In spite of their simultaneity, the relationship between the play's success and the audience's new behaviour is not one of immediate causality. The question is not what poetic aspect incited the audience's response to this specific play, but rather why it reacted with a call for the author at all. As David Saunders has cogently argued, intellectual property is not innate to human society but developed out of technological advances, new philosophical relationships between writers and texts, and the legal arrangement among commerce, government and culture.[26] Like literary property, to which it was intimately related, the call for the author was not fated to take place in Spanish culture, but was the result of specific social, economic, political, and artistic stimuli.

As Romantic works had been staged to great success before 1836, the reasons for the public call for the author to have happened on that date are logically non-artistic.[27] Moreover, if *El trovador* was truly the consummation of Romantic artistic and philosophical ideals and, therefore, it was the inner perfection of the play that inspired this unprecedented reaction in the public, it remains unclear why the custom of calling for the dramatic author continued and was eventually executed indiscriminately. In a period in which audience behaviour was increasingly restricted and the parterre disappeared, it is surprising that this sort of unconventional behaviour was deemed appropriate.[28] Moreover, in spite of the poet's marginal role in performances, there had previously been some demonstration of interest in poets. Carmen Iranzo has pointed out that the 1924 edition of the Espasa-Calpe dictionary named Moratín as the first poet called out on stage by the public (at the conclusion of his play *El barón* in 1814).[29] The *Boletín del comercio* reported in 1833 that at the 29 January performance of *Los celos infundados, ó el marido en la chimenea* at the Príncipe Theatre, 'quisiéramos que el autor hubiera estado presente á la representacion para preguntarle si quedaba satisfecho de ella; si los actores habien espresado debidamente, etc. ... En fin, á pesar de que la ejecucion no ha sido mas que mediana, el público, al caer el telon celebró al autor con triple salva de universales aplausos' [we would have wished that the author had been present at the performance so that we might have asked him if he was satisfied with it, if the actors had presented their lines as they ought to, etc. ... In any case, in spite of the fact that the execution was not more than average, when the curtain fell the public lauded the author with a triple *salva* of universal applause].[30] In this case, the public knew that the prominent Martínez de la Rosa had written the play, so what was new about the call for García Gutiérrez? Why did the call for the author at the end of *El trovador* mark a new era in Spanish theatre?

The call for the author was an articulation of public opinion and a new understanding of the dramatic poet's place in the production of Spanish theatre. Plays had long been attributed to specific poets in Spain; but the perceived value of the creative process and responsibility for a poetic creation had become nuanced by Romanticism and the perception of the theatre as an expression of the nation's poets, rather than a tool of the Crown. The call for the author was not a feverish reaction by an enraptured audience, although its approval of *El trovador* is not in question here. Throughout the nineteenth century, the claque was a powerful force in the theatre whose reactions directed audience responses and interpretations. There is no written record of claques' interventions, but their ubiquity is documented in contemporary texts. In Wenceslao Ayguals de Izco's novel *Los pobres de Madrid* from the mid-century, Lucas (the son of a chambermaid) is a paid member of the public and, as instructed, applauds, boos, or calls for authors to appear on stage. He proudly declares that he personally creates reputations and that his mercenary voice determines who is deemed Spain's leading poet.[31] Navas Ruiz has credited Eugenio Ochoa (who later petitioned María Cristina for dramatic copyright) with the introduction of the customary call for the author. He reports that Ochoa was present at the Paris premiere of Dumas's *Anthony*, where he witnessed the author step forward. It is likely that vocal proponents of theatre copyright like Ochoa and Larra directed public response at the premiere of *El trovador*.

The relationship between literary Romanticism and political liberalism is complex and uneven, but in the case of *El trovador*, the production of the Romantic play and liberal policies drew them together. García Gutiérrez's piece was premiered as the government was legislating land reform: a fertile context in which to re-present the case for dramatic copyright as authors' rights (*derecho de autor*). The proponents of intellectual property (principally, the *Parnasillo* circle) took advantage of political circumstances favourable to property and employed Gutiérrez and his play as an illustration of their argument. The poet became a personal protagonist in the political comedy of copyright to convince the government to extend the scope of intellectual property to dramatic poetry. At the same time, García Gutiérrez demonstrated how the 'liberation' of land that had traditionally been held in common could theoretically create new deserving property holders and inscribe more people of talent and hard work into the nation.

Set in the political turmoil of civil war in fifteenth-century Aragon, *El trovador* stages the story of a poet-warrior pulled between duty to his gypsy mother, Azucena, and devotion to his aristocratic lover, Leonor. Politically, socially, and racially, Manrique is an outsider. But through the cultivation of both arms and letters, the dashing, honourable, and lyrical troubadour strives to acquire both a name and a legitimate social identity. This desire for a name underscores all of Manrique's actions and is a motif repeated throughout the play. To a nineteenth-century public, the similarities between Manrique and García Gutiérrez as poets, social outsiders, and self-made men were unmistakable. The call for the revelation of the author's name at the end of the play was to a certain degree prompted by a desire to complete the protagonist's quest and know Manrique's identity. In his review of *El trovador*,

Larra conflated the two into a single figure whose identity and role in society are yet to be recognized and appreciated by his peers. In the play, Manrique is thwarted by the jealousy of his rival in love and the desire for vengeance by his (foster) mother: the troubadour dies moments before Azucena reveals that he was not her son but rather the oldest child of the noble Artal family and the brother of the rival who kills him. Manrique lived with several identities just beyond his reach, but he died bereft of even a self-knowledge. In contrast, Larra argues that Gutiérrez could and should earn a name and fame through the cultivation of poetry. Intellectual property would reward Gutiérrez for his excellence, and talent should become a revolutionary way of entering the 'aristocracy,' as Larra calls it. Because he lives in modern Spain and not medieval Aragon, Gutiérrez has possibilities unavailable to his protagonist.

The plot and characters of *El trovador* raised the issues of individualism, identity, legitimacy, and the poet's place in society. The *mise en scène* of the call for the author staged the implications of these same questions for the art of theatre. The public's call for the author at the end of the performance required the actors to step aside literally and figuratively from centre stage to allow the dramatic poet to be deemed responsible for the success of the production. Several accounts point out in great detail that the leading actors (who were onstage to receive the applause when the call began) ceded their position to Gutiérrez. The public's decision, as likely directed by Ochoa and a claque, to consider the poet, among all of the producers of the spectacle, to be the most deserving of praise and thus most responsible for the piece was an argument for the expansion of the natural-law model of property into the realm of intellectual property – by considering García Gutiérrez to be the intellectual source of the play and the labourer who created it.[32]

Gutiérrez's involvement with intellectual property did not end on 1 March but continued in his highly stylized presentation by the press as the exemplary landless (but intelligent) young man who merited an opportunity to advance socially in post-absolutist Spain. Both after 1 March and throughout the century, he was cast as 'un jóven patriota alistado voluntariamente en los ejércitos de la libertad (lo cual constituia el mejor pasaporte en aquellos dias)' [a young patriot voluntarily enlisted in the armies of liberty (which served as the best passport in those days)],[33] and as a young celebrity he progatonized the need for dramatic literary property up to and through its presentation to the Regent, María Cristina.

The version of the premiere written by Mariano José de Larra, the foremost cultural critic of the 1830s, was one of the first and most influential: his persuasive essay was printed in *El español* on 4 and 5 March – precisely the same days when the arguments for and against *desamortización* filled the columns of the Madrid papers. The political and economic questions of private property that textually encircled the reviews of the play wove a paratextual context. Given the extra-textual dialogue with contemporary politics and the inherent stylistic complexity in all of Larra's articles, even his theatre reviews must be analysed with care.[34] His review of *El trovador* commented much more than the quality of the production or the structure of the piece. Larra recounted Gutiérrez's introduction to the public in a variety of tones, including that of the quasi-mythological birth of the representative of the future of Spanish society – an author whose nobility stemmed from talent:

> El autor del *Trovador* se ha presentado en la arena, nuevo lidiador, sin títulos literarios, sin antecedentes políticos; solo y desconocido, la ha recorrido bizarramente al son de las preguntas multiplicadas: *¿Quién es el nuevo, quién es el atrevido?*; y la ha recorrido para salir de ella victorioso; entonces ha alzado la visera, y ha podido alzarla con noble orgullo, respondiendo a las diversas interrogaciones de los curiosos espectadores: Soy *hijo del genio, y pertenezco a la aristocracia del talento*. ¡Origen por cierto bien ilustre, aristocracia que ha de arrollar al fin todas las demás! (Original emphasis)[35]

[The author of *El trovador* has presented himself in the arena, a new warrior, without literary titles, without political backing, alone and unknown, charged through it gallantly to the echo of questions *Who is this new person, who is so daring?* and he surveyed the arena in order to come out from it victorious; then he raised his visor, and he was able to raise it with noble pride, responding to the various interrogations of the curious spectators: I am the *son of genius, and I belong to the aristocracy of talent*. An unarguably illustrious origin, the aristocracy that will rout all others in the end!]

In this first description, Larra intertwines a revolutionary image of a new aristocracy with the language of war, and although he refers to the 'author of *El trovador*,' his description could easily apply to either the poet Manrique or the dramatist Gutiérrez. The social message that Larra sees in this play is as much about the hero's creator as it is about the hero. Larra portrays the dramatic poet as the intellectual equivalent of a soldier in battle against Carlism and a challenger to its royalist and aristocratic regime. His titles, and indeed his identity, are not a legacy bequeathed by his ancestors, but born of his talent. Moreover, he appears alone; the individual hero will acquire a name without the benefits of political protection or inherited privileges. This stylized account of Gutiérrez's presentation to the public idealizes him as the exemplary modern dramatic poet who has transferred contemporary social reforms to the space of dramatic writing: although only partially realized in the realm of government, talent and merit do triumph in the world of letters.

Larra then relates the same events in a different tone at the conclusion of his article: the proud aristocrat is replaced by a modest poet who is revealed as the source of the spectacle behind the curtain:

> Felicitamos, en fin, de nuevo al autor, y sólo nos resta hacer mención de una novedad introducida por el público en nuestros teatros: los espectadores pidieron a voces que saliese el autor; levantóse el telón y el modesto ingenio apareció para recoger numerosos *bravos* y nuevas señales de aprobación.
>
> En un país donde la literatura apenas tiene más premio que la gloria, sea ése siquiera lo más alto posible; acostumbrémonos a honrar públicamente el talento, que ésa es la primera protección que puede dispensarle un pueblo, y ésa la única que no pueden los Gobiernos arrebatarle.[36]
>
> [We conclude by congratulating the author yet again, and all that remains is to mention a new custom introduced by the public in our theatres: the spectators called out for the author to enter the stage; the curtain was raised and the modest genius appeared to receive the numerous *bravos* and new signs of approval.
>
> In a country where literature has barely more reward than glory, let it at least be as resounding as possible; let's get used to publicly honouring talent, as this is the primary protection that a community can grant it, and this is the only one that Governments cannot take away.]

Larra deems the call for the author as a recognition of talent by the public and a 'protection,' but he contrasts this with the scant financial recompense afforded to dramatic poets and suggests that there could and should be more 'premio que la gloria.' The responsibility of the nation ('En un país ...') to grant greater reward than glory to its poets is an idea that Larra returned to in other essays. In this article, he does not stipulate the protection and reward that the government could or has taken away, but in an essay from 1833 (echoed in many of the phrases of the *Trovador* review), Larra directly had specified it to be 'el derecho de propiedad' [property rights].[37] The proponents of literary property (as discussed in chapter 2) believed that it had been established by previous laws and was presently being circumvented. Authors' rights reframed the question of property around the individual and raised the issues of moral rights, talent, private ownership, and personhood.

Gutiérrez dramatized the campaign for a liberal law to recognize dramatic poets' writing as work and property. As Flórez Estrada was accusing the ruling liberals of excluding the poor and uneducated from the benefits of *desamortización*, *El trovador* demonstrated that the fundamental benefits of private property should include a young genius and poor labourer like Gutiérrez. Moreover, *derecho de autor* was also nationalistic: Isabel II's Spain was to be a country in which the intellect was assured prospects for individual progress. The public subsequently learned that the *niño mimado de la escena* [beloved boy-wonder of the stage] had discovered that he couldn't financially survive solely through the cultivation of poetry and had instead turned to the army, which promised rapid advancement in the ranks to enlisted men with an education.[38] In contrast to Carlism, portrayed as an anti-intellectual regime and a continuation of the court life of favouritism, liberalism promised young luminaries a better future than a place in the military. *Derecho de autor* held the possibility of transforming poets from landless labourers into property-holding individuals with a name and political identity.[39]

Larra's stylized characterization of Gutiérrez has been taken as fact and embellished by later critics, although it is almost completely contrary to historical evidence. Before the premiere of *El trovador*, Gutiérrez had already been active in the Madrid literary scene as a translator and contributor to periodicals. The highly respected poet José de Espronceda had publicly approved of the younger poet's work, and Gutiérrez moved within the circle of influence of the powerful Juan de Grimaldi. However, the truth of Larra's account lay in its charm: a bright young foot soldier who was also a talented dramatist was the ideal figure not only to represent dispossessed labourers to the liberal public in wartime, but also to demonstrate generally that versification was labour, cultivated not only by high officials like Martínez de la Rosa, but also by poor provincials. In his role as a marginalized outsider (much like his character Manrique), Gutiérrez did serve to draw the analogy between physical and intellectual labours and convinced the government to extend the natural-law theory of property to dramatic literature.

The second lesson of the *Trovador* premiere was the analogy drawn between the huge dominions of the Church and municipalities and the cultural heritage of the nation. With *desamortización*, the physical land of Spain was to be the property of individuals who would support capitalist ideology; with literary property, the intellectual terrain of the Spanish kingdom was likewise to be repartitioned according to the various liberal doctrines of work, labour, and the individual. There was to be no public domain during a poet's lifetime: this property was tied to the personality of its creator.

Propiedad literaria was not literally land, but it functioned figuratively as if it were. Quite simply, a cultivation of literary property was analogous to the appropriation and cultivation of land. In this way, Romantic literature was nationalistic by its very existence, as well as in content. Whereas the territorial limits of Spain were not only finite but, as a consequence of the recent independence of the former American colonies, severely reduced, literary property was, in contrast, infinite and existed for anyone with sufficient talent and merit to create it. The expanse of Spain's cultural property was theoretically endless. The nation's communal territories that were to be auctioned off could therefore expand onto a virtual plane: the stage, the glory of the national image, and the fruits of literary labour were an uncharted field of property.

Literary property law embued new intellectual creations with an immediate exchange value and removed them from the traditional commonwealth of a shared theatrical repertoire. Moreover, literary property would not only create new property but also, like *desamortización*, would redistribute fields of culture traditionally considered a shared good. Like the municipal lands seized and auctioned by Mendizábal and Espartero, the long-shared works of dramatic poetry from the sixteenth, seventeenth, and eighteenth centuries were commodified and circulated as private property. Editors (including poets) established definitive texts of famous works and claimed them as their own property.[40]

The political mood at the *Trovador* premiere continued through the summer: the dominance of radical liberalism was politically guaranteed after the rebellion at La Granja in August 1836 (five months after the premiere of *El trovador*) forced the Regent to sign allegiance to the

Cadiz Constitution. Now a professional poet, Gutiérrez continued to dramatize the need for the recognition of the poet's craft as labour and property, and for the liberal regime to embrace this branch of Spanish culture. The arguments for the transposition of liberal ideals of work and property onto dramatic literature were ultimately successful, and the disentailment of physical land did indeed lead to the privatization of the text produced on the Spanish stage. This same privatization provides the organizing principle behind the relationship between the public and the popular theatre, media, and visual arts today. Mendizábal's critics would agree that even two hundred years later, only a select few benefit from a liberal definition of performance works as property, as copyright conglomerates dictate taste and determine the cultural flavour of Spain.

2 Performative Appeal: From *El trovador* to the Royal Decree

On 5 May 1837, one year after the audience in the Príncipe Theatre had called for García Gutiérrez, María Cristina declared dramatic works by contemporary Spanish poets legal property. While this decree was presented to the nation as a rational act in accordance with the 'enlightened benevolence' of its royal Regent, it was in fact prompted by a petition by Antonio García Gutiérrez, Juan Eugenio Hartzenbusch, Manuel Bretón de los Herreros, Gregorio Romero, and Eugenio de Ochoa on 4 February 1837. Their arguments survived debates by government ministers, were developed in several rough drafts, and ultimately evolved into a royal decree that retained much of the original language and ideological underpinnings of the initial petition. An analysis of the manuscripts of both the petition and the law demonstrates the link between the concept of intellectual property for dramatic works and the project of the construction of the Spanish nation. Moreover, attention to the ideological justification of the petition's premise shows it to have been the logical outcome of the designation of the poet García Gutiérrez as author, following the premiere of his most popular play.

The dates of the strongest liberal governments, 1835 to 1842, coincided with the period that Susan Kirkpatrick has defined as the height of Spanish Romanticism, a movement whose literary development was punctuated in the theatre by the works of young authors like Hartzenbusch and Gutiérrez.[1] Hartzenbusch earned his celebrity a mere two weeks before he petitioned the Queen for recognition of his rights as author. On 19 January 1837, his play *Los amantes de Teruel* had been premiered in the Príncipe Theatre and, like Gutiérrez, he was also hailed by the audience as 'author.'[2] Decorated with popularity, the two young poets were the symbolic envoys of all Spanish dramatists. Indeed, as the public of the Príncipe Theatre had already designated them as authors, they became a bridge between the voice of national sovereignty (in the articulation of public opinion in the theatres) and the royal will, whose confirmation of their authority they sought.

The royal order they requested was a particular type of law. The muted revolution that followed the death of Fernando VII had led to a weak constitution, the *Estatuto* of 1834, replaced by a radical constitution in 1837. During these three years, the head of state could simply decree through royal orders or present laws to the *Cortes* [Parliament] for confirmation. The Parliament's role was not to initiate legislation but rather – theoretically – to represent and articulate the will of the nation. In the case of dramatic literary property, this model was slightly altered, as the 'people's' wish to recognize a poet's work as property preceded the law and was first expressed in the theatre, rather than the *Cortes*.

Traditionally, the stage had projected the image of the state, but in the new modern nation, the nature of this cultural identity was transformed, as both the theatre and constitutional government became spaces of national representation. Spaniards were to see themselves both in the content of popular Romantic plays and in the voices of the *Cortes*. This paradigm especially held true in the case of works by Bretón de los Herreros, one of the petitioners. Although chronologically part of the Romantic generation, his comedies represented contemporary middle- or upper-class Spaniards. At the premieres of *El trovador* and *Los amantes de Teruel*, the analogy was realized: the nation was represented not only in the spectacle presented on the stage, but also in the voice of the public whose call for a recognition of author(ship) approximated the chorus of votes that would be intoned in Parliament if the national will of the citizens were to decide the issue of literary property for dramatic works. As the *Cortes* could not propose this – or any – law, representatives of the 'Nation' instead vociferated their desire for intellectual property for dramatic works within the theatre. With the will of the nation regarding literary property thus demonstrated, García Gutiérrez and his cohorts petitioned the Regent, María Cristina, for its confirmation through a royal decree. The royal will and that of the people seemingly converged in this issue as both the public and the Crown found *derecho de autor* to be just and necessary.

In spite of their celebrity, Hartzenbusch and Gutiérrez were of meagre social standing and ineligible to address the head of state directly. Accordingly, the pets of the Príncipe Theatre were flanked by the important cultural broker Eugenio de Ochoa (poet, editor of several anthologies of Spanish writers, and translator of the laissez-faire economist Joseph Garnier), the highly respected *literato* Manuel Bretón de los Herreros, and Gregorio Romero (lawyer and director of literature in the Liceo).[3] The composition of the petitioners suggested that the representatives of popular enthusiasm for the theatre were inseparable from those officially responsible for the nation's cultural matters.

The eight poets most directly involved in the legislative process at this point (the five poets named in the petition, and Mariano José de Larra, Francisco Martínez de la Rosa, and Antonio Gil y Zárate) span the literary spectrum. Although many of the arguments in favour of dramatic copyright rested on Romantic concepts of authorship and a cult of the individual, not all of these writers ascribed to Romantic ideologies, and their more conservative positions on intellectual property demonstrate the widespread appeal that this new idea had in the 1830s. Larra most symbolically incarnated the Spanish brand of high Romanticism that, at first, seems to run contrary to the values of recognition by the law and financial security that grounded the struggle for copyright. It bears remembering his initial adulation of, and subsequent virulent opposition to, Mendizábal and his financial and electoral agendas. Gil y Zárate, as discussed below, was alternately a neoclassical dramatist, radical Romantic, anticleric and liberal, and, later in life, conservative, as demonstrated by his remorse at having attacked religious communities in his plays and in his politics. At the other extreme, their contemporary Mesonero Romanos (not involved in this process, but vocally in favour of literary property) ridiculed Romanticism for what he considered its juvenile tendencies. Romantic and 'non-Romantic' authors held similar positions regarding copyright as a panacea to cure Spanish theatre of its creative and financial woes and to promote original writing. Thus, intellectual property was radical in its promise to change the future of Spanish theatre and implement the new economic theories of authorship, even while it harkened back to the traditional model of writers and theatre in Spanish society and the glory of the Early Modern stage. The Romantics saw in intellectual property a means to reinvent Spain through a new empowerment of the individual intellectual and writer in society according to the ideologies of the new economy, although they had no idea where it would lead them. But, certainly, not all writers and politicians in favour of intellectual property were liberals or Romantics; rather, copyright is a useful lens for examining differences among their ideological stances. The way each one argued for intellectual property revealed the direction that he hoped Spain would take in the near future.

Poets and politicians often held opposing views on the commercial status of theatre; but during these first years of the liberal period, all parties agreed that intellectual property would civilize Spain, recognize the work of poets, protect texts from piracy and unauthorized modifications, and improve the general state of affairs. In a word, it was all things to all parties. After property rights were granted for dramatic literature, poets generally wanted to avoid its commercializing effects, whereas politicians still saw theatre as industry.[4] The complete social and practical implementation of *derecho de autor* for dramatic works only occurred later in the century, but its legal and ideological foundation was officially established during the heady days of Romanticism by royal decree on 5 May 1837.

A transcription of the manuscript text of the poets' initial petition to María Cristina is reproduced in the Appendix; *minutiae* and other papers regarding the government's response to it are reproduced below.[5] Through these records, the development of the campaign for literary property for dramatic works during the regency of María Cristina can be traced from its beginnings in November 1833 to its culmination in 1837.[6] Popular events, such as the *Trovador* premiere and Larra's widely read articles, complemented official action by the government. When read in context with contemporary social occurrences, the court manuscripts present a comprehensive picture of the issues involved in the legal transformation of dramatic literature into commodity. The first document from this chapter of the commercialization of dramatic literature is the petition by Gutiérrez, Hartzenbusch, Ochoa, Bretón, and Romero.

In the Western tradition, the creation of law tends to be conservative, with attempts to present new regulations as legitimate continuations of established laws and customs rather than as revolutionary departures from them. The poets opened the petition with a reminder of the Queen's prior pledge to address literary property. This was emphasized later in the petition through reference to current (already legislated) laws that indirectly allowed an author to control his written words as property.[7] Both the Regent's intent and current law were shown to predate the new measure that the poets petitioned from her.

In order to attenuate the radical nature of their request, the supplicants reviewed the Queen's position in 1833 regarding the decline of Spanish theatre and incorporated much of her original wording. The supposed state of decadence of Spanish drama was to be repeatedly bemoaned by artists and cultural critics throughout the nineteenth century, but the petitioners employed the term with shrewd political acumen. If the theatre (a cultural thermometer of the nation, according to a subsequent decree) was in decadence, Spain was likewise in decline.[8] The Queen Regent had stated in the royal decree from 1833 that she found the theatre to be in 'mal estado' [poor state]. But whereas many other phrases from her earlier proclamation were reproduced exactly, the poets transformed this term in 1837 into the stronger 'decadencia' [decadence], or decline from previous grandeur. In the context of the petition, the word reassured María Cristina that if she were to grant their request, the poets would not employ *propiedad literaria* to create a new or progressive theatre; but rather, they would work conservatively to restore the theatrical glories of Spain's past. As, apparently, culturally conservative, this tactic allowed Gutiérrez, Ochoa, Romero, Bretón, and Hartzenbusch to present a modern, revolutionary measure as the means for the Queen to head off the sort of radical, avant-garde, and powerfully influential popular theatre that sprang up in France following the execution of her royal relatives and the promulgation of *droit d'auteur* there.

In associating *derecho de autor* with the need to lift Spanish theatre out of its decadence, these five representatives of contemporary dramatic poetry subtly vowed to fix their gaze upon the past and build a bridge with their productions to the pre-decadent Golden Age culture of the theatre written by Lope de Vega and Calderón de la Barca. The veracity of their alleged intent is debatable; however, the politics of legislation and the Queen's unease regarding social progress required them to pitch their case along the lines of tradition: an example of the compromises between the absolutist Queen and her liberal supporters in their union against Carlism. In a general sense, the Romantic-era reinvention of the nation was guided by a historicizing imagining of a fictionalized past. The literary and spectacular grandeur of Spain's formidable Golden Age theatre provided the government with a finite goal for the cultural renaissance that was to result from the measures on dramatic *derecho de autor*.

In her decree of 1833, immediately following the death of Fernando VII, the Queen Regent formed a council to address the poor state of the theatre. It was reproduced, like all official royal statements, in the Madrid daily *Boletín del comercio*.[9] (It had been preceded for several weeks by heated debates in the same paper over the validity and necessity of intellectual property and, indeed, of literature itself for the success of a nation.) The reasons that María Cristina had offered for favouring this art in 1833 were twofold, and fundamentally political. She expressed her wish to see the theatre increase the degree of 'civilization' in Spain, a gesture symptomatic of Spain's inferiority complex vis-à-vis its neighbours, and to promote national industry.

As discussed in the Introduction, the theatre had long been a tool of the Hapsburgs and the Bourbons (on both sides of the Pyrenees) to proclaim their political status internationally. State power was projected through the grandeur of stage spectacle, which was understood to 'da[r] tanto lustre a las naciones' [shed such lustre upon nations].[10] This idea also informed the Queen Regent's treatment of theatre; however, the evolving political environment of the period was infused with Enlightenment ideas that conceived of theatre as culture and of culture itself (*civilización*) as something done by and found in the people, instead of exclusively by and in the Monarch. The Regent's second reason for promoting renovation of the theatre redirected the focus of its benefits from the royal head of state and onto to the nation, by means of its individual citizen-subjects. The theatre was an industry that employed them. This economic rationale for Spain's need to revolutionize its theatre was based on the assumption that industry is the best way to stimulate the wealth of a nation, whose glory no longer lay exclusively in the person of an Ancien Régime Monarch, but rather in its measurable economic growth. Accordingly, in 1833, eight weeks into her regency, María Cristina ordered the *Junta* to propose a reform of the theatre (including an investigation into the creation of intellectual property for dramatic poets) as a means to foster that wealth and civilization. However, the government changed before the *Junta* made any official recommendations, and the subject was set aside.

The Regent used the term *civilización* to describe the artistic and economic enrichment brought about by a healthier theatre – a word that would eventually be replaced in common parlance with *cultura*. Stephanie Sieburth (following the lead of Raymond Williams) has mapped the evolution of these terms in nineteenth-century Spain. Whereas 'culture' had previously defined an agricultural process, she notes that, in the early nineteenth century, it began to be used to identify intellectual activities and attained its current usage in Spain sometime around 1870. In contrast, 'civilization' was 'understood as an increase in material prosperity.'[11] In the documents examined here, the primary advantage of an industrious theatre was its potential to encourage financial prosperity in Spain: civilization. However, the goals of material civilization and artistic culture were related: the economic promotion of the industry of theatre was closely seconded by a concern for the level of artistic achievement that Spain could demonstrate both to itself and to its European neighbours. According to the 1833 decree, this wealth in the dramatic arts was to be encouraged through a variety of means, including literary property. In its final articulation, dramatic *derecho de autor* was developed upon the model of the disentailment and redistribution of agricultural lands – which, in turn, had built upon the concept of responsibility for the culture (in its older meaning as the cultivation of land) of Spain. The cultivation of dramatic literary property paralleled the agricultural processes to be controlled by private landholders and was intended to enhance national prestige through both economic strength and good theatre.

On 4 February 1837 the supplicants reminded the Queen that her intention in convening that council in 1833 had been to address the issues of literary property for dramatic works, schools for actors, laws that defamed the author's profession, and the policing of spectacles, in general (public behaviour and censorship). As noted above, a comprehensive law or decree regarding the theatre was not promulgated. The petitioners pointed out that although its lack was felt in every element of the realm of theatre, in the intervening three years, all but one of the proposed law's topics had been moderately remedied through some other means. They do not mention specific actions; however, in 1831, while still Queen Consort, María Cristina had founded an *escuela de declamación*, from which Julián Romea and other actors of note emerged during the Romantic period.[12] (In contrast, her husband had established and patronized a tauromachy school.)[13] The profession of the dramatic poet had risen in social standing, as it had begun to be considered an appropriate arena for future politicians to demonstrate their intellect. Censorship had been reformed several times after the death of Fernando VII, and the legal restrictions on audience behaviour had been drastically increased.

Gutiérrez, Bretón, and the others were not the first to solicit the Queen for theatre reform, or even literary property. However, whereas recent discussions of *derecho de autor* had been based solely upon either a recognition of the rights of the poet to remuneration or the question of whether or not fictional ideas could enter the marketplace as property, the argument in 1837 was more complex. Engaging with both the Romantic ideas of individual genius and the conservative view of poets' role in the royal administration, the petition underscored the changing nature of the institution of the theatre and of the poets who wrote for it. Although much of the petitioners' argument for literary property recycled previous ideas, it differed by deploring the state not only of the dramatic poet and the stage but also of the dramatic poem in a nation without literary property. The modest improvements made in actors' training and audience conduct in the mid-1830s had ameliorated elements of the *spectacle* of stage productions, but the protection of the *text* of the play had heretofore not been a matter of concern. The poets took an unusual stance in suggesting to María Cristina that the means to improve the theatre – and consequently Spain – were to be found specifically in the privileging and protection of the linguistic element of the stage, in treating it as an entity separate from the whole of the theatrical spectacle. *Derecho de autor*, it was argued, would elevate Spanish theatre by establishing an authorized version of a text.

In order for literary property for dramatic works to have any practical application, the poet's verse had to be considered a unique intellectual creation, produced through labour and inseparable from his mind and character: the natural-law model of ownership. This recognition of the relationship between author and product could have allowed poets to control their property without having to sell it outright. (However, as discussed in chapter 3, most poets ultimately did choose to sell their property rights.) Under the literary property law proposed by the petitioners, an inseverable tie between poet and play was to survive the public's initial consumption of the piece. According to the proposed arrangement, poets – now authors – would retain ownership of their plays and receive royalties upon their use: literature was no longer to be ceded to an *autor de comedias* like the merchandise of a painter, tailor, or other artisan of the theatre. Literary property thus signalled the end in Spain of a centuries-old concept of a common cultural repertoire in which, once sold and performed, dramatic texts were staged in any manner, by anyone, in any place without the owner's knowledge.[14] Once redefined as legal property and removed from the shared heritage of the nation, the texts were to be controlled by the author: only he could grant or refuse the right to perform or print them.

Appealing to the relationship between modern property, individualism, and Romantic subjectivity, the petitioners employed a discourse of bodily pain and injury to argue that the uncontrolled circulation of 'their' texts wounded their persons. Of course, the mutilation and disfigurement referred to in the petition was to a conceptual body. The intellectual entity parallel to the poet's anatomical body was, in turn, a product of Romantic ideas in which a poet's expression in verse is a manifestation of his subjecthood. Without authors' rights, they claimed, those who wrote for the theatre were personally at risk of 'incalculables perjuicios' [incalculable risks]. Poets were not only financially damaged by the current practices of stage production and play publication, but their dramatic works appeared 'disfigured' and 'mutilated' because of them. In the context of the contemporary civil war and turbulent age, the words were well chosen: Spain's young men (such as Gutiérrez's former colleagues in the army) were being physically wounded in the battle to defeat absolutism and defend Isabel's claim to the throne. María Cristina could employ various policies of the modern state to rectify both sources of personal injury (Carlism and the weak protection of individual property), and the physical and social reality of one group of young men transferred easily onto the argument of another. According to the young dramatists, to have one's words and works disfigured and mutilated, no matter what the reason, was a metaphorical injury and a perversion of the sacred individuality and inviolability of each person – so fundamental to both Romantic and liberal ideologies. In sum, the petition suggested that the disfigurement and mutilation of private persons that took place without *derecho de autor* was socially retrograde in an enlightened age.

The trope of the body presented literary property as a crucial necessity for Spain's writers and as a guarantee to advance the nation's theatre to its former pre-eminence. The objective to modernize and civilize Spain gained urgency when the imperialist project imploded early in the century and Madrid began its preoccupation with the 'civilization' of its citizen-subjects inside Iberia. A splendid, traditional theatre would evidence the recovered glory and culture of Spain upon the recent loss of its colonies, while an appreciation of property was fundamental to the modern definition of 'civilization.'

As the government's response to the petition developed, it was convinced that the extension of literary property to plays would ensure the growth of Spain's civilization (relative to that of its neighbours – specifically France). The Ancien Régime perception of the theatre as a gauge of the grandeur of the state gave way to the idea of a propertied stage as an external marker to foreign countries of the degree of civilization in Spain. Literary property for dramatic works would supposedly improve the nation's theatre by guaranteeing that the performance and circulation of a play text would be executed according to the Romantic fantasy of 'author's intent.' Logically, if dramatic poetry were protected, more and better young poets in Spain could be enticed to write for the theatre. As argued by Hartzenbusch, Gutiérrez, Romero, Ochoa, and Bretón de los Herreros in 1837, the civilizing effects of literary property were nearly boundless.

Echoes of Larra

The political and economic advantages of intellectual property were presented logically and convincingly, but the petition on 4 February 1837 was only one element of a lengthy campaign strategy. On 1 March 1836, the day of the premiere of *El trovador*, Mariano José de Larra, the most widely read writer in Spain, published an article in the Madrid paper *El español* in which he discussed the poor state of the theatre in Spain, assessed the various stances taken by Spanish rulers and governments regarding the theatre, and offered recommendations as to how it should be reformed.[15] In particular, he addressed the administration of theatres, the formation of acting companies, and literary property for dramatic works. His article rekindled interest in intellectual property, authors, and theatre as a public tool and framed the initial reception of *El trovador*.

Many of the most significant images and phrases of Larra's article were echoed, first, in the 1837 petition; second, in the royal ministers' response to the poets' petition (discussed below); and third, in the definitive version of the royal order promulgated on 5 May 1837 (several months after Larra's death). Larra was not among the petitioners to the Queen on 4 February 1837, yet his participation was crucial. In both tone and language, the texts of the petition and his essay are strikingly similar and, at times, identical. Among the strongest arguments in both is the relationship between the state and the institution of the theatre. Larra argued that the association between civilization and theatre within a nation is natural and that modern Spain required a more artistically accomplished theatre in order to demonstrate its already superior degree of civilization.[16] Looking back to its use and abuse by previous rulers, he then suggested that the theatre had suffered without legal protection and was instead 'considerado la mayor parte del tiempo como un mal inevitable por el mismo Gobierno que lo toleraba'[considered most of the time as an inevitable evil by the Government that tolerated it].[17] Moreover, the government even used it to repress society: 'en el [teatro el Gobierno] persigió las luces, en él trató de ahogar una manera de expresión de la opinión pública' [in the theatre, the Government persecuted knowledge, in the theatre, it tried to drown a means for the expression of public opinion].[18] The logical and indeed lexical parallels of these and other passages with the Gutiérrez petition are not coincidental. Larra was a prominent and well-respected writer and a member of the same literary circles as Gutiérrez and Hartzenbusch's protectors. His publication of what is, essentially, a draft of their petition places Larra at the centre of the political campaign for literary property in the theatre. The appearance of his essay on the morning of the *Trovador* premiere suggests that the emerging protagonism of García Gutiérrez from unknown poet to famous author in need of intellectual property was not fortuitous, but rather a step in the process outlined by Larra and his colleagues.

The Ministerial Mesa

The Queen Regent's ministers summarized and commented on the petition by Gutiérrez et al. and counselled her accordingly.[19] Their language was heated, and their remarks exhibited a unanimous desire to protect the rights of dramatic poets. Their commentary begins forcefully, by 'calling her attention' to the 'escandaloso abuso que se hace de la propiedad literaria, en lo relativo á obras dramáticas' [the scandalous abuse that is being done to literary property, regarding dramatic works]. Foremost, they urged María Cristina to ameliorate the currently appalling state of affairs for dramatic poets and poetry by issuing to the political chiefs of each province, without delay, a royal order forbidding the staging or printing of plays without the author's permission. The royal ministers also advised the Queen Regent on five interrelated key points. The official recognition of literary property would perpetuate established laws and practices, stabilize Isabel's throne by exemplifying María Cristina's *ilustración* [Enlightenment] as opposed to her predecessor's (and, indirectly, the pretender's) absolutism, draw the theatre out of its decadence, end a system of abuse and privilege, and defend the most fundamental of all properties – as her 'wise' neighbours in France had already done.

The advisers emphasized that the theory behind *derecho de autor* for dramatic works had been previously introduced in Spain. The assurance that it already '[g]arantizado está en nuestras leyes' [is guaranteed in our laws] was confirmed by a lengthy citation from the *Novísima recopilación* (1804–6) dealing with a writer's printing privilege and his right to bequeath it, as he would any other possession.[20] It is interesting that while most of these ministers had participated in the Cadiz regency to some extent, they did not invoke its Constitution (restituted after La Granja and in force in winter–spring 1837) or any other modern rulings, but instead chose a solidly absolutist precedent to convince the Regent. The importance of this legal conservatism extends beyond mere convention to family ties and legitimacy: María Cristina had to ensure continuity with the reign of Carlos IV and Fernando VII, as certain segments of the kingdom (and Europe) contested the legality of Isabel's claim to the throne. The ties (imaginary or otherwise) to tradition were vital to the demonstration of the authenticity of María Cristina's royal power as the custodian of the natural heir to the Bourbon line.

Nevertheless, the ministers' primary strategy of argumentation was based on a fundamental differentiation between Enlightenment and Absolutism, favourably contrasting the intelligence and efficacy of María Cristina and Isabel with the corrupt culture of privilege in the court of King Fernando VII. According to the ministers, Enlightenment was a modern, progressive philosophy wholly divorced from Absolutism, defined as an anti-intellectual government. At several points in their commentary, the ministers presented *propiedad literaria* for dramatic works as a vehicle for María Cristina to prove herself to be an Enlightened ruler committed to modernization by ending a 'disgraceful mistreatment' of poets and dramatic poetry in Spain. They described in striking terms the restrictive circumstances – nurtured by an 'injudicious' Absolutist ruler who repeatedly refused to recognize the value of literature – under which previous generations of dramatic poets had attempted to create culture: '... la tendencia constante del Gobierno-absoluto á sofocar todo germen de ilustracion y vida para los pueblos, le hacia mirar con desden y aun con repugnancia toda proteccion concedida á los ingenios españoles ...' [... the constant tendency of the absolutist Government to suffocate any germ of enlightenment and life for the people made it look upon any protection conceded to Spanish intellectuals with disdain and even disgust].

Thus established that poets had been severely neglected, it was then proposed that poetry had likewise deteriorated under the crippling circumstances enforced by the unenlightened regimes. The ministers turned their attention from the crimes against individual rights to the mistreatment of art, and elaborated their subjective view of the current state of the theatre in Spain. Whereas the petitioners had demoted the condition of the stage from 'mal estado' [bad state] to outright 'decadencia' [decadence], the ministers turned to an even more forlorn image of the theatre: forgotten and buried under the sands of time. The ministers traced the sources of the allegedly deteriorated state of the stage to the abuses of authors' rights allowed by Absolutism: 'tan arraigado, tan sancionado dejó el absolutismo un abuso que á la ilustracion de V.E. toca aniquilar, sacando del polvo un elemento de civilizacion al cual está enlazada la prosperidad de muchas industrias' [so rooted, so sanctioned did Absolutism leave an abuse that the Enlightenment of your Excellency must annihilate, dusting off of an element of civilization that is tied to the prosperity of many industries]. Through this Enlightened ruling, María Cristina could aggressively promote her nation's industries, as an effective modern ruler was expected to do.

The Absolutist government, they argued, had not only allowed the theatre to decay, but it had also dishonoured it outright by considering 'al teatro como una condescencia que era forzoso tener con la relajacion pública, tolerandolo solamente, del mismo modo que á las mugeres públicas, como una concesion hecha á la flaqueza humana' [the theatre a necessary evil that it was forced to allow for public relaxation, merely tolerating the theatre, in the same way as it did public women, as a concession made to human weakness]. In calling the eighteenth-century theatre a 'public' woman, the ministers effectively deemed it a space of pornography (the artistic depiction of painting or writing about prostitutes).[21] The ministers proclaimed that theatre had not even been acknowledged as a space of art since the end of the seventeenth century, but rather had been denigrated as a site of vice barely tolerated by indulgent kings. The unspoken outcome of the Regent's potential recognition of *derecho de autor* reads like the plot of a melodrama: a beneficent royal takes pity upon a dishonourable woman, protects her, and transforms her into the jewel of the kingdom. If the theatre was to be a traditional representation of monarchical power, the image evoked by the ministers was antithetical to the representation of female royalty projected by the young Queen and her mother and thus urgently required attention. If María Cristina, the 'maternal' Queen, were to promulgate *derecho de autor*, she could convert the theatre from a virtual prostitute into a respectable element of bourgeois society and, like a domesticating angel, reform her nation – as she would her family – into the modern ideal: useful, industrious, and purged of courtesans, privileges, and other leftover vices of the Ancien Régime. A 'public' woman was representative not only of societal immorality, but also of the perversion of the modern ideology of property within the family unit, for she is considered a shared good and the opposite of the private property that an ideal wife was to a man in nineteenth-century Spain. This image of a nurturing, virtuous woman was nearly synonymous with the new bourgeois society. As Catherine Jagoe has argued, this 'notion of true womanhood' was symbolic of the nineteenth-century bourgeois reaction to the Ancien Régime and its immoral aristocratic behaviours and values.[22] A rejection of the prostitution of the theatre and the general licentiousness permitted under the Absolutists would identify María Cristina as an Enlightened reformer and advocate of a new system of property-based society.

Less melodramatic, but equally timely, was the argument based on Romantic personality and the protection of the expressions of the individual self. After considering versification as labour, her ministers then instructed the Queen that an author's right to control his verse was a property claim even more fundamental than that over land. They equated land and poetry as terrains of labour in order to differentiate them and argue the superiority of intellectual creation over material toiling. Property of the mind was, in their view, more pure than that from commercial exchange and interests, and closer to that of aristocratic ownership based on merits recognized by kings. The time for literary property to be rewarded to persons of merit such as Larra's aristocrat-poet of talent (as he described him in the review of *El trovador*) had arrived:

> [P]uede considerarse como la primera, como la propiedad por escelencia, por que no es producto de combinaciones ó modificaciones materiales, como las demas, sino que es una creacion, y su taller está en el entendimiento; esta propiedad está esperando todavía la mano ilustrada que estienda hasta ella la egida que proteje á las demas. No se trata de ningun privilegio; no se trata de crear un derecho, sino de que la voz poderosa del Gobierno haga respetar uno que ecsiste ...

> [(It) can be considered as the first, as property *par excellence*, because it is not the product of material combinations or modifications like all of the rest, but rather because it is a creation, and its workshop is in understanding; this property still awaits the enlightened hand that will extend to it the Aegis that protects other properties. This does not concern a privilege; this does not concern the creation of a law, but rather the powerful voice of the Government that will enforce the respect of a law that already exists ...]

Following a line of argumentation close to Larra's, the ministers suggested that the government produce a law comparable to that recently passed in France and realize these potential benefits of literary property. In particular, they proposed that the Queen and her council consult 'el informe presentado poco há al Gobierno francés por el sabio Conde de Segur' [the report recently presented to the French government by the wise Count de Segur]. Although they assured the Queen that Spanish laws and customs provided the legal foundation for *derecho de autor*, the *Progresista* ministers encouraged the espousal of foreign models to modernize Spain.[23]

Finally, the ministers insisted that the Queen Regent not be advised exclusively by aristocratic poets, as previous committees had been. For, the 'altas notabilidades literarias, que alejadas, años há, del ejercicio de la poesía dramática, no pueden conocer á fondo el actual estado de nuestros teatros' [high literary notables, long since distanced from the exercise of dramatic poetry, cannot thoroughly know the current state of our theatres]. Literary property was intended to overhaul the working conditions of dramatic poets and the process of producing a dramatic text, and, in the ministers' opinion, preparation of the law required an immediate knowledge of the industry.

The Queen Regent Responds

Convinced by the petition and her ministers, in May of 1837, María Cristina not only issued a royal order that provisionally established *derecho de autor* but also appointed three prominent poets to a committee specifically designed to prepare the law of literary property for dramatic literature.[24] Whereas the popularity of Gutiérrez and Hartzenbusch had socially justified their presence among the February petitioners, they were not sufficiently influential to merit inclusion among the Queen's advisers on this committee. Instead, and in spite of her ministers' admonition, she selected poets of a high social standing who, most importantly, claimed they did not (and did not intend to) live from their verse: Manuel Bretón de los Herreros, Antonio Gil y Zárate, and Francisco Martínez de la Rosa. The poets whom María Cristina appointed were, moreover, her servants. The first was a librarian in the National Library as of 1836, and the latter two were royal ministers. Martínez de la Rosa, the head of the council, had even repeatedly indicated that he composed dramatic works in his leisure, without intending for them to be staged.[25] Stylistically, these three poets were reliably conservative. Bretón wrote comedies as a disciple of Moratín; Gil y Zárate would go on to stage his shocking dramatization of the exorcism of the last Hapsburg king, Carlos II, seven months later, but as of May 1837, had established himself as a neoclassical writer whose plays stood in contrast to those of high Romanticism. While Martínez de la Rosa's *La conjuración de Venecia* (1834) was an early piece with Romantic characteristics, it did not gesture to the excesses of the next generation of writers. They were not, however, opposed to modernization: all three writers served as a bridge between neoclassicism and the new Romanticism and were committed to the renovation of Spanish theatre. Bretón, in particular, was recognized throughout his life (by Hartzenbusch and Larra, among others) for the zeal with which he worked to reinvigorate Spanish theatre, and he was well aware of theatre's political, social, ideological, and economic contexts.[26] He wrote countless newspaper articles proposing means to stimulate the theatre. In his essay 'Proyecto de estímulo y subsistencia para los autores dramático' [Project for the motivation and subsistence of dramatic authors] from 1833, he had argued for treatment of plays as property so that authors ('poetas dramaticos' and 'autores de comedia') would necessarily be remunerated with royalties for their use. Although not usually considered part of the Romantic school, his ideas on individualism and property strongly allied him with writers as varied as Larra and García Gutiérrez.

In her convocation of the council, the Regent reiterated the importance of theatre in the cultivation of an increased degree of culture among the people of Spain, but implied that this theatre was certainly not to be popular in nature. María Cristina was disposed to display an Enlightened attitude even as she resisted modernization. The composition of the committee continued a traditional configuration in which a select few determined the content and the means of the creation of culture for the majority. That is, three ministers with positions in the royal bureaucracy were to decide the working conditions for hundreds of commercial dramatic poets.

The three distinguished *literati* were notified of their appointment in a letter framed by a version of the Queen's cultural concerns that contrasted with the nationalistic and liberal tone of both the petition and the royal order.[27] What María Cristina claimed in the published decree and what she directed Bretón, Martínez de la Rosa, and Gil y Zárate to do were indicative of her overall political philosophy: an absolutist at heart, she was obliged to present herself as a modern reformer to garner support among those opposed to the pretender Carlos:

Al Sr. Dn. Francisco Martinez de la Rosa
Madrid 5 de Mayo de 1837

Excmo. Sr.

Habiendo llegado á oidos de la augusta Reina Gobernadora las quejas de varios literatos de esta corte sobre la usurpacion que se hace del derecho de propiedad literaria, señaladamente en lo relativo á obras dramáticas; y deseosa S.M. de remover todo obstáculo al desarrollo y fomento de un arte que tan inmediatamente influye en la cultura y civilizacion de los pueblos, se ha dignado resolver que una comision compuesta de VE, de Don. Antonio Gil de Zárate, Oficial de este Ministerio, y de Dn. Manuel Breton de los Herreros, Bibliotecario de la Nacional, presente á la mayor brevedad un proyecto de la ley que declare

[next page]

deslinde y afiance los derechos respectivos de la propiedad literaria en todos sus accidentes.

Los ingenios españoles, que tan ardientemente reclaman esta ley, no podran menos de ver una garantía de acierto, al contemplar al frente de la comision que ha de formarla, un nombre por tantos títulos respetable, y que ademas descuella entre los que mas lustre y honor han dado á la poesía ~~nacional~~ castellana. De orden de S.M. lo comunico a VE para el indicado objeto. Dios VG

[no signature]

La misma, menos el último parrafo, á Dn. Antonio Gil de Zárate
Yd. á Dn. Manuel Breton de los Herreros

[To Sr. Dn. Francisco Martinez de la Rosa
Madrid 5 May 1837

Esteemed Sir,

The august Queen Regent having heard the complaints of various writers of this court about the usurpation of the right of literary property that is being done, specifically as concerns dramatic works; and as Her Majesty desires to remove all obstacles from the development and promotion of an art that so immediately influences the culture and civilization of her people, she has deigned to resolve that a commission, composed of Your Excellency, Don Antonio Gil de Zárate, an Official of this Ministry, and Don Manuel Breton de los Herreros, National Librarian, presents as soon as possible, the project for a law that will declare,

(next page)

demarcate, and affirm the respective rights of literary property in all its incidents.

Talented Spanish writers, who so ardently clamour for this law, will certainly find a guarantee of success, by seeing at the head of the commission that will formulate it, a name respectable for its innumerable titles and that moreover, stands out among those who have given the greatest honour to ~~national~~ Castilian poetry. By order of Her Majesty I communicate this to your Excellency for the indicated reason. May God keep you.

(no signature)

The same, excepting the final paragraph, to Don Antonio Gil de Zárate Idem to Don Manuel Breton de los Herreros]

In contrast to the petition, in this notice there was very little attention given to the liberal aspects of *propiedad literaria* for dramatic works as modern property, save in two curious terms. 'Usurpation' is a synonym for theft and was the (criminal) act that Don Carlos was attempting on Isabel II's throne: just as he hoped to steal her name and title as Monarch, the title of author was being stolen from poets. Deslinde is a similarly interesting choice. The word denotes a clarification between two concepts or a division between, for example, two parcels of land. While the committee was to clarify the rights to be included or excluded from protection under dramatic *propiedad literaria*, it was also to divide up a traditional shared cultural heritage of dramatic poetry and delineate the extent of a poet's rights over his verse. The insertion of the term '*deslinde*' into the letter is yet another marker of the development of literary property upon the terms and models of landed property. Apart from those two words, however, the letter of appointment focused primarily on the benefits of literary property for the nation: the appointees were not directly charged to contemplate the natural rights of individual authors over their works, but rather the potential cultural gain for Spain promised by *derecho de autor*. Finally, the letter identified Bretón and Gil y Zárate only by their official roles in the government and not as poets, an indication of the reserved attitude with which they were to approach the case.

Only Martínez de la Rosa, the head of the committee, was addressed as a poet. The draft of the letter had noted his contribution to 'national' poetry, but the term was later eliminated in favour of the linguistic modifier 'Castilian.' The first term was modern and Romantic and reflected the idea of poetry as essential to Spain's cultural identity. In contrast, the second adjective removed Martínez de la Rosa from the political moment and from the collective construction of the modern state and shifted him into the space of tradition, inhabited by other poet-grandees who wrote in the same aristocratic language and who dated from before the post-imperial, Romantic reinvention of the nation. As a minister, Martínez de la Rosa had contributed to the progress of the nation; however, as a poet he had cultivated the linguistic heritage of Garcilaso and Quevedo. This distinction echoed contemporary views on the importance of literature in defining a nation and also clearly separated his duties as minister of state from those as a Castilian poet. He was to invoke public confidence in the committee because he was a poet himself, but was to proceed as a disinterested official member of the royal ministry.

At the same time (5 May 1837), the Queen published a royal decree. This royal circular served as a temporary measure to address literary property, and it both responded to and indeed publicized the literary crisis which had been protagonized by García Gutiérrez on 1 March 1836, narrated in the press in the intervening year, and presented by him and other poets to the Queen in Febuary 1837.

This royal order was the culmination of three years of deliberation on theatre reform, in general, and literary property, in particular. Attitudes had ranged from the relatively conservative 1833 decree regarding spectacle to the radically liberal responses to the poets' petition by the ministers, but all involved had concurred that authors' rights were vital to the rehabilitation of the national theatre. The hugely uneven language of the various manuscript versions of the decree reveals the ferocity of the debate over the issues of property, nationalism, theatre, and authors' rights – in essence, the nature of the state itself. The ministers' opinion (seen in non-public court documents) was only awkwardly reconciled with that of the Queen Regent, evident in the bizarre and sometimes contradictory mix of phrases and voices in the royal order. The apparent difficulty in selecting an ideological position is not surprising as this decree was to impose revolutionary modifications on the practices of an ancient and traditional theatre industry throughout Spain. Just one day before its proclamation, several of the most emotive elements of the argument were cut from the decree (per the draft from 4 May reproduced in the Appendix). The horrifying evocation of 'mutilations' on the stage (one of the strongest images in the petition) was suppressed, and only the term 'disfigured,' rhetorically more distant from the body, remained to illustrate the poets' claim of truly treacherous conditions in a theatre industry without authors' rights. The ideas of 'lucro' and 'just reward,' central to Flórez Estrada's brand of liberalism, as well as the definition of a poet's verse as a product, were also cut. The latter was transformed into the more artistic 'obra' or 'opus.' The removal of these three terms de-emphasized the natural-law model of intellectual property, which was too progressive for the Queen Regent's more tepid embrace of moderate liberalism but nevertheless provided the ideological foundation for the decree. That is, the new concept of Romantic authorship and writing as labour, which had been intertwined with the traditional definition of the theatre as wholly an element of the royal bureaucracy, was eliminated. The 'economic model' for copyright, with its intent to foment social welfare and entice more poets to create for the theatre (and its confirmation of the supremacy of the nation's benefit over those of individuals' needs), provided the justification here. The Queen Regent did not engage with the concept of a natural right (the Lockean 'natural-law model' favoured by the radical liberals). Likewise, the charged 'usurpation' was eliminated, and poets' income under the previous Bourbon kings was redefined as 'reduced' rather than 'stolen.' Authors' rights were certainly established by this decree; however, the primary justification was not the recognition of property rights of individual labourers or even the protection of Romantic selves, but rather the importance of the theatre to the culture of Spain. María Cristina simply facilitated poets' attempts at serving the state on the stage.

Several elements from the earlier stages of the measure, however, were retained and more fully developed in the decree. Although the extremely harsh condemnation of absolutism that characterized the ministers' commentary was diminished overall, as María Cristina projected continuity and improvement upon previous regimes, her husband did not escape unscathed in the circular and was still condemned as anti-intellectual. However, just as the royal right to rule passed from the eighteenth-century Bourbons to Isabel II, the legitimacy of María Cristina's royal order is based upon laws created by her husband's grandfather, recalled in the opening phrases of the decree.

The fact that absolutism had granted perpetual *privileges*, whereas the Queen Regent was sanctioning a *right* recognized by society, is simply not addressed. Rather, through the reformulation of the impersonal verb 'se aprueba' [is approved] into the active 'aprueba' [she approves], the Queen claimed personal responsibility for the passage of this act. As an Enlightened despot, more effectual than the *Cortes*, she could personally alleviate the poets' troubles, while her ministers and the Parliament elaborated a more permanent law. As reflected in the above revisions to the decree, in spite of public opinion, the poets' 'quejas' [complaints] were not 'justas' [just and justifiable] until deemed so by the Regent.

The definition of the theatre as the apex of national culture remained essential to the decree. The Queen confirmed its civilizing contribution to Spain and its ties to many of the nation's industries. But the decree's central tenet was its promise to lift the theatre from its decadence and eradicate the former abuse of poets' rights. The 'Golden Age' alluded to by the petitioners and in the ministers' evocation of decadence and dust is clearly articulated as the new regime's objective: the era of liberty and reinvention of the nation held the promise of a 'new' Golden Age, linking the reign of Isabel II with that of Spain's glorious past. Indeed, in the royal order, the poetry that will be staged under its protection is considered 'nacional' rather than Castilian, and tied to the wealth and culture of the collective polity. The imminent benefits of *derecho de autor* to individual property owners are, it is implied, to be matched by those to be shared by all Spaniards.

As Ronald Bettig has noted, histories of intellectual property law tend to be teleological and present the rise of authors' rights as a logical step in the evolution of modern civilization. In this approach, the particularities of their emergence have been altogether disregarded.[28] The royal order of 5 May 1837 presented that same teleological fiction within its text. According to its own narration, the decree not only recognized poets' property rights, but also self-consciously reversed the dismal trajectory of an 'abandoned and abused' theatre in a nation that was desperate to promote both culture and industry. In it, María Cristina claimed to have afforded dramatic literature with the theoretical and legal groundwork to flourish in a modern economy. The Regent suggested her 'Enlightened' consternation at the complaints presented by 'varios literatos' to have been the source of the decree and presented herself as mediator between the nation's theatre and the *Cortes*. Her decision was offered as the rational and utterly logical response to the institutionalized 'theft' of poets' rights – and her sensitivity to the importance of culture to the nation distinguished her from her absolutist predecessors, who had simply overlooked both the specific abuse and culture in general. With its mythological allusions (the Aegis of literary property transformed María Cristina into Minerva), this explanation corresponded to legal discourse of the early nineteenth century but masked the measure's social and cultural determinants.

The birth of literary property for dramatic works in Spain was not an inevitable step in the nation's advancement toward modernization, but rather a response to myriad circumstances specific to the brief historical period of its genesis. The *Progresismo* of the Queen's ministers in spring 1837, María Cristina's tenuous hold on the regency, the drive to modernize Spain, the Romantic reinvention of the nation, the spectre of the Golden Age stage, the centrality of the theatre to national identity, Spain's attempt at a cultural renaissance, the social, political, and economic realities of the Carlist war, and the *cause célèbre* of *El trovador* were all used to great advantage by Larra, Bretón, Ochoa, and the poets of their circle. A product of the almost accidental confluence of these various issues – most of which have little currency in present society – 'propiedad literaria ... en lo relativo á obras dramáticas' has legislated the way that dramatic poetry has been written, printed, produced, and read in Spain since.

STAGE TWO

Poets and Publishers

When members of the audience in the Príncipe Theatre called on 1 March 1836 for the author of *El trovador* to present himself, writers for the theatre acquired a new legal, social, and political identity. The public's question, '*¿Quién es el autor?*' would concern critics, from various vantage points, through the end of the next century. The legal outcome of the redefinition of *what* and *who* a theatre writer is began in 1837 with a modern idea of authorship. The law placed the poet and his text at the heart of stage production and, naming him owner of its immaterial property, considered him responsible for its creation. This section addresses earlier constellations of authority between poets and acting companies and between text and performance, as mediated by royal power and audience expectations, in order to clarify exactly what was modern about dramatic authorship. The second stage of literary property saw the rise of the dramatic *editor*, who stabilized and guaranteed the new legal and theoretical concepts and the practical arrangements of textual authority. The relationship between authors and *editores* evolved significantly over the course of the century, but during the early years of copyright their intimate relationship formalized the alienable rights of literary ownership. After an examination of the legal relationship between poets and *editores*, this section analyses the consequences of an alienable authorship on a national scale and the means by which *editores* represented and exercised their ownership rights outside of Madrid.

3 Authors between Stage and Page

The modern definition of a dramatic poet as author rested upon the treatment of a play as a fundamentally poetic and literary creation, rather than an inextricable element of spectacle, and granted the text an authority in performance.[1] The modern relationship between poets and their plays was initially resisted, because it stood in direct opposition to established practices. Nevertheless, copyright did take effect, and the dramatic *autor* did attain a brief tenure of supremacy in Spain over the next hundred and seventy years, until challenged by early-twentieth-century theories of the stage. Indeed, the tyranny of the text that would soon be vehemently attacked by the European vanguard was not an ancient tradition in Spain, but rather, a relatively recent phenomenon, tied to bourgeois property.

In contrast to this poetic authority, which was enshrined by law in the nineteenth century, twentieth-century theorists and practitioners, from a number of ideological positions, have argued that such authority should be wrested away from the poet and placed in the hands of a director, the public, or any number of agents in the performance. An early example is 'Oriental and Occidental Theatre,' in which the French playwright, critic, and director Antonin Artaud strongly advocated a reintegration into performance of other scenic languages that, in the Western tradition, had been devalued as a result of the exclusive attention to the linguistic aspect of stage productions. In his assessment of Western theatre, 'the Word is everything, and there is no possibility of expression without it; the theatre is a branch of literature ... The idea of the supremacy of speech in the theatre is so deeply rooted in us, and the theatre seems to such a degree merely a material reflection of the text, that everything in the theatre that exceeds this text, that is not kept within its limits and strictly conditioned by it, seems to us purely a matter of *mise en scène*, and quite inferior in comparison with the text.'² Although Artaud's proposed reforms were far-reaching in their radical departure from the dominant practices in European theatre more generally, what he presented as avant-garde was actually traditional Spanish practice. In the Spain of the sixteenth, seventeenth, and eighteenth centuries, the poet's text was understood to be in service of the larger art of theatrical production controlled by the performers and their director, and – a precedent of Artaud's theatrical liberation from the word – the writer's contribution was easily changed. While 'speech' was unarguably central to nineteenth-century Spanish theatre stagecraft, its supremacy over other scenic languages was the product of prolonged artistic and legal reforms.

The nineteenth-century development of poet-as-author was a result of an understanding of the relationship between writer and text based on 'natural law,' but it was neither fundamental to the nature of theatre as an art form nor necessarily an enduring concept. Contemporary critics who debate the treatment of plays as either theatre or literature would do well to bear in mind that intellectual property law and the 'birth' of the dramatic author have ensured that text will remain firmly entrenched in its privileged position in performances – as long as copyright law continues to exist as we know it today.

The challenges to the poet as author (owner and executor of the discourse of the stage) that took place in Spanish theatre were similar to what Michel Foucault formulated in his theoretical and historical analysis of the impersonal construct of the author-function in modern European literature.[3] In the pages that follow, I examine *who* and *what* a dramatic author was in Spain during the nineteenth century, both at the time of his legal construction, and at his deconstruction a century later.

'¿Quién es por acá el autor de una comedia?'

The nature of dramatic authorship received comparatively minimal attention in Spain during the first decades of the nineteenth century. Although indirectly implicated in the concerns about the quality of dramatic works, censorship, and the art of performance that were frequently raised during the first third of the century, the task of the dramatic poet was not fully re-evaluated until the 1830s. In '¿Qué cosa es por acá el autor de una comedia?' [What is the author of a play around here?] and its continuation, '¿Quién es por acá el autor de una comedia?' [Who is the author of a play around here?], from his series of articles on theatre, Larra offered an investigative essay on the ambiguous identity of 'the author of a play' in nineteenth-century Spain.[4] Unlike the audience at the Príncipe Theatre on 1 March 1836, his objective was not to discover the name of an individual author, but rather to assess the changing concept of a creator of a dramatic text. But, as with much of the reform advocated in his articles, the recognition of a dramatic author's property rights that Larra outlined here was frustrated by resistance to innovation at the time of its composition.

In these articles from 1832,[5] Larra unequivocally identified the poet and his text as the sole source of theatre. 'Supongamos por un momento que se retira el público, que no existen actores que representen, y que desaparece el local; todavía quedará la comedia escrita e impresa, que, si es buena, deleitará e instruirá a las gentes de casa en casa' [Let us suppose for a moment that the public steps away, that the actors don't exist and that the auditorium disappears; what will still remain is the written and printed play which, if it is good, will still entertain and instruct in each person's house].[6] Theatre's success was, in Larra's Enlightenment-inspired view, not dependent upon the agents of performance, but rather on the text's ability to fulfil the Horatian dictum to please and profit. Larra raises the possibility of reinventing theatre as an event that could easily and even preferably take place in private homes and gestures toward a negation of its collective, public nature. Larra's comments point not only to a new arrangement between text and reader and stage and audience, but also to the supremacy of the individual and his interpretive power over the communal and shared experience.

Larra's objective in the second, and longer, article – '¿Quién es por acá el autor de una comedia?' – was to argue aggressively the necessity of intellectual property for dramatic literature. The dramatic poet-author was a relatively ill-defined figure in the pre-Romantic period, whose legal and social authority was contingent upon the legislation and enforcement of literary property. Indeed, Larra opened his article (itself entitled with a question) with a second question, '¿Qué cosa es el derecho de propiedad?' [What are property rights?] – confirming the inseparable link between literary property and authorship as both emerged as complementary legal concepts in Spain in the 1830s. At the time of the composition of this article, Spanish society did not hold either the individual dramatic poet or the profession, in general, in great esteem. By highlighting the rights that contemporary poets did *not* have over their dramatic works, Larra illustrated why they needed literary property to materialize and to prosper as authors. Teasing out the logic of a property-based culture, Larra concedes that in spite of its philosophy of individualism, authorship is not an autonomous act: the modern dramatic author can only exist when his society recognizes and respects his property rights and his text cannot be changed by others.

In the first article ('¿Qué cosa es por acá el autor de una comedia?'), Larra pointed out the disparity between the public's (correct) perception that a poet was the source of a play and the lack of a law that recognized his authorship. Although most people probably supposed he already enjoyed the protection of his natural right, they were unaware that the law did not concede this to him:

> El mayor número de las gentes, cuando concurre a la representación de una comedia, y la aplaude si le parece buena, cree que el autor ha sacado el fruto de sus vigilias y del don rarísimo que de agradar a los más recibió de la Naturaleza; discurre espontáneamente y sin trabajo que aquella entrada y cuantas produce aquel drama son debidas al talento del autor, y que saliendo de aquellos fondos cuanto gasto se ocasiona, el autor aquel y los demás autores de comedias son los que dan de vivir a los actores, a las empresas y a todos los dependientes y sanguijuelas, que no son pocas, de semejantes casas. Esto parece natural a primera vista, y no se necesita haber cursado en Salamanca para conocer que a no haber dramas que representar, sean de la clase que se quiera, inútil sería el teatro con todas sus consecuencias. Pero como hemos nacido en el siglo de los prodigios, ha de saber el mayor número de las gentes que no sólo no es así, sino que se equivoca groseramente al pensarlo de esta suerte.[7]

> [Most people, when they attend the performance of a play and applaud it if it seems good, believe that the author produced it through careful study and the rare gift of pleasing others that he received from Nature. Likewise they assume spontaneously and easily that the receipts from that evening and in the future are a result of the talent of the author, who, like the authors of all other plays, provides a living for the actors, the theatre companies, and to all the dependents and leeches, of which there are more than a few, of such houses. This would seem natural at first glance, and it isn't necessary to have studied in Salamanca in order to know that without dramas to stage, whatever kind they may be, the theatre and all of its consequences would be useless. But, as we were born in the age of wonders,

most people should know that, not only are things not this way, but that in believing that they are, most people are grossly mistaken.]

Thus Larra concludes that until the labour of a poet is appreciated as the source of a performance, 'el autor de una comedia no es nadie por acá' [the author of a play is a nobody around here].[8]

Engaging with the Romantic idea of an author's work as an expression of his personality, and therefore part of his own being, Larra argues that the application of the rights of property, as they functioned elsewhere in society, to literary works in dramatic form would transform the poet into author and strengthen his relationship with his text. If property, as opposed to privileges, was the foundation of a new political economy, then dramatic authors were to acquire theirs through a recognition and respect of their authorial identity by their peers.

Larra broached the issue of literary property forcefully in his second article, posing as an innocent to challenge the rules of society and note the illogical exclusion of the labour of a poet from the general protection afforded to other labourers and their products. 'No comprendemos en realidad porqué ha de ser un autor dueño de su comedia; verdad es que en la sociedad parece á primera vista que cada cual debe ser dueño de lo suyo; pero este no se entiende de ninguna manera con los poetas' [We don't understand, really, why an author should be the owner of his play; the truth is that in society it seems, at first glance, that everyone ought to be the owner of his or her own things; but this in no way applies to poets]. Modern society had formalized the status of every other person vis-à-vis their possessions.[9] As a result of this exclusion from the system of property, poets were seen as somewhat less than human, as 'un animal que ha nacido como la mona para divertir gratuitamente á los demás, y sus cosas no son suyas, sino del primero que topa con ellas y se las adjudica.' [an animal born, like the monkey, to entertain everyone else for free, and his things are not his but rather belong to the first person to find them and claim them].[10] In the scene depicted by Larra, the dramatic poet is not simply marginalized from his Romantically appointed role as a privileged voice in society, but he is also incapable of executing it because he has yet to be fully accepted as a peer and humanized within Spain's new property-based economy.

The arguments for the necessity of a fundamental right of literary property in a rational liberal society and for financial recompense in order to save poets from becoming circus animals were followed by an even stronger description of other property rights that the Spanish dramatic poet did not enjoy: the authority to control the proliferation of his dramatic text and to intervene in the staging of the play. The tone of the essayist in the following passage is agitated, but not hyperbolic: until 1837, Spanish poets truly held no legal recourse to concede or negate permission for the performance of their texts, and plays were rarely staged in the form penned by the poet.

The campaign for property rights that would acknowledge a poet as an 'autor de una comedia' was fundamentally a battle over the control of the stage. In Larra's arrangement, actors trained in the art of spectacle would be displaced by men of letters armed with the authority of property rights as the individuals responsible for the content, composition, and success of theatrical productions. The current exclusion of the poet was presented as injudicious and detrimental to Art:

> Ved cómo corre su comedia de teatro en teatro; en todas partes gusta, pero acerquémosnos un poco mas. Aquí el corifeo de la compañía le despojó de su título, y le puso otro, hijo de su capricho, porque, ¿qué entienden los poetas de poner títulos á sus comedias? Allí otro cacique de aquellos indios de la *lengua* le *atajó* un *parlamento* ó le suprimió una escena, porque, ¿qué actor, por mal que represente, no ha de saber mejor que el mejor poeta dónde han de estar las escenas, y cuán largos han de ser los parlamentos y los diálogos, y todas estas frioleras del arte, particularmente si en su vida ha visto un libro, ni estudiado una palabra? Porque es de advertir que en materia de poesía, el que mas lee y mas estudia es el que menos entiende. Y gracias si la cuchilla de aquel bárbaro victimario no le suprimió entero el papel de un personaje, aunque fuera el del protagonista, que era el que menos falta hacia y mas fuera estaba de su lugar.[11]

> [See how his play moves from theatre to theatre; it is enjoyed everywhere, but let's get a little closer. Here, the Corypheus of the company stripped the play of its title and gave it another one, the fruit of a whim, because, what do poets know about giving titles to their plays? There another tribal chief of those Indians of *language lopped off* a *speech* or suppressed a scene from it, because, what actor, however poorly he may perform, isn't going to know better than the best poet where scenes should be and how long speeches and dialogues should be, and all these trifles of Art, in particular if he has never seen a book nor studied a word in his life? Because, mind you, the person who reads and studies the most is the one who understands the least. And thank heaven if the knife of that victimizing barbarian didn't

completely eliminate the role of a character, even if it were that of the protagonist, which was the least necessary and the most out of place.]

In this sarcastic description of the fate of a dramatic text under a system of actors, Larra decries the subordination of the poet's voice to the skills and needs of other agents of the production. Until society at large recognized the poet to be an *autor*, not only were his verses a shared good, but also even his name was not his own property. Larra reports that in provincial theatres the names of known authors were capriciously removed from playbills by crafty impresarios and replaced with poet's names of higher market value.[12] Because of this carnavalesque confusion of identities, the tie among name, fame, and literary value was severed, and a poet's name circulated and accrued value independently from the literary words or social deeds executed by the actual person with that name. According to Larra, in the view of the provincial theatre impresarios

> todos los hombres y todos los autores son iguales, y desde el ápice de sus ficticios tronos ven á todos los mayores ingenios tamaños como menudas avellanas, y hacen justicia de unos y de otros, y una masa comun de todas sus obras, fundados en que si tal autor no hizo tal obra, bien pudiera haberla hecho; y en el supremo tribunal de estos nuevos dispensadores de la fama lo mismo vale un Juan Perez que un Pedro Fernandez.[13]

> [all men and all authors are equal, and from the heights of their fictitious thrones they see all of the greatest minds the size of small hazelnuts and they pass judgment on every one, and they make a jumbled mass out of their works, based upon the idea that if a certain author didn't write a certain work, he might well have; and in the supreme tribunal of these new granters of fame, a Juan Perez is worth the same as a Pedro Fernandez.]

Larra's complaints might be expected, given that as a 'high' Romantic, he shared in the modern celebration of the individual. However, these same concerns were raised in the early 1830s by Larra's colleague and sometime rival Manuel Bretón de los Herreros (1796–1873), who is not usually considered a Romantic. Indeed, in many of his comedies, Bretón parodied Romantic sensibilities. The desire for a fixed text in performance and the moral right of attribution were not simply Romantic ideals but specific actions that impacted writers' working conditions.[14]

The King's *autores de comedia*

The rearrangement of the relationship between a poet and his text proposed by Larra and Bretón might seem painfully obvious to a twenty-first-century reader and, indeed, a commonplace to be challenged by avant-garde writers; however, in 1832 it suggested a radical departure from established practices. The tasks of staging (including the sanctioned custom of modifying dramatic texts according to the resources of the company) were traditionally executed by the head of an acting troupe, but not by the author of the text, except in the few cases they were the same person, such as Lope de Rueda in the sixteenth century. Before the legal reconfiguration of the dramatic poet into the 'autor de una comedia' in the later 1830s (as predicted and advocated by Larra), there was a distinct but nearly homonymic figure of the *autor de comedias* (that had existed in Spain for several centuries), as well as earlier meanings of the term 'autor' itself.

In nineteenth-century Spain, an *autor* was any person who was the source or responsible party of an event or entity. The meaning was certainly not strictly, or even primarily, an artistic one. The second definition of the term offered by the Spanish Royal Academy in their dictionary from the 1830s was a metaphoric application of the primary definition to lyric poets who penned a body of verses, since (as their activity approximated that of a creator) they could arguably be seen as the source, origin, and person responsible for the verses. This is the common meaning of the word 'author' today (a writer, in relation to his work, is an author), although the metaphor upon which this meaning of the term is based has been elided in common usage. While the designation of poets as authors was not novel in the nineteenth century, its regular application to dramatic poets vis-à-vis their *dramatic* texts was.

In Spain, the stage had traditionally been considered to be the appropriate venue for a theatrical spectacle in which the poet's text was simply one element among many. Before 1836, and well into the 1840s, those who wrote the verses of a play in Spain were generally not called '*autores*' but rather '*poetas dramáticos.*' As Hugo Rennert explains, in the Golden Age system of marketing and circulation of dramatic texts, the poet played only a very minor part: 'Having bought a play from its author [dramatic poet], it was of course to the interest of the purchasing manager [*autor de comedias*] to prevent its appearing in print and thus becoming common property. Besides, plays were often acquired surreptitiously by some individual possessing a good memory, who visited the theatre and noted down what he could, filling in the rest from memory or *de su cosecha*, and then disposing of them to some bookseller or theatrical manager.'[15] That is, it was in the interests of an *autor de comedias* to *prevent* the circulation of printed editions – the opposite of Larra's suggestion of individuals privately reading and interpreting authors' printed texts at home. In addition, the designation of an 'autor' as creator or originator in sixteenth-, seventeenth-, eighteenth-, and early nineteenth-century Spanish theatre was applied to the person deemed responsible for the entire stage production – not just the text. The same person was also financially responsible for the acting troupe.[16]

The official application of the term *autor* for an agent of the theatre evolved substantially over two hundred years. The ancient title 'autores de comedia' was destabilized in the 1830s as an appreciation of the composition of the text supplanted an appreciation of the task of coordinating the spectacle, and poets (theoretically) acquired the right to perpetual financial recompense (royalties, instead of the one-time payment they had traditionally received) according to the success of the production. After 1836, the term was more ambivalent when used in reference to the theatre, as can be seen in contemporary newspapers and even in articles by Larra and others in which it referred to both the old and new models of authority. But by the beginning of the twentieth century, writers of dramatic texts were consistently called authors, and the older agent called 'autor,' disappeared.[17]

The role of *autores de comedia* in pre-Romantic theatre was substantially different from that of poets – a distinction that has led to confusion by some modern literary historians ever concerned with the act of writing.[18] Some *autores* did write, but as most of the tasks of an *autor de comedias* were contrary to those of a modern creative literary author, we should be careful to not read the terms anachronistically.

In theory, from the sixteenth through the eighteenth century, anyone could write for the stage (although, as Herrera Navarro has pointed out, many did so anonymously).[19] In contrast, from the late sixteenth century through the end of the reign of Fernando VII, only a select few could be an 'autor.' They were producers of spectacles named by the Crown, and their activities were highly regulated by it. In 1603, the royal decree of the reformation of *comedias* had authorized only eight companies. In 1615 the number of authorized companies (each with an 'autor de título') rose to twelve.[20] During the Cadiz regency, the *autor de comedia* was no longer accountable to the Monarch but instead reported directly to the *ayuntamiento* of the 'pueblo' in which he worked. His authority, like that of all persons during the regency, was granted and recognized according to the will of the people rather than appointed by the Crown.[21]

Under the reign of Carlos III, José Antonio de Armona, the *Corregidor* of Madrid and the *Juez Protector general de todos los teatros y representantes del Reino* codified and enumerated the responsibilities of these royal agents.[22] The royally authorized *autores* were responsible to the Monarch (and his representatives) for the visual and linguistic content of the productions and also for the financial solvency of the company.

After 1777, all *autores* in the kingdom received an identical annual budget and were required to keep strict accounts, furnish the physical space of the theatre, provide actors with costumes, and procure other necessary supplies (e.g., 'alumbrado, soldados, iluminacion de faroles, adehalas de compania, velas de los musicos, cartels de apuntador [etc.]' [house lights, stagehands, torch lighting, gratuities, candles for the musicians, prompter's cards]). Moreover, Armona dictated, in a four-page list, the props that each *autor de comedia* was required to provide for performances by his company. These 'standard' props ranged from the expected 'coronas' [crowns], 'bandejas' [trays], and 'tapices' [tapestries] to 'ataúdes y paños para cubrirlos' [coffins and cloths to cover them] and 'abanicos ridículos' [ridiculous fans].[23] Thus, the stage production organized by the *autor* was the result of the strict material contingencies (stage properties and money) imposed and normalized by the state, the number of actors (arranged by royal command and custom), and the malleable text.

Once authorized to organize and originate performances, the *autor* was legally responsible for both the company's activities and its well-being, as well as controlling audience response to performances. In sum, the *autor de comedias* was financially and ideologically responsible for all aspects of theatrical discourse (both textual and spectacular) until literary property law transformed and transferred legal authority and originality onto the dramatic poet – a move that would have tremendous consequences for the treatment of the text in the theatre and in print.

Qué est-ce qu'un auteur?

Whereas the audience in the Príncipe Theatre asked 'who' a particular author was, and Larra had asked why he was not who he should be,

Michel Foucault, in his essay on authorship, described 'what' the author was in modern European society. He outlined the relationship between the privatization of knowledge and the individualization of property rights in literature in terms of power and the control of discourse. His 'author-function' is an impersonal construct that bears legal and social responsibility for the content and circulation of literary works pertaining to it. This authorial responsibility was most often attached to the person of the *writer*, but could (and did) develop and function independently from a human figure. Foucault argues that later readers have understood this fusion of social and juridical persons into the legally recognized author to be sacrosanct, indivisible from the text or from either the juridical or the social persons, without a full awareness of its construction. Along these same lines, Martha Woodmansee has successfully challenged the universally held modern conception of the author, defining it instead as a recent 'reconceptualization of the creative process that culminated less than 200 years ago in the heroic self-presentation of Romantic poets.'[24] The protection of 'originality' has since served as the justification for the rights and responsibilities of ownership and literary property law (in the title of authorship). However, the seemingly transparent title of 'author' given to a dramatic poet, based on a consideration of his proprietary relationship to his text, sidesteps the network of political and economic relations of power that were inextricable from the creation, dissemination, and consumption of dramatic texts in the first years of copyright. As much as Larra might have dispensed with actors, he was keenly aware of the power of the stage and its position at the heart of cultural life. A new, but nevertheless complex, system quickly developed to bring texts from poets to readers.

Individual authorship was debated and literary property laws (re)legislated in 1833, 1837, 1844, 1848, and 1879. However, although these laws were successfully passed multiple times, in practice they did not create a large number of propertied poets or greatly increase the number of individuals authorized to control dramatic discourse. Instead, as will be discussed in the next chapter, the laws of *derecho de autor* consolidated the property of dramatic literature into the hands of fewer than a dozen non-literary businessmen, as most poets chose to sell their property rights to publishers or 'editores.' Also, the high *derecho de licencia* (fee paid to the government to run a theatre) effectively kept the institution of the theatre under the control of impresarios with substantial economic, social, or political power. Nevertheless, the dramatic author began to exist in name in the nineteenth century: both under the law and on the title pages of printed dramatic literature.

In contrast to the relative paucity of discernible eighteenth-century dramatic authors (and anonymous ones at that), a cult of authorship exploded in the middle decades of the nineteenth century.[25] After the passage of intellectual property laws in the 1830s and 1840s, the title of authorship itself would become commodified along with the author's property rights, but the practice of consistent attribution only slowly took hold. The novelty of the relationship between name and authorship, or between individual identity and private literary property, was evident in the ritualized calls by the public for a play's unnamed author to reveal his identity. The literary personality of the nineteenth-century dramatic author became a precious construct, ritualistically created by the public and the poet. His identity was the product of cultivated fame and deftly manipulated advertising (such as the journalistic narratives surrounding García Gutiérrez, as discussed in chapters 1 and 2) that enticed audiences to clamor for the author's mysterious identity to be revealed.

For example, one week before the premiere of *Don Juan Tenorio*, the journal *El laberinto* offered a flattering portrait and generous biography of José Zorrilla, promoting his literary personality and advertising his printed works to subscribers (fig. 1). The promotional article closed with the following remark: 'Tambien el teatro ha sido campo de sus victorias literarias ... *D. Juan Tenorio*, drama que ha de representarse en breve ornará sin duda con nuevos lauros la coronada frente del poeta' [The theatre has also been an arena for his literary victories ... *Don Juan Tenorio*, a drama that will be staged very soon, will undoubtedly adorn the poet's brow with new laurels].[26] Before the theatre public called for the poet to reveal his supposedly 'unknown' identity one week later, the periodical, owned by Ignacio Boix (the editor of some of Zorrilla's lyric poetry), had generated interest in the literary personality of a rising young star by publicizing his name.

In yet another article dealing with authorial identity, Larra described the public's creation of Juan Eugenio Hartzenbusch as author after his name was pronounced at the premiere of *Los amantes de Teruel*. Larra saw this ritualized call for the author as not merely a game among writers, theatre publics, and publicity agents, but rather a process by which writers – and theatre, in general – was to be regenerated. Larra began his review of the premiere by exaltedly describing the *birth* of a poet as author:

Venir á aumentar el número de los vivientes, ser un hombre mas donde tantos hombres; oir decir de sí: es un *tal fulano*, es ser un arbol mas en una alameda. Pero pasar cinco ó seis lustros oscuro y desconocido, y llegar una noche entre otras, conovocar á un pueblo, hacer tributaria su curiosidad; alzar una cortina, conmover el corazon, subyugar el juicio, hacerse aplaudir y aclamar, y oir al dia siguiente de sí mismo al pasar por una calle ó por el Prado, *aquel es el escritor de la comedia aplaudida*, eso es algo; es nacer; es devolver al autor de nuestros dias por un apellido oscuro un nombre claro ...[27]

[To increase the number of the living, to be another man among many men; to hear others say of you: he is just *some guy*, that is to be just another tree in the forest. But to spend twenty-five or thirty years in the shadows and unknown, and then to arrive one night, bring together a public, dominate its curiosity; to raise a curtain, move hearts, conquer judgments, be applauded and acclaimed, and hear others say of you the next day as you stroll down the street or through the Prado, *there is the writer of a successful play*, that is something; it is to be born, it is to return to authors of our day an honourable name.]

According to Larra, the dramatic author is conceived by and born of both legal and public recognitions of a writer's talent and labour. Authorship is not an absolute identity applied to all who write, but rather a marker of success and a means to economic recompense.

In 'El Romanticismo y los Románticos' [Romanticism and the Romantics], Mesonero Romanos, the essayist and social critic from the mid-nineteenth century whose attitudes reflected more conservative bourgeois values,[28] parodied this indulgent treatment of dramatic authors and the public fascination with their names. His essay satirizes the craze about their sacred identity and suggests that the ceremonial call was losing its value as it had begun to be done indiscriminately for any new play.[29] The essayist reproduces the fictitious playbill for the dramatic piece written by his supposedly Romantically ailing nephew. Below the title there appears a note that teases: 'Por ... *Cuando el público pida el nombre del autor*' [By ... *When the public asks for the author's name*]. In spite of his sarcasm, Mesonero precisely questions the limits of authorial identity by insinuating that if the public does not ask, '¿Quién es el autor?' upon the conclusion of the play, the *autor* and his publicly created authority do not exist.

Mesonero presents the possibility of a public that is well aware an individual 'genius' had created an original play text but, without interest in his person or personality, refuses to perform its role. Clearly, the play discussed by the narrator is very poor, and the public is right not to call for the author to appear. By withholding public authorship, a theatre audience invalidates the classification of the play as worthy of value, as a property that should be owned. Who creates an immaterial property: writers, the law, or the public?

In contrast, when the public called for the poet indiscriminately, the theatre itself suffered, for the distinction between good and bad literature was effectively erased. According to the 1837 royal order, legal authorship was intended to elevate the quality and quantity of original dramatic literature produced in Spain during its 'new Golden Age.' The legal rights of authorship were certainly to be extended to all poets, but not every author of a play deserved public admiration. The tension between 'high' and 'low' or 'artistic' and 'popular' theatre, and between poets who wrote plays of a high literary quality versus those who wrote for the public's entertainment and pleasure, was yet another ill-defined aspect of the identity of the dramatic author. What was an author? A democratically applied legal definition or a marker of literary elitism? The journal *El entreacto* attempted to train the public to realize its obligation and to designate poets as authors judiciously.[30] According to this journal, authorship was not only ownership but also a title of the aristocracy of talent, to be bestowed by the public only upon creators of works of superior merit. Literary property could rejuvenate the stage, but a public with a poor aesthetic education was, in the opinion of the writers at *El entreacto*, jeopardizing the quality of theatre in Spain. José Zorrilla was the first poet to be announced as author on theatre posters, before performance. In his memoirs, Zorrilla writes that this was seen as an audacious challenge and an affront to the public, and he relates how other dramatic poets studied the play for weaknesses in order to ensure his downfall during performance and punish him for his vanity. The play, *Segunda parte de El zapatero y el Rey* was a sequel, and therefore Zorrilla's authorship was evident.[31] Nevertheless, the publication of the poet's name as author before performance flouted the new conventions of authorship and the public's role in it.

The new authorship of the poet in the theatre would remain merely a legal and artistic theoretical construct, with little change in actual performance practices, until the 1840s. However, Spanish poets working in Madrid in the 1830s were eager to assume responsibility for dramatic discourse – although many were reluctant to engage with the financial aspects of legal authorship. The gradual metamorphosis of Spanish poets into *autores* was evident in the 1839 *refundición* of Larra's article 'Una primera representación' [A premiere], originally printed in April 1835. Whereas Larra had proposed theatrical agency for poets and then despaired of its possibility, later in the decade, it was presented as a hopeful, if not completely certain, future.

In Larra's original 'Una primera representación,' the poet does not see himself as responsible for the success of the performance, but rather as utterly powerless over the dramatic discourse. He pleads for help from actors 'en ademán de pedir perdón' [in a gesture of begging forgiveness], imploring them to select costumes appropriate for their roles, to declaim their lines with art, and ultimately to recognize their profession itself as an art. During the performance, the actors perform abominably, the audience mills about the auditorium, and all of the other aspects of the production are executed dreadfully. As no one had respected the poet's authority over the production, these other people ruined the representation of the literary work. But, Larra's narrator bemoans the irony that when the performance is a failure, the author is deemed responsible – when it is a success, the poet is not mentioned.

Larra's article was rewritten four years later (after copyright) as 'La primera representación' by an unnamed writer at *El entreacto*.[32] There have been changes from the situation described by Larra: now the poet does retain authorial supremacy, and his labour is recognized when the play is a *success*. However, the tone remains negative in spite of the moderate improvements. In the new version (written in first person), the poet is still fearful of the audience, but he does not beg the actors to do his bidding. In spite of the fact that actors are not dressed moments before the play is to begin and that the costumes of the extras are 'una porquería, el público los va á silvar …' [are a mess, the public is going to hiss at them], the beauty of the text supersedes these flaws. The poet thanks the actors and the extras, but ultimately he regards himself as responsible for the favourable reception of the play. Thus, the article presents a positive example of what *El entreacto* considered appropriate treatment of the poet, leading to a successful stage production. At the end of the performance, 'muchos aplausos le siguieron, se pidió el nombre del autor, y sin embargo salí del teatro descontento y aun enfermo. Esto le pasa al autor que escapa bien ¡ay del silbado!' [it was followed by lots of applause, the author's name was called for, but nevertheless I left the theatre unhappy and even sick. This is what happens to the author who escapes – woe to the one who gets hissed at!].

Although both the poet and the public recognize his authorial responsibility for the piece, the actors, stagehands, and agents of *spectacle* do not. Their utter disregard for his authority has not sabotaged the play in this case – although it might the next time.

Copyright was argued for by poets, authorship was realized by theatre audiences, but the source of authority between page and stage remained unresolved. Theatre copyright led to the definitive transformation of the *autor* from the 'authorized director' to the 'poeta dramático.' However, centuries of established customs in the theatre industry and a Romantic poets' ideological rejection of lucre and materialism left unclear, for several decades, just exactly who an author was. Out of the disjuncture between established practices and legal impositions, a new agent would emerge to replace the old *autor de comedias* in mediating between play and production (stage and print). However, instead of modifying or rearranging the verses, his primary task would be to protect the new identity of the author, the inviolability of the text, and the value of intellectual property. A modern writer could not own authorship without either the public or his publisher.

4   *Editores* and Owners

Spanish literary property laws recodified authorship according to ownership and proprietary claims and transformed the meaning of the term 'autor dramático' and the understanding of the poet's contribution to the spectacle. As a result, copyright laws for theatre guaranteed that not only poetry, but also authorship itself, should become a commodity, available for exchange in the literary marketplace. The figure who bought and sold dramatic copyrights and authorships was the new literary entrepreneur of the nineteenth century, the 'editor.' Indeed, his presence was so great that according to Spanish historian Jesús A. Martínez Martín, the nineteenth century should be considered 'el tiempo de los editores' [the epoch of the *editores*].[1] He was born, like the dramatic author, out of intellectual property law but, for the most part, disappeared by about 1900, when the majority of dramatic poets began to retain both their copyrights and their legal authorships. During his period of influence of nearly seventy years, the impact of the *editor* on the production of nineteenth-century dramatic literature in Spain was decisive, but, because of a scholarly tradition of author-based criticism, his role has generally been overlooked.[2]

Poets and novelists had long turned to booksellers, printers, and other literary agents to purchase their manuscripts and to administer the dissemination of their works. However, the *editor* was unlike his predecessors in many ways. As opposed to the situation in the seventeenth century, described in chapter 3, copyright theoretically stabilized the text, and the ties between the play and the author's personhood were rendered nearly inseverable.[3] When he bought a dramatic copyright, the *editor* became the owner of the immaterial property and, in essence, a double of the author, as authorship itself became a commodity. The *editor* existed as a function of a reconciliation of ideological incompatibilities between poets as removed from society and modern ideas of property. He was, as Christine Haynes has argued, 'not a natural outcome of technological and economic change, but a construction of law and literature.'[4] The activities of this new copyright agent included serving as an exclusive patron-figure to the poet, providing a one-time exchange of money for verse (thus appropriating the perpetuity of literary property), and collecting the legally stipulated royalties. He buffered the writer from the commercial world of a nascent market economy and its ever-growing theatre and reading public. However, he was different from today's publishers in that he legally assumed the name 'autor.'

Before literary property, the duties of the *editor* in book production had not constituted an independent profession, but were part of a larger process of textual creation that included printing and selling by several people. The technological, educational, and economic advances of the modern era prompted an individualization of this aspect of book production as printers, *editores*, and booksellers evolved into three separate professions.[5] Indeed, linguistically, the modern *editor* first appeared officially in the Royal Academy dictionary of 1803, where he was defined as, 'el que saca á luz, ó publica alguna obra agena, y cuida de su impresion' [he who brings to light or publishes some work not his own and watches over its printing]. Specifically, he was in charge of supervising its reproduction for readers; that is, its printing. But as novel as the role of the *editor* was in the beginning of the nineteenth century, part of this definition was taken from an earlier entry for 'autor.' In the 1732 dictionary, the second definition of an *autor* was '... el que escribe libros, y compóne y saca á luz otras obras literarias' [he who writes books and composes and brings to light other literary works]. The definition of *editores* from 1803 highlights the importance of the *editor* in 'bringing to light' (into the space of knowledge) or presenting to consumers literary works written by authors (others) and was the first blurring of the distinction between the functions of the author and the *editor*.

In addition to the arguments for writers put forth by Larra and the petitioners, others, informed by the philosophy behind Fernando VII's 1826 measure for *propiedad industrial*, reasoned that literature should be treated like other industries. This would, they argued, foster its aesthetic rejuvenation and economic modernization. Writing in London in 1834, Antonio Alcalá Galiano discussed what he considered to be the most effective means of improving the quality of literature written in Spain, including a free press and cessation of censorship. But beyond these more obvious measures, Alcalá Galiano added *capital* to the classic triad of readers, authors, and texts, as an element that would come from a new, outside source to increase the quantity and quality of new literature in Spain: 'La escasez de lectores, la falta de capital en el negocio de libros, el limitado número de autores, y el no menos pequeño numero y baja calidad de sus obras...' [the scarcity of readers, the lack of capital in the book business, the limited number of authors and the equally small number and low quality of works ...][6] were, according to Alcalá, the primary reasons for poor literature in Spain. Alcalá Galiano believed that commercialization of the book trade was necessary for literature, itself subject to industrialization, to grow.

Similarly, in the March 1837 essay 'Costumbres literarias,' Ramón de Mesonero Romanos offered a fictionalized account of the Spanish poet's complex relationship with the market in the period immediately preceding the rise of the dramatic *editor*. His portrayal illustrates the evolving – and contradictory – attitudes toward literature in a capitalist society that led writers to literary *editores*. Written during a period when poetic treatises calling for reforms in composition were common, 'Literary Customs' stands out as an appeal for an extra-literary reform of the market such that capital would stimulate the field without compromising the poet's Romantic image. As seen in chapter 3, Mesonero had little patience for the preciousness of dramatic authorship, but he did approve of copyright as a way to support literature more generally.

His essay is composed of four sections. Each describes an element of literature that Mesonero considered wanting in modernization before more accomplished works could be created in Spain. The first, 'Literatura' [Literature], defines the place of this art in society during the Golden Age, during the eighteenth century, and in contemporary Spain. During the seventeenth century, a successful poet had to be graced with literary talent and be adept at *intriga cortesana* [courtly intrigue] in order to create great works; during the second period, only high-placed ministers wrote poetry. As a result of literature's association with power and elitism, Mesonero's contemporaries mistakenly saw literature merely as a vehicle to a position in the government bureaucracy. Because they wrote solely for career advancement (and were rewarded), Spain had facilitated a *prostitucion de las letras* [prostitution of literature]. The second section, 'El Manuscrito' [The Manuscript], discusses the aesthetic and thematic freedom available to writers since the end of Ancien Régime censorship. However, as literature is seen as a means to a government position, rather than as an end unto itself, contemporary poets practise self-censorship, avoiding artistic themes and instead choosing to write about current events in the newspapers. That is, Mesonero Romanos suggests that writers are already functioning within the confines of a market and are eager for rewards – it is simply that direct monetary compensation had not been available.

The third and fourth sections directly call for an industrialization of the literary world. 'La librería' [The Bookstore] describes both the unmodern, belaboured process by which a manuscript slowly becomes a book and the dismal appearance of bookstores. Indeed, because of writers' supposed ineptitude in the commercial realm and their responsibility for the creation and marketing of their own books, it was difficult for Mesonero's readers to procure good-quality texts. Enumerating the tasks involved in bringing a literary work from the pen of the writer to the hands of a reader, Mesonero depicts a tortuous process, one to which a writer is ill-suited.

However, Mesonero does not suggest that poets should learn the technical skills necessary to deal with accountants and booksellers in order to produce a book; rather, writers should deal exclusively with poetic composition. Merchants of literature must assume responsibility for all of the commercial and material aspects of book production and distribution in order for quality texts to be produced in Spain. This separation of labour that Mesonero proposed reflected an ideological framework in which Romantic poets, disenchanted by the material aspects of modernity, could remain dedicated to their art, while printers and booksellers concerned themselves primarily with profit. The Spanish *editor* arose out of this gap.

Whereas Larra had qualified the *theatre* as the thermometer of the nation's degree of civilization, Mesonero measures Spain's cultural status according to the bookstore and literature's commercial health. The status of literature in Spain was manifest in the bookstores' sorry physical aspect. Mesonero saw Spanish bookstores as anti-commercial, and booksellers as opposed to the innovation, enterpreneurship, and industrialization that had revolutionized other small businesses. Instead of encouraging the sale of texts and the dissemination of ideas, booksellers were hidden away in a pre-modern squalor. Equating commerce with civilization, Mesonero argues that a greater commercial spirit ('good' business practices) on the part of booksellers would allow literature to achieve the degree of civilization found in other aspects of modern Spanish life.[7]

1 Front page of *El laberinto* with portrait and biographical sketch of José Zorrilla (Madrid, 16 March 1844).

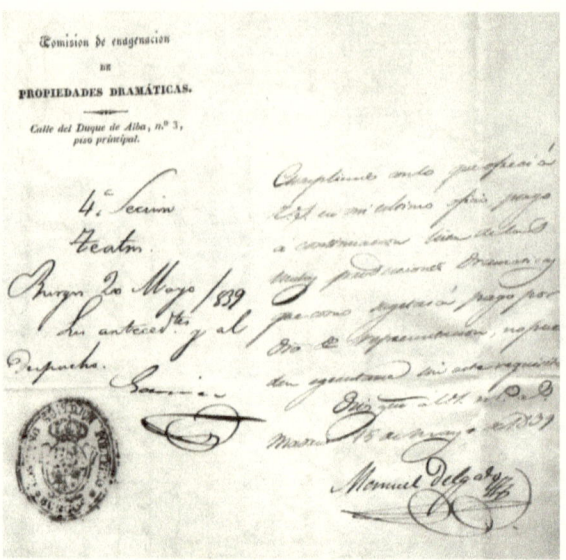

2   Letter from Manuel Delgado to the Censor of Burgos confirming that copyright will be paid to his 'Comision de enagenacion de propiedades dramáticas' before the Censor will permit performance.

3   Censor's approbation of performance of *La escuela de los periodistas*, Valladolid, 26 January 1842: 'Puede representarse en calidad de que esté pagado el derecho de propiedad' [May be staged on the condition that copyright is paid].

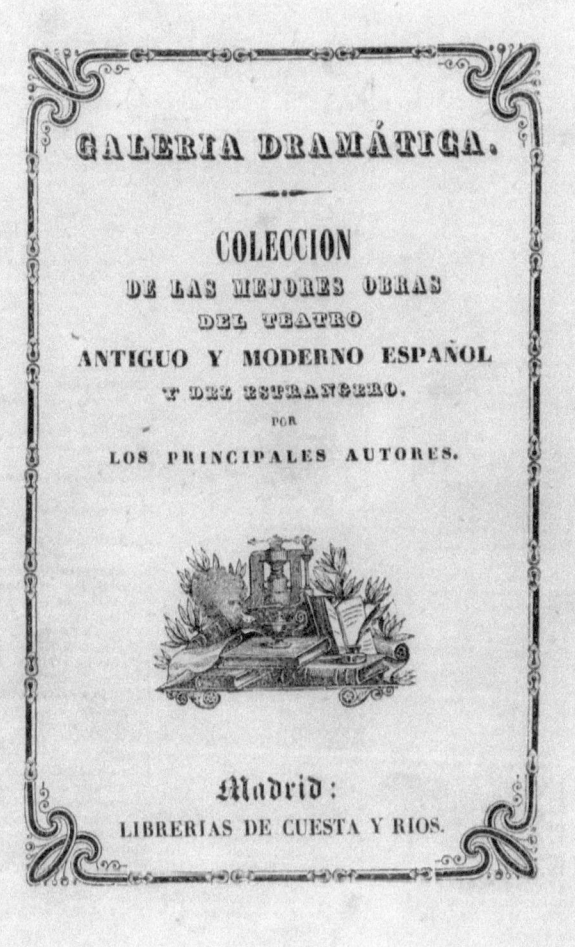

4 Galería Dramática wrapper from 1842.

*Se halla en Madrid en las librerías de Es-
camilla, calle de Carretas; en la de Cuesta,
frente á las Covachuelas, y en las provincias en
las siguientes:*

Habana............	*Alegría.*
Cádiz...............	*Hortal y compañía.*
Barcelona........	*Piferrer.*
Valladolid........	*Rodríguez.*
...a...............	*Yagüe.*
...ia.............	*Sanz.*
...encia..........	*Mallen.*
Coruña............	*Pérez.*
Burgos.............	*Arnaiz.*
Vitoria.............	*Hormilugue.*
Santander........	*Martinez.*
Santiago..........	*Rey Romero.*
Sevilla.............	*Caro Cartaya.*
Oviedo.............	*Longoria.*
Salamanca.......	*Moran.*
Málaga.............	*Viuda de Aguilar*
Murcia.............	*Benedicto.*
Pamplona........	*Suarez.*
Córdoba...........	*Berard.*
Badajoz............	*Viuda de Carrillo y sobrinos.*
Alcoy...............	*Cabrera.*
Jerez................	*Bueno.*
Palencia...........	*Pastor.*

5   Back cover of play edition from 1840 with a list of the cities and bookstores throughout Spain and Cuba where the play was sold.

Propiedades de que consta la Biblioteca Dramática.

TRADUCCIONES.

EN UN ACTO.

El paje de Woodstock.
La Barbera del Escorial.
El derecho de primogenitura.
Un buen marido!
La vida por partida doble.
Percances de la vida.
El maestro de escuela.
La hija del bandido.
La muger eléctrica.
El confidente de su muger.
La viuda de 15 años.
La pupila y la péndola.
Mas vale tarde que nunca.
La cocinera casada.
Tom-Pus, el marido confiado.
Dos contra uno.
El marido de la Reina.
Con todo y con ninguno.
Perder y ganar un trono.
El hijo de mi muger.
Invertir, bravo y barbero.
Un tio rico con dos camas.
Muerto civilmente.
—El doctor Capirote.
—Los dos maridos.
—Amante y hermana á un tiempo.
El mudo por compromiso ó las emociones.
Un Juan Lanas.
Las camaristas de la Reina.
—Una muchachada.
El usurero.
Una cabeza de ministro!
El raptor y la cantante.
Una noche á la intemperie.
Memorias de dos jóvenes casadas.
Un diablillo con faldas.

EN DOS ACTOS.

El rey de los criados y acertar por carambola.
La ja de mi tio.
César ó el perro del castillo.
Un pintor millonario.
Los soldados del rey de Roma.
La modista alferez.
Un avo.
El lazo; Margarita.
El Guarda-bosque.
El diablo nocturno.
Un casamiento con la mano izquierda.
Un padre para mi amigo.
La probada sin saberlo.
Una broma pesada.
El Corredor de Madrid.
El caballo de Griñon.
Ni ella es ella, ni él es él, ó el capitan Mendoza.

El robo de un hijo.
Los pasteles de María Michon.
Dos noches, ó un matrimonio por agradecimiento.
—Las dos épocas, ó restauracion y terror.
Cuando quiere una muger!!

EN TRES ACTOS.

Mi vida por su dicha.
Un dia de libertad.
La Abadia de Penmarck.
El vivo retrato.
El diablo y la bruja.
Casarse á oscuras.
Deshonor por gratitud.
La heredera.
El novio de Buitrago.
El guante y el abanico.
Clara Harlow.
Uno de tantos bribones.
Julian el carpintero.
El zapatero de Lóndres.
Los templarios, ó la encomienda de Aviñon.
Reinar contra su gusto.
El tarambana.
Los mosqueteros de la Reina.
Vencer su eterna desdicha ó un caso de conciencia.
Luchar contra el destino.
Una cura por homeopatía.
Un casamiento á son de caja, ó las dos vivanderas.
—La boda y el testamento.
No ha de tocarse á la reina.

EN CUATRO ACTOS.

Jorge el armador.
La mano derecha y la mano izquierda.
El doctor negro.
—Beltran el marino.

EN CINCO ACTOS.

La hermana del soldado.
Fausto de Underwal.
Los prusianos en la Lorena, ó la honra de una madre.
Las intrigas de una corte.
El agiotage ó el oficio de moda.
La hermana del carretero.
La Corona de Ferrara.
En la falta vá el castigo.
Las huérfanas de Amberes.
Las colegialas de Saint-Cyr.
—París el gitano.
Maria Juana, ó las consecuencias de un vicio.
El diablo en Madrid.
Nuestra Señora de los Avismos, ó el castillo de Villemeuze.
La hija del Regente.
El castillo de S. Mauro.
Fuerte-Espada el aventurero.

La noche de S. Bartolomé de 1572.
El nudo Gordiano.
—Juana Grey.
La Alqueria de Bretaña.
Gustavo III ó la conjuracion de Suecia.
Nunca el crimen queda oculto á la Justicia de Dios, 6 cuadros.
Los mosqueteros, id.
El pacto sangriento, ó la venganza corsa, id.
El leñador y el ministro, ó el testamento y el tesoro, id.
El médico negro, 7 cuadros.
El mercado de Lóndres, id.
Martin y Bamboche, ó los amigos de la infancia, en 9 cuadros.

ORIGINALES.

EN UN ACTO.

Perder el tiempo.
Un error de tipografia.
La joven y el zapatero.
La herida de Clavijo.
Engaños por desengaños.
Una conspiracion.
Tanto por tanto, ó la capa roja.
Un casamiento por poderes.
Estudios históricos.
La posada de Gurrillo.
Dos y ninguno.
Jai que jembra.
Una accion improvisada.
—Cosas del dia.
—El marinero, ó un matrimonio repentino.
José María, ó vida nueva.
La feria de Ronda.
De Cádiz al Puerto.
Es el demonio!!
El andaluz en el baile.
Un tio como otro cualquiera.
—El cautivo de Lepanto.
El tio y el sobrino.
Ilusiones.
La cantinera.
La ley del embudo.
La Perla sevillana.

EN DOS ACTOS.

En la confianza está el peligro.
Si acabarán los enredos?
Juan de las Viñas.
Mateo el veterano.
El premio grande.
El hermano del artista.

EN TRES ACTOS.

El médico de su honra.
—Yo por vos y vos por otro!!
Los infantes de Carrion.
La reina Sibila.
Un motin contra Esquilache.

---

6   Biblioteca Dramática catalogue from 1848: 'Propiedades de que consta la Biblioteca Dramática' [Properties held by the Biblioteca Dramática].

EL TESTAMENTO.

DRAMA EN UN ACTO,

TRADUCIDO DEL FRANCÉS

POR

DON VENTURA DE LA VEGA.

Representado en el teatro del Príncipe el 26 de Agosto de 1831.

SEGUNDA EDICION.

MADRID.

IMPRENTA DE REPULLÉS.

1842.

7   Title page of *El testamento*, with Manuel Delgado's initials in laurels.

Artículos de los Reglamentos orgánicos de Teatros, sobre la propiedad de los autores ó de los editores que la han adquirido.

«El autor de una obra nueva en tres ó mas actos percibirá del Teatro Español, durante el tiempo que la ley de propiedad literaria señala, el 10 por 100 de la entrada total de cada representacion, incluso el abono Este derecho será de 3 por 100 si la obra tuviese uno ó dos actos.» *Art 10 del Reglamento del Teatro Español de 7 de febrero de 1849*

«Las traducciones en verso devengarán la mitad del tanto por ciento señalado respectivamente á las obras originales, y la cuarta parte las traducciones en prosa.» *Idem art. 11.*

«Las refundiciones de las comedias del teatro antiguo, devengarán un tanto por ciento igual al señalado á las traducciones en prosa, ó á la mitad de este, segun el mérito de la refundicion.» *Idem art. 12.*

«En las tres primeras representaciones de una obra dramática nueva, percibirá el autor, traductor, ó refundidor, por derechos de estreno, el doble del tanto por ciento que á lo misma corresponda. *Idem art. 13*

«El autor de una obra dramática tendrá derecho á percibir durante el tiempo que la ley de propiedad literaria señale, y sin perjuicio de lo que en ella se establece, un tanto por ciento de la entrada total de cada representacion, incluso el abono. El máximum de este tanto por ciento será el que pague el Teatro Español, y el minimum la mitad.» *Art. 59 del decreto orgánico de Teatros del Reina, de 7 de febrero de 1849.*

«Los autores dispondrán gratis de un palco ó seis asientos de primer órden en la noche del estreno de sus obras, y tendrán derecho á ocupar tambien gratis, uno de los indicados asientos en cada una de las representaciones de aquellas.» *Idem art. 60.*

«Los empresarios ó formadores de Compañias llevarán libros de cuenta y razon, foliados y rubricados por el Gefe Político, á fin de hacer constar en caso necesario los gastos y los ingresos.» *Idem art 78.*

«Si la empresa careciese del permiso del autor ó dueño para poner en escena la obra, incurrirá en la pena que impone el art. 23 de la ley de propiedad literaria.» *Idem art. 81.*

«Las empresas no podrán cambiar ó alterar en los anuncios de teatro los títulos de las obras dramáticas, ni los nombres de sus autores, ni hacer variaciones ó atajos en el testo sin permiso de aquellos; todo bajo la pena de perder, segun los casos, el ingreso total ó parcial de las representaciones de la obra, el cual será adjudicado al autor de la misma, y sin perjuicio de lo que se establece en el artículo antes citado de la ley de propiedad literaria.» *Idem art. 82.*

«Respecto á la publicacion de las obras dramáticas en los teatros, se observarán las reglas siguientes:

1.ª Ninguna composicion dramática podrá representarse en los teatros públicos sin el previo consentimiento del autor.

2.ª Este derecho de los autores dramáticos durará toda su vida, y se transmitirá por veinte y cinco años, contados desde el dia del fallecimiento, á sus herederos legítimos, ó testamentarios, ó á sus derecho-habientes, entrando despues las obras en el dominio público respecto al derecho de representarlas.» *Ley sobre la propiedad literaria de 10 de junio de 1847, art. 17.*

«El empresario de un teatro que haga representar una composicion dramática ó musical, sin previo consentimiento del autor ó del dueño, pagará á los interesados por via de indemnizacion una multa que no podrá bajar de 1000 reales ni esceder de 3000. Si hubiese ademas cambiado el título para ocultar el fraude, se le impondrá doble multa.» *Idem art. 23.*

8   Copyright statement in play edition from 1849.

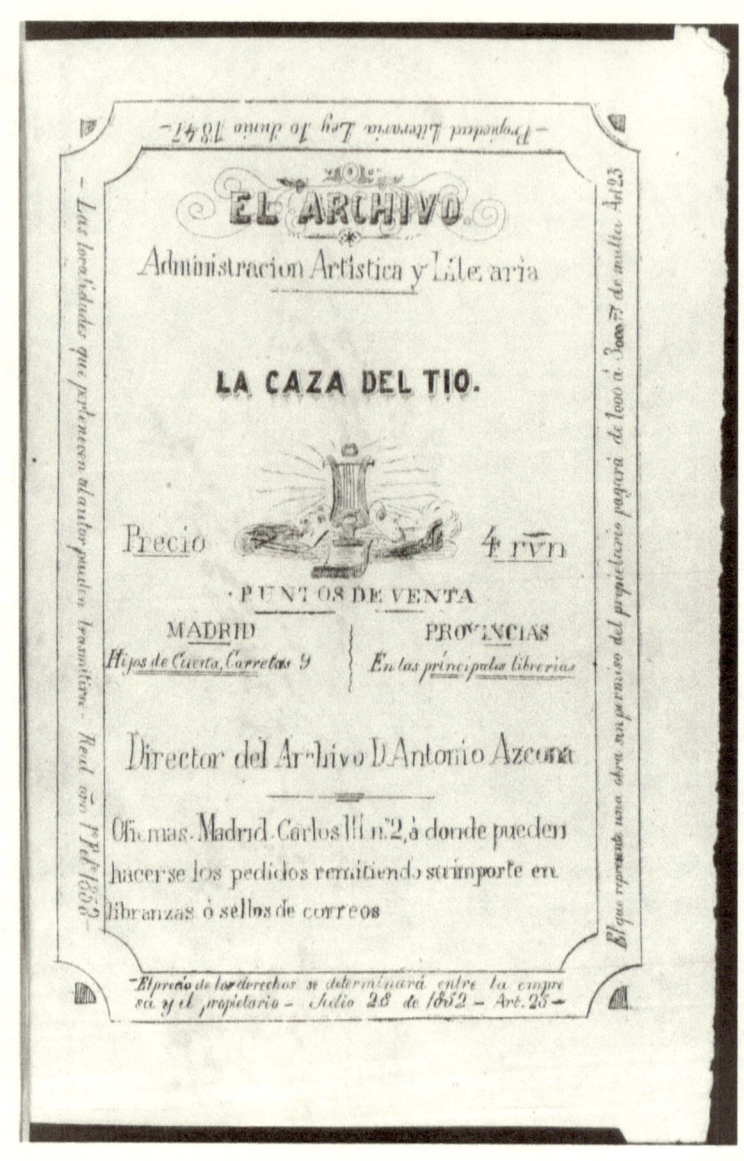

9 Lithographed title page from 1870.

The injection of economic thought and practices into the literary field is most evident in the final section of the essay, 'El autor.' In 1837, Mesonero employs the idiom of economic liberalism to describe the impossibility of a poet remaining dedicated to 'su sagrada y única mision' [sacred and unique mission] and surviving in his modern society dominated by capital and greed:

> El desdichado autor cae entonces bruscamente desde su cielo ideal en este mundo *mecánico* y *positivo*; mira con dolor que el ingenio es un *capital pasivo* que no empieza a *producir* hasta despues de la muerte; que la sabiduria no tiene *cosecha*, ó que si *siembra* ideas es para *recoger* unicamente desengaños; que *hacer* libros donde nadie lee, es ponerse á *fabricar* rosarios en Pekin; que aquella individualidad, aquella sublime escepcion á que ha aspirado por resultado de sus tareas le ha constituido en una situación exótica en medio de una sociedad *material* y *positiva*. (Emphasis added)[8]

> [The unfortunate author then harshly falls from his ideal heaven into this *mechanical* and *positivist* world; he sees, with pain, that talent is a *passive capital* that doesn't begin to *produce* until after death; that knowledge has no *harvest*, or that to *sow* ideas is to *harvest* nothing but disillusion; that to *make* books where no one reads is to *manufacture* rosaries in Beijing; that individuality, that sublime difference to which he has aspired as a result of his work, has made him exotic here, in the middle of a *material* and *positivist* society.]

Hence, in spite of their talent and fame, poets in Mesonero's bleak world quit literature and become bureaucrats (where they will endlessly transcribe the useless documents and papers of others). Its exact nature is left unsaid, but Mesonero indicates that there should be an alternative, a clear division of labour that would protect the writer from the material aspects of his trade. The poet who writes good literature would be financially rewarded, better literature would be written, and more people would read. While Mesonero does not mention copyright or *editores* by name, both the legal structure and commercial function are sketched out here with great appeal. It was out of this sort of aesthetic and entrepreneurial indigence that the nineteenth-century *editor* arose in Spain.

Nineteenth-Century Troubadours

Some poets saw commercialization as a means of improving literature, and literary property was part of Spain's larger attempt at a modernizing, industrial revolution. But a disparity between poetic and economic conceptions of the individual poet in society problematized the relationship between the poet and his reading public. The arguments that had led to the legislation of *derecho de autor* were philosophical, legal, and practical, and the notion of poet as labourer was necessary to the whole justification of literary property after 1837. By legally transforming literary pursuits into labour and poem into commodity, *derecho de autor* obliged the poet to be remunerated by the public at large for their consumption of his verse. Thus, whereas Romanticism offered the poet the liberty to rhetorically exist as a privileged voice outside the establishment, economic liberalism forced him to exist rhetorically within the market.[9] According to Larra, modern society marginalized writers: 'un literato es un vago sin oficio ni beneficio, y el que vive de su talento es menos todavía que el que vive de sus manos' [a writer is a vagabond without a job or quality, and he who makes a living from his talent is lower than he who makes a living from his hands].[10] The idealized paradigm proposed by Mesonero was impossible unless poet and worker, and sacred art and profane market, could be reconciled; or, to employ Bourdieu's terms, poets be allowed to deal exclusively with 'signification' and the 'symbolic values' of their goods, distancing themselves from those writers who publicly worked for hire and dealt openly with 'merchandise' and market values.[11] Victor Carrillo has called the Spanish *editor*, specifically, 'un industriel du livre,' and Christine Haynes, discussing French *éditeurs* of the same period, has defined their role as speculation and innovation in the book trade after 1830.[12] Within about a decade, poets began to see *editores* as a necessary nuisance, and this is the sentiment most often remembered.[13] But poets' initial reactions to the effects of copyright ranged from ambivalence to uneasiness with the alienating effects of modernity, and they welcomed the intervention of *editores*.

A Western view of poets as both privileged and marginalized was elaborated during the Romantic period. The ideal poet was a genius whose talent was innate, granted by God or a muse, and revealed by his ability to create in isolation. He created verse as an extension of himself and generated art that was independent of imitations of anything or anyone. The idealized model of the Romantic poet as a voice on the margins of, and misunderstood by, his society and graced with the creative power of God (authorship) was celebrated in Salas y Quiroga's journal *No me olvides*, reproduced here in part:

Poeta, ser privilegiado por Dios, hombre independiente, alimentado de esperanzas y sensaciones, flor que crece en el desierto! Para él todo es ilusión, todo porvenir, ama y odia con entusiasmo, y guiado por solo su talento eleva sus ideas hasta el trono de Dios y escribe en la bóveda celeste con carácteres de fuego, sus primeras sensaciones; rasga el velo que cubre su destino, que el poeta es el único ente á quien es dado adivinar su suerte. Sublime en las ideas, profundo en el saber, paseando su mirada desdeñosa y ardiente sobre las cabezas estúpidas que le rodean y que vegetan a su lado, el poeta es sin embargo el juguete de un envidioso a quien mortifica su genio.

Después de penosos estudios, después de haber admirado y penetrado los profundos conceptos de los mas sublimes ingenios, despues de haberse empapado en saber y ciencia, el que nació poeta se halla un día inspirado, toma la pluma y vierte conceptos, pensamientos, sentencias, en una palabra estampa los sueños de su imaginación ... Respira un aire puro en su atmósfera, atmósfera donde no es dado a los demás respirar. Después llega el momento en que concibe y crea, ya es poeta; ya puede enseñar á sus semejantes! Sigue! ... no te detengas en el camino, inmortalízate, llega al templo de la gloria, y cuando los laureles ciñan tu abrasada frente, cuando el aplauso del triunfo resuene en tu corazón, ten lastima del pueblo estúpido que te cerraba el paso para llegar a la cumbre ... compadécele, lastímate de su ignorancia, enséñale, sé generoso, olvida sus injurias ... No le humilles, reflexiona, que si primero te detuvo en tu rápida carrera, después te ha ensalzado, te ha aplaudido, le has arrebatado! ... Miserables criaturas de barro no han podido resistir a la magia de tus palabras; ha llegado hasta su corazón, ha conmovido su alma! Los has enseñado, ahora te comprenderán![14]

[Poet, a being privileged by God, independent man, nourished by hope and feelings, flower that grows in the desert! For him everything is fascination, everything is a future, he loves and hates passionately, and guided only by his talent he elevates his ideas unto the throne of God and writes in that celestial vault with letters of fire, his first feelings; he tears away the veil that covers his destiny, for the poet is the only being to whom it is allotted to divine his fortune. Sublime in his ideas, profound in his knowledge, casting his disdainful and fiery eye over the stupid heads that surround him and vegetate at his side, the poet is nevertheless the toy of one envious of him whom his wit mortifies.

After painful study, after having marvelled at and penetrated the profound ideas of the most sublime geniuses, after having immersed himself in knowledge and science, he who was born a poet finds himself inspired one day, he takes his pen and ideas, thoughts, judgments pour out, in a word, he makes an imprint of his imagination ... He breathes a pure air in his atmosphere, an atmosphere where others are not permitted to breathe. Then comes the moment in which he conceives and creates, now he is a poet, now he can show his peers! Hurry! Don't delay on the path, immortalize yourself, go to the temple of glory, and when the laurels crown your burning brow, when the applause from triumph resounds in your heart, have pity for the stupid masses that cut off your path to the top ... sympathize with them, pity their ignorance, teach them, be generous, forget their offences. Don't scorn them, consider that if first they held you back in your rapid career, later they have exalted you, have applauded you, you have crushed them ... Miserable creatures of clay, they were unable to resist the magic of your words, it went to their heart, and it moved their soul! You have taught them, now they will understand you!]

José Zorrilla was one of the many Spanish poets who performed this persona. According to both his contemporaries' accounts and his own memoirs, Zorrilla's versification was not studied, he claimed to have no models, and he created in solitude, with verse verily bursting forth from his being. Most well known are his adamant claims of originality for his play *Don Juan Tenorio*, a Romantic version of the 'Don Juan' story, composed in harried, but inspired, circumstances.[15] Although a highly prolific writer, he famously lived in perpetual poverty and, not uncoincidentally with respect to his successful projection of the Romantic ideal, maintained constant ties with his principal *editores*, selling every last literary property to them.

By codifying the values of singularity, personality, and originality in a poetic composition as the qualification for its recognition as property by natural law, *derecho de autor* irrevocably burst the bubble of creative solitude in which the Romantic poet supposedly existed. It unequivocally established a financial relationship between the author and the public, commanding the public to pay and the author to collect. In order to dispense publicly with *derecho de autor* and simultaneously maintain his public posture of pre-capitalist distance, the poet privately negotiated with the *editor*. Of about four thousand plays written between 1837 and 1860 that I surveyed for this study, the *derechos* of only less than a dozen pieces were fully retained by their authors. Therefore, it would seem that the 1837 law had almost no practical impact on the older arrangement whereby the writer sold his play to a printer and relinquished control. However, the apparent incongruity between legal authorship and sale of rights to *editores* in fact illustrates the strength of legal authorship as a new, alienable commodity. Copyright law did not fully bind the rights and title of authorship to the historical person who wrote the play, as happens today. But, unlike the situation in previous centuries, the sale of copyrights to publishers did guarantee attribution to authors and integrity of the text.

Mark Rose has argued that the centrality of original genius to Romanticism and its veneration of creativity as the original expression of self 'not only obscures the fact that cultural production is always a matter of appropriation and transformation, but also elides the role of the publisher.'[16] The role of the nineteenth-century *editor* has been underestimated in Spain, in part, because he was successful in camouflaging the fact that poets were like every other member of nineteenth-century society: labourers in a market economy. Because the *editor* appropriated the many realities of cultural production and diverted them from the idealized and aestheticized figure of the poet, writers maintained an elevated position in society and the role of the *editor* was gradually minimized. In the market economy of the modern nineteenth century, the poet represented for his readers an imaginary fetishized space beyond the realm of commodification.

The poet-*editor* relationship joined two idealized roles: one wholly poetic and the other wholly financial. A fictionalization of their relationship maintained a division between the first two agents and defined the interaction of each with the market, with the poet cast as a troubadour and the *editor* as his patron or benefactor. That is, in order to represent his marginal relationship with the market in pre-modern terms, the writer adopted the persona of the troubadour, found within Romantic works such as José Zorrilla's *Cantos del trovador*, José de Espronceda's *El diablo mundo*, or Antonio García Gutiérrez' *El trovador*; and in contemporary journals themselves entitled *El trovador* (Madrid, 1841, and Barcelona, 1846) that first published the works composed by these same poets and their contemporaries.

Ricardo Navas Ruíz explains that many of the historical works of Romanticism testify to the problems or anxieties of the nineteenth century and that their reinterpretations of history reflect contemporary preoccupations, effectively converting the historical past into a mirror of the present.[17] The same is true of the Romantic poets' feigned distance and rhetorical rejection of the market. This performance masked the realities of the arrangement after copyright but was predicated upon an idealized misinterpretation of the past. That is, the troubadour was a useful metaphor that allowed the nineteenth-century poet to perpetuate a pre-modern model in which a poet was free from the desire for profit and freely gave of the divinely inspired knowledge that he had been granted through inspiration. Cast as an extra-societal troubadour, the poet was deemed divine by his aversion to, or freedom from, the fiscal in modern liberal society.

Although the 1837 and 1839 petitions for literary property for dramatic works cast the poet's craft as labour only independent writing – supposedly uncompromised by the market – was understood to reflect faithfully the personality of the poet and be worthy of serious consideration, or protection by copyright. The distinctions between high/low and original/reproduction were related to questions of poetic identity and authorship. Solitary creativity was the foundation of literary property, and the existence of a unique literary personality (revealed in a text) was fundamental to the logic of the new system.

The growth and appreciation of the role of the *editor* as intermediary in the circulation of literature are evident in articles from Romantic magazines of the period. For example, the task of the *editor* was celebrated in October 1837 by the literary journal *No me olvides* (Madrid, 1837–8), run by Jacinto Salas y Quiroga. The highly specialized readership of this journal would have been keenly aware of the difficulty of procuring quality editions of literature, much as Mesonero had described. Manuel Delgado would become the most important *editor* and José Zorrilla among the most widely read Romantic dramatists. Here, the journal commented on Delgado's purchase of the copyright for Zorrilla's poetry, an early phase of their relationship. Salas y Quiroga's notice is striking to a twenty-first-century reader, for it challenges modern assumptions regarding the source of literature:

> [Nota:] El muy conocido editor de las obras de Larra, del teatro moderno español, y de otras producciones de mucho mérito, DON MANUEL DELGADO, á quien, en honor de la justicia, debemos confesar que es deudora la literatura de muchas y muy cuidadas publicaciones, acaba de comprar el permiso de imprimir, formando cuerpo de obra, los escritos poéticos de DON JOSE ZORRILLA. A la hora en que esto escribimos están ya en prensa, y tenemos entendido que, antes de concluirse este mes, verán la luz pública. Felicitamos al SEÑOR DELGADO por tan dichosa idea, y le pronosticamos buena venta, pues el bien merecido renombre que tiene el SEÑOR ZORRILLA de ser uno de nuestros primeros poetas, á pesar de sus

pocos años, despertará ciertamente sumo interés y curiosidad hacia sus obras. Nosotros deseamos buen éxito al SEÑOR DELGADO, tanto para que sea una recompensa de los servicios que le deben los escritores y el público, como con el fin de que le sirva de estímulo para emprender otras obras.[18]

[(Note:) The well-known *editor* of Larra's works, of modern Spanish theatre, and of other productions of great merit, DON MANUEL DELGADO, to whom, in all honesty, we must confess, literature is indebted for a great number of carefully made publications, has just bought the right to print, and form into a body of work, the poetic writings of DON JOSE ZORRILLA. As we write this note, the works are already at press, and we understand that before the end of the month, they will be available to the public. We congratulate SEÑOR DELGADO for such a fortunate idea, and we predict a good sale for him, since the well-deserved reputation that SEÑOR ZORRILLA has of being one of our best poets, in spite of his youth, will certainly spark great interest and curiosity in his works. We wish SEÑOR DELGADO a great success, not only as a repayment that writers and the public owe him for his services, but also so to encourage him to undertake future works.]

Salas y Quiroga (or his anonymous writer 'S.') announces to his readers that new Literature is indebted for its existence to the intervention of the *editor*. As *No me olvides* presents it, poets create poetry, verse, or fine art, but *literature* is the materialization of this same verse as an aesthetically pleasing good, whose alluring paratext rivalled that of the text in the eyes of the modern consumer. Literature, then, is the result of an economic reality overseen by the *editor* and a social phenomenon whereby he transmits the poet's voice to a public sphere, and it becomes shareable and knowable. The poet's voice is given a 'cuerpo' [body] as modern editions of literature unite the spiritual (Romantic, poetic) and the corporeal (financial, material) in a book. Just as the Romantic poet was a mouthpiece of the sublime visions that he received through inspiration, the *editor* was a parallel conduit between poet and reader, safeguarding the verses' passage through the market.

According to Salas y Quiroga, without Delgado's acquisition of authorship, Zorrilla's verses would have remained unread, languishing with the poet and isolated from society. What is of 'note' in Salas y Quiroga's notice is not the fact that Zorrilla had composed poetry (his poetry had already appeared in the pages of *No me olvides* and other literary journals), but rather that Delgado had prepared them in a new volume and separated them from the person of the poet and his immediate circle, introducing them into a wider world of readers. Supposedly, Zorrilla could not have done this himself. The notice approaches advertising, for it urges the readers of *No me olvides* to show their approval with their pocketbooks: if Delgado does not make money, he may not agree to future ventures, and readers may not have access to future verse written by other aspiring poets. The supposed stagnation of literature (as had been described by Galiano and Mesonero Romanos) might persist, to the detriment of Spanish civilization. Thus, the subscribers to *No me olvides* are to purchase responsibly and guarantee that the works of the next Larra, or the next great poet or dramatist, will receive the same estimable treatment as those already published by Delgado. Notices like this both promulgated and perpetuated the myth of the creative Romantic poet as isolated from, yet responsible for, the entire nation's cultural wealth.

In recognition of the task of the *editor*, his corresponding right to profit, and modern authorial ownership, Delgado, instead of Zorrilla, is the sole recipient of Salas y Quiroga's wishes for success. The poet is seen as bereft of all agency in the publication and material preparation of the volume, and the journal does not need to wish him a favourable critical reception. Salas y Quiroga instead predicts good fortune of the the *editor*: 'le pronosticamos buena venta.' Although Salas y Quiroga asserts that Zorrilla's reputation 'despertará ciertamente sumo interés y curiosidad hacia sus obras' [will certainly spark great interest and curiosity in his works] (presumably in those who are reading this notice), the readers are not really encouraged to purchase the volume primarily in order to appreciate the poetry in it, but rather to reward Delgado. The *editor* is indispensable: he is presented as the sole conduit of verse from poet to public and responsible for its existence in print.

Writing over sixty years later, the Nicaraguan poet and essayist Rubén Darío expressed the same observation regarding the vital role of the *editor* in the production of Spanish dramatic literature. Darío credits Delgado and his colleagues with the transformation of dramatic poetry into a desirable commercial good and its aesthetic renaissance. Modern Literature was, to some degree, created by these merchants, who provided the reading public with plays:

> [E]n la época romántica se fundaron las «Galerías dramáticas», y creo que el editor Delgado fue el primero que intentó el negocio ... Así como ahora lo que sobra en las galerías son títulos, al principio faltaban, y para pre-

sentar un catálogo copioso de obras nuevas y nombres nuevos, Delgado ofrecía buenas pesetas por todas las obras que le llevaban los principiantes. Imprimía los originales sin leerlos siquiera. Sólo así se concibe que hayan llegado a publicarse muchas obras ...[19]

[In the Romantic period the 'Galerías dramáticas' were founded, and I believe that the *editor* Delgado was the first to undertake the enterprise. Although now the *galerías* have too many titles, in the beginning there weren't enough, and in order to present a copious catalogue filled with new works and new names, Delgado offered good money for all of the works that new poets brought him. He printed the originals without even reading them. It is only in this way that he could conceivably have published so many works.]

Darío's central idea in his discussion of Spanish dramatic *editores* in the Romantic period is that even if Delgado barely read the plays he published, he made them accessible in great quantity for the first time to a public eager to read them: 'Las ediciones de los románticos – algunas muy bien hechas y muy parecidas a las de los franceses – debieron ser numerosas. Demuestran más que el valor de los poetas, el entusiasmo del público' [The editions of the Romantics – some very well done and similar to those of the French Romantics – must have been numerous. They show, more than the worth of the poets, the enthusiasm of the public].[20] Delgado's negotiation with young poets and his ever-growing catalogue were the foundation of nineteenth-century Spanish dramatic literature, through the creation of a readership for dramatic literature that rivalled that of novels. This statement echoes the *Nota*: in the Romantic period, literary quality was not vital for publication; rather, it was of greater urgency simply to circulate a great quantity of works in print, and to grant readers the opportunity to select texts. Salas y Quiroga and Darío depict the dramatic *editores* of the Romantic period less as cultural gatekeepers than as indispensable facilitators who furnished readers with a heretofore inconceivable variety of dramatic literature. Literature was subject to the demand of the market, and the readers' aesthetically informed purchases ideally would direct the future production of dramatic verse.[21]

In Darío's view, before the first *editor*, Spanish dramatic literature scarcely existed. In the beginning, there was almost nothing: few titles were available to readers ('al principio faltaban'). Darío defines the eras of 'before' and 'after' in Spanish theatre history, not as one of authorship or copyright, but according to the related absence or presence of the *editor*. Darío wrote this article in 1899, as a lament over the disappearance of this assertive agent, who was, in his opinion, responsible for the proliferation of dramatic literature in the Romantic period. 'No hay duda de que del año 1840 al 1860 se publicaba y leía más en la Península que lo que ahora se publica y se lee' [There is no doubt that from 1840 to 1860 more was published and read in the Peninsula than is published and read today]. For, as Darío goes on to explain in the rest of the essay, poets continue to write, but the task of the *editor* changed, and that is why, tragically, less is published and, consequently, read at the end of the century.

Manuel Delgado officially presented himself as a legal and financial agent who facilitated the poet's interaction with the market and the public. Whereas later editorial houses (*galerías*) bore names that portrayed them as spaces of art, the first one was an agency that treated dramatic literature as property. Delgado's was called 'Comisión de enagenación de propiedades dramáticas' (Commission for the alienation of dramatic properties). Its name confirmed that dramatic literary property in nineteenth-century Spain could – like all other property – be possessed, used, and legally alienated. As David Saunders has already argued, in its earliest instance, European copyright law never 'assumed or required any equivalence between the person of the copyright holder and the moral or aesthetic personality of the writer; rather, it delineated and attributed the legal capacity to own copyright in a manner designed for the regulation of a specific economic activity – the making of and trading in a printed commodity.'[22] Dramatic authorship was a construct that by the 1830s in Spain had combined with the illusion of author as owner of discourse and placed Delgado in the position to defend both the law and the philosophies of individualism and private property by organizing himself as an economic entity. (See fig. 2.)

The director (*editor*) of the *comision* made possible the process (*enagenacion*) by which a poet divested himself of the property, claimed that the acquisition of such property by Delgado was equally legitimate, and that he had the right to use and possess the goods transferred to him by the poet. The poets' decision to sell their *propiedades dramáticas* to Delgado was not a confused, accidental, or misinformed loss of an unrecognized right of ownership, but rather a real engagement with the recognition of verse as property. Later apologists for poets like Zorrilla suggested that they simply did not understand the law (just as

Mesonero's poets were supposedly incapable of dealing with and were thereby swindled by printers and booksellers). In doing so, they infantilized writers and dismissed the role *editores* played in the larger shift in Spanish theatre from a spectacle-based to a text-based art. Representative statements, such as those by Marciano Zurita early in the twentieth century, portrayed poets as naïve, foolish, and fooled – either like the grasshopper of a children's fable who was so enamoured of his song that he failed to save, or the modern equivalent of the biblical Esau, stupidly surrendering a spiritual inheritance to satisfy immediate material (physical) needs.[23]

Although the poets' identity as creators or the source of plays was not effaced through the transfer of property, the alienation of this aspect of authorship neatly separated the act of writing from the responsibilities of ownership. Moreover, the act of selling actually replicated the Romantic definition of the act of writing, namely, the embodiment of the author's will in his text. Thus, an *alienation* of their works (*obras*) – understood to be an expression and externalization of their will – to Delgado was a second expression of it. The philosophy behind this arrangement was indirectly Hegelian:

> It is possible for me to *alienate* my property, for it is mine only in so far as I embody my will in it. Thus I may abandon (*derelinquere*) as ownerless anything belonging to me or make it over to the will of someone else as his possession – but only in so far as the thing [*Sache*] is external by nature.
> Addition: While prescription is an alienation of property without a direct declaration on the part of the will, true alienation is a declaration by the will that I no longer wish to regard the thing as mine. The whole issue can also be viewed in such a way that alienation is regarded as a true mode of taking possession. The first moment in property is to take possession of something immediately; use is a further means of acquiring property; and the third moment is the unity of the first two, namely taking possession of the thing by alienating it.[24]

The alienation of property was effectively, then, an externalization or expression of the will and fully consonant with a Romantic attitude toward writing. But, to do this is also to reflect one's self onto an other; for *bienes mostrencos* [ownerless goods] were prohibited in liberal Spain.[25] This *other* for the Spanish Romantic dramatic poets was, of course, Manuel Delgado, who, as *editor*, allowed them to divest themselves of their property and appropriated, possessed, and used their rights as authors. As the legal owner of the immaterial *propiedad literaria*, he exercised the author's right to negotiate with theatre companies, printers, and booksellers and be financially compensated for the use (reading or performance) of his *propiedad literaria* by yet a third other.

Delgado as Patron

The dramatic *editor* also grew prominent as modern dramatic authorship failed to be accepted in the nation's provinces. The new authorship that had been reshaped around the dramatic poet in the 1837 royal order was resisted by actors and impresarios in theatres outside of Madrid, who continued to modify texts, change titles, suppress authors' names, and simply refuse to recognize literary property, much as Larra had described earlier in the decade. Each *editor* represented a multitude of individual authors who had created a handful of commodities and thus centralized authorship into a single figure of considerable importance. Analogous to the government's attempts to impose its political measures (formulated in Madrid) throughout Spain, the *editor*, through his agency, endeavoured to guarantee that the words and images of all his plays premiered in the capital were accurately reproduced (and literary property heeded) on the national stage.

The 1837 petition for literary property for dramatic works had been presented by 'varios literatos' (Bretón, Gutiérrez, Hartzenbusch, Romero, and Ochoa). Two years later, on 27 February 1839, Manuel Delgado presented a second petition, repeating many of the same arguments and asking for a repromulgation of the same royal order. He spoke in the name of authors' rights and posed the same questions of responsibility for dramatic discourse and literary property that had been put forward before, expressly framing his request as a continuation of the poets' case. The single difference between the first and second petitions lay in the person who represented *authorship*, as the signifier for the control of dramatic discourse slipped from the person of the poet to more generally any owner of the property of the play. Because of its fundamental transferability, legal authorship became tied to a set of legal rights and was transmissible to anyone who bought or became vested with them.

María Cristina's ministers also treated Delgado's petition as a continuation of the process begun by Gutiérrez et al. in 1837, even presenting their commentary to the Queen on the same folios first used two years before. The poets' petition for dramatic copyright became a palimpsest for their successor and guarantor. The previous narrative and arguments regarding the theatre's relationship to national industry, civilization, and literary glory (discussed in chapter 1) were directly invoked as the Queen was presented with a second opportunity to rectify the 'escandaloso' theft of authors' property in Spain's theatres.[26]

The ministers agreed with Delgado's arguments and maintained nearly all of his ideas in their commentary on his petition.[27] They recommended a second royal order by contrasting the justice of royal law, the associated social order, and literary property for dramatic works with rebellion, theft, and disorder, pitting capital against periphery. Openly defying ('quebrantando abiertamente' [openly breaking] the Queen's royal order, the theatre impresarios in the provinces had also disregarded the officially protected poetic images of Spain to be represented on its stages, held as private property by *autores* or *propietarios* in Madrid. Both individual authors and the system of property, but also the Crown's authority, had been 'attacked' through the unauthorized performance of plays classified as dramatic literary property.

The source of the 'abuso escandaloso' [scandalous abuse]) of authors' property and the challenge to the Queen's authority shifted from the legacy of the Ancien Régime (where it had been found in the 1837 commentary) to contemporary actors and impresarios. This distinction further divorced the art of the poet from the art of the stage, by differentiating his rights and wishes regarding the text from those of actors and impresarios, and instead allied the poet with the government and its policy on property and its emphasis on writing. Interestingly, in this way, the rebellious, individualistic, and anti-establishment poet represented a politically conservative rejection of spontaneous and authentically unique interpretations by actors and artisans in the periphery. In opposition to the poets and the royal government who created power in literary and juridical texts and represented the new regime, the actors and impresarios of the provinces (who refused to relinquish the theatrical space of improvisation) were characterized as criminals in their defiance of the propertied plays and royal orders emanating from Madrid. The ministers suggested that provincial theatres actually did understand the law but chose to elude and break it. Twice repeating Delgado's qualification of the amount owed to authors as 'mezquina' [meagre] and the financial returns to the *editor* as 'intereses de pequeña cuantía' [interests of a small sum], the ministers implied that the issue involved was less economic than ideological. In addition to condemning the theft of the author's small, but just, recompense, the ministers found 'duro que la codicia de un empresario esponga á un desaire público á un jóven autor' [terrible that an impresario's greed exposes a young author to public insult]. The young poet – like the 1837 royal order itself – was being personally attacked and affronted by insolent actors and impresarios in the provinces. Because the poets and Delgado could not defend themselves alone, the Crown (which had recognized dramatic authorship) must mediate to defend both them and the concept of literary property itself. According to the ministers, the most efficient means of doing this would be through a second royal order and active intervention in the process of authorizing performances in the provinces.

In order to encourage María Cristina to respond to Delgado's petition, the ministers declared that the Queen had ruled wisely in her 'justo decreto' [just decree] on 5 May 1837, by conservatively recognizing a law supposedly already present in Spain's legal tradition. As discussed above, in that royal order she had stated her intent to recognize literary property for dramatic works in order to combat the theft of property and the proliferation of incorrect copies of poets' texts, to increase the number of young poets composing works for the stage (consequently enhancing Spain's literary and cultural glory), and to stimulate the various industries related to it. Although, two years later, many theatres in the provinces did not heed the law, the ministers nevertheless assessed its effects to have been favourable. The number of poets who were writing dramatic literature had increased (stimulated by hopes for glory for both themselves and the nation), and their activity had become a new industry. Although the 'recompensa pecuniaria' [financial recompense] was 'mezquina todavia' [still meagre] it was greater than it had ever been before. Thus, not only was versification seen as labour rather than *ocio* [leisure], but also it became effectively commercialized as a *negocio* [occupation], realizing the arguments presented by the poets in 1837.

Once again, her ministers presented literary property as a means for María Cristina to seize control of society and to present herself as a modern ruler. Whereas in 1837 she had protected the dramatic poet and his poem, in 1839 her decision to repromulgate the royal order would preserve literary property (and a belief in the inviolability of this 'sacred' concept itself) intact and 'unharmed' (*ilesa*). Indeed, the fact that young poets were being defrauded of the fruit of their labour was perceived as producing disorder in the theatre. If the words declaimed in performance differed from those written by poets and owned and controlled as individual private property, then it was unclear exactly who owned the image of the nation on the stage.

Order in the theatre would be established if provincial impresarios were forced to pay the owner of the literary property for the performance of a play and could not change the text or title. The situation in the theatre reflected a larger resistance to the modern regime. As persons accustomed to the old system of privilege and shared cultural patrimony, the impresarios metaphorically represented other persons in contemporary society resisting both the wholesale reclassification of all possessions, labour, and products in Spain as private property, and María Cristina's authority more generally. A fear of chaos in both dramatic discourse and the new social order of property informed the ministers' advocacy for a royal enforcement of the *derechos de autor* recognized in 1837.

Ultimately, the *mesa* suggested that the Queen order the provincial theatres to obey the 1837 order and that she deploy her regiment of provincial censors to ensure their adherence to it. The royal order of 9 April 1839 was María Cristina's response to the ministers' account of the need to protect the industries related to the theatre, halt the open rebellion against her orders in the nation's provinces, and implement order in dramatic discourse. On 9 April 1839 the Regent ordered that all performances first had to be authorized by the owner of the *propiedad literaria* and that a document attesting to this approval would have to be presented to the censor of the province before performance could be permitted. Subsequently, regional censors would not only monitor the social morality, religious tone, and political tenor of the pieces they approved, but also confirm that the performance and public consumption of these plays were carried out with recognition of the owners' rights. Figure 3 shows the manuscript approbation by the censor of Valladolid, who permits the performance of Ventura de la Vega's *La escuela de periodistas* on the condition that the *derecho de autor* is paid to the play's owner. Slowly, the legally stipulated control of performance through literary property did take effect nationally.

Dramatic Literary Property as a Nationalizing Agent

Gregorio Martín has argued that copyright in Spain was repressive.[28] Indeed, it did restrict the circulation of dramatic texts, for although their consumption was encouraged (through the marketing of the work as a commodity, to ensure a favourable economic return for the investments of *editores*, as Mesonero had anticipated), this same consumption was vigilantly monitored by both its owners and the Crown.[29] Whereas the eighteenth-century Protector of Theatres, Armona, had stipulated the material stage properties that each theatre company had to own and employ (when theatre was understood as fundamentally a spectacle-based event), after the promulgation of literary property for dramatic literature, the author's text was the most scrutinized and controlled element of the stage. The Romantic period was a time of innovation in set design, and the art of acting was given serious consideration by the public and critics; however, over the course of the century, an appreciation of the aesthetic project of Romanticism and the active intervention of *editores* served to cultivate a public demand for original, authentic pieces of *literature* performed on stage.

In 1839, María Cristina directed censors to ensure that owners authorized (and received payment for) performances of texts in the provinces, but the *editores* were ultimately responsible for verifying the conformity of the lines declaimed to the words printed in the authorized edition. Most poets in the nineteenth century sold their rights to one of six principal dramatic *editores*: Manuel Delgado, Alonso Gullón, Vicente Lalama, Ignacio Boix, Eduardo Hidalgo, and Pablo Avecilla (and their inheritors or successors), although there were others with smaller collections. Usually, poets retained the *derechos* pertaining to performances in Madrid (where most of them lived), and the *editores* acquired the *derechos* to print editions and control performances in the provinces. The concentration of nearly all dramatic copyrights in the hands of a few investors provided them with a centralized authorial power over the stage that the Crown did not possess. In order to protect their investments, the publishing houses that owned nearly every dramatic copyright in the nineteenth century developed a network of agents throughout the Peninsula and colonies (particularly in Cuba). Over the course of the century, they solidified their far-reaching power to ensure that every play performed on any stage in Spain matched the printed text that they owned. By the 1860s, there was a branch of the principal Madrid dramatic editorial houses in all of the main Spanish and colonial cities, dedicated to collecting *derecho de autor* royalties and attempting to regulate adherence to the legal text in stage performances.[30]

As the observance of literary property law became more extensive and literature completed its conversion into a commodity for mass consumption, the poet's work was increasingly fossilized in the version that was realized in the first printed edition. According to Ronald Bettig, the 'fixing' of the literary work that took place in Europe and the Americas during the nineteenth century was the consequence of the belief that ideas should be regarded as property and, hence, treated as capital.[31] Likewise, the copyright laws legislated by the governments of María Cristina and Isabel II did serve to systematize the circulation of literary works as privately held capital. The assumptions of a liberal political economy that were codified in literary property resulted in the dual process of the textualization of a cultural heritage (by subordinating the traditional conventions of the stage to the modern laws of property) and the transformation of Spanish theatre into what was understood to be a nationally uniform system of performance. Functioning as capital, the entire content of the play text was rendered immutable, and the circulation of a work in print or representation was restricted to an exact copy of the version of the text owned by the holder of the *derecho*.

In the 1840s, dramatic *editores* had only relative success in executing these two main objectives in the theatre. In 1844, Hartzenbusch founded the Sociedad española de autores dramáticos [Spanish Society of Dramatic Authors] to try to influence those in power to further guarantee copyright.[32] In the *Real decreto orgánico* of 7 February 1849, a lengthy royal decree reforming theatres throughout Spain, Isabel II continued the measures begun by her mother and addressed the place of 'autores dramáticos' in the theatre.[33] Twelve years after the initial royal order for literary property for dramatic works, *derecho de autor* and the text were given priority over the agents of performance in theatrical productions. First, Article 60 resolved the question of the poet's right to attend performances of his plays, by according the author of the literary property the right to attend every performance of his play in order to ensure that the dramatic text was faithfully reproduced on stage as he had written it.

Since its first instance in 1837, literary property was conceived and developed as an immaterial parallel to land; this understanding also informed the royal decrees and effectively cast the author or owner of the dramatic literary property as a landlord. As an absentee owner cannot properly verify the appropriate use of his domains nor oversee his economic return, Article 60 precluded the possibility of an absentee author, owner, or metaphorical landlord. After the royal decree, the poet or his agent was to be present at the performance of a text in order to police the actors and the impresario, and safeguard the purity of the printed, authorized text. In contrast, impresarios and actors (increasingly divested of any poetic licence as artists to improvise or modify even a poorly written text) became mere tenants of the words they declaimed. Like other disenfranchised segments of society without the rights of property, they were subject to its laws, while simultaneously dispossessed of the power to wholly control the texts they cultivated or to intercede politically on their own behalf to challenge the laws that directed their relationship to that property. As described by José Zorrilla in his memoirs, throughout this period poets often wrote for specific actors and collaborated with them. But once a play was written, copyright changed the legal relation between actors and texts.

According to the 1853 royal order, not only could a *derecho de autor* be sold or exchanged an infinite number of times, but the associated rights of authorship and the execution of these rights could be transferred to and performed by any authorized agent. In addition to the physical presence of the poet or owner in the theatre during a performance, there were a number of other means available to the owner of the *propiedad* for protecting his investments. All of these authorial activities could be performed either by the owner of the *derecho de autor* or by any person whom he named as his representative. The authorship born from the mind of the *ingenio* was, usually, sold to an *editor*, who remained in Madrid. He, in turn, hired an agent in each provincial capital to act as a representative of his authority as owner of the *derecho* and to oversee the consumption and reproduction of the text. Although invested with authorial powers, the provincial agents did not directly represent the poets as legal *autores*, but rather the legal authorship owned by the *editor*. The wholesale imposition of national literary property onto a previously province-specific theatrical system was only realized through the transfer and fragmentation of the rights of authorship onto these various agents. Bretón, Gutiérrez, Zorrilla, and other poets wrote thousands of plays during the nineteenth century; the stability of their identity as the authors of these works was maintained through the transmission and distribution of the rights associated with authorship onto hundreds of agents they never met.

In Article 82 of the *Real decreto*, the Queen once again prohibited unauthorized changes to the literary text in performance and to some degree answered the complaints made by Larra several decades before:

> Las empresas no podrán cambiar ó alterar en los anuncios de Teatro los títulos de las obras dramáticas ni los nombres de sus autores, ni hacer

variaciones ó atajos en el texto sin permiso de aquellos; todo bajo la pena de perder, segun los casos, el ingreso total ó parcial de las representaciones de la obra, el cual será adjudicado al autor de la misma ...

[The companies may not change or alter the titles of dramatic works nor the names of their authors in the theatre's notices, nor vary or abridge the text without the permission of the former, at the risk of losing, according to the individual case, all or part of the box office receipts, which will be turned over to the author of the work.]

Authenticity of the original work was contingent upon an immutable textual property, and anyone who challenged that concept in a single work could undermine the whole system. If practices such as described in the law were permitted to continue, they would have left a work's readers and the theatre public confused as to which version was the *real* or *correct* play that the poet had truly intended to articulate (the one created in solitude or the one reworked after audience reactions). Contemporary theatre journals satirized this possibility endlessly, but the implications for property law and the traditionally tight control of the stage were real.[34] To some degree, literary criticism and textual editing have followed the lead of property laws and are built upon the idea of a 'true' original and uncorrupted text.

After the *propiedad literaria* of a play was sold, a poet with the right to rework it could only be a potential corruptor of the value of the property of the *editor*. Some poets took advantage of this right.[35] But the *editores* were eager to protect their financial investments and soon adroitly circumvented this hypothetically harmful aspect of the law. In the bills of sale drawn up between poets and *editores*, the purchasers of the title of authorship employed the force of contract law to supersede provisions in the royal decree and prevent the uncontrolled creation of economically subversive variations of their properties. For example, in 1862, Bretón de los Herreros ('como dueño y propietario que es de las obras Dramaticas tituladas') [as owner and proprietor of the Dramatic works titled] sold over two dozen plays to Vicente de Lalama. Part of Bretón's contract (written in standard language and formulae) stipulated that he ceded full ownership to Lalama, 'no pudiendo refundir ni corregir estas obras sin permiso del Editor' [not being able to rewrite or correct these works without the permission of the *editor*]. The contract then concluded with a phrase in which Bretón swears to not 'reclamar ni pedir cosa alguna contra este contrato bajo ningun pretesto' [protest or call for anything counter to this contract under any pretext].³⁶ The literary property and all of its accompanying rights wholly became the property of Vicente de Lalama. In an attempt to protect his literary capital, the *editor* thus prohibited Bretón from plagiarizing his own work.

Parodies were one type of imitation and adaptation that was allowed. Nineteenth-century Spanish theatre was replete with these works, which, in many ways similar to *refundiciones*, did not claim to rival the original play or harm the economic interests of their owners. Perhaps the most curious example is the parody of *El trovador* written by Antonio García Gutiérrez himself less than a decade after the original premiere. In *Los hijos del tío Tronera*, the author satirizes the core themes of Romantic love, race, marginality, and identity from his original play but highlights their very fragility in the original piece.

In reality, the nature of theatre as an art form always entails some variation in performance, but through the intervention of *editores* and their agents, dramatic propriety was redefined as *propiedad dramática*: by the 1860s, it was deemed both aesthetically and legally proper that a stage production not significantly alter the author's text, which, in turn, was understood as the source of the production. As a result, as the author's original became the only valid version, different stage productions of the same text were perceived as representations of the poetic idea created by the dramatic *autor*.

This 'fixing' of the text became visually manifest in the new printing formats that Manuel Delgado and his colleagues developed. Constructed upon the concept of a sacred, unique text (much like a painting), their collections highlighted the poet's originality, just as their emphasis on legal authenticity restricted both modifications to the text and illicit copies. The propertied text thereby 'fixed' the role of their collections in the nationalization of culture and capital.

STAGE THREE

National Literary Galleries

In the third stage of dramatic property, copyright was materialized in printed editions, and it imposed a series of controls on both private readers and collective audiences. This section addresses the impact of theatre copyright in the new models for marketing, printing, and reading. First, the novel development of *galerías dramáticas* in the 1830s as a print phenomenon is read in conjunction with the contemporary opening of the Prado Museum to the middle class. *Editores* attempted to market dramatic literature as a textual museum: a means for the general populace to access Spain's celebrated theatre and new national art gallery by proxy. Second, a reading of the entire paratext of the *galería* editions analyses the interplay between intellectual property and state power in order to address the twin processes of Spain's internal colonization and the formation of a national culture through theatre. Every aspect of the paratext functioned to direct or restrict reception. In addition to long, poetic copyright declarations that prefaced theatre books, stage directions (didascalia) first began to be included in *galería* editions – a novelty that changed the way that the verses were not only read as literature but also staged. (Because they were part of the author's original copyrighted words, directions on lighting, costume, and other 'stage languages' were subjected to the supremacy of the text.) Reversing the ancient tradition of actors' improvisation and response to audience reaction, copyright fixed the performance, just as it had fixed the text, and imposed a nationally uniform theatrical experience, independent of local tastes. The theatre again served the state as its colonizing gaze turned inward after the loss of the greater American empire, and it began to regularize policy with the disparate regions of Iberia. In conjunction with direct legislation, the Crown outsourced the execution of its nationalizing project to the *editores*, whose attempts to enforce copyright law carried out cultural policy for the modern nation.

5 Textual Museums

After poets exchanged manuscripts for money, these became books within collections called *galerías* that, in turn, determined the way in which literature and theatre were read and understood over the course of the century in Spain. Manuel Delgado first launched the term 'galerías' as a brand name in 1839 for his set of titles.[1] Delgado's initiative was quickly imitated by other *editores*, and the word was eventually generalized to describe all compilations of editions of dramatic literature, until their decline at the end of the century. Large numbers of printed plays began to be published in the seventeenth century, but the marketing of the *galería* system marked a new framework for the public's interaction with theatre as culture in the nineteenth century.

The word *galería* itself illustrates the marketing of dramatic literature as textual art during the Romantic period. The original name of Delgado's firm, Comisión de enagenación de propiedades dramáticas [Commission for the alienation of dramatic properties], publicized his merchandise as dramatic property, not literature, and his business was contingent upon the poet's right to divest himself of his original *derecho de autor*. By presenting his editorial house as a commission for the alienation of dramatic properties, Delgado had first articulated his business of the transfer of artistic commerce within the economic and political project of *desamortización* [disentailment]. The philosophy of 'enagenación' continued to inform the entire *galería* system, even after the name was slowly replaced. In 1839 the concept of intellectual property was still contested, and only after dramatic literary property law was repromulgated on 8 April 1839 (at Delgado's insistence) was the corporation renamed Galería dramática.[2] The new designation shifted the advertised focus of the corporation's services from the trade between poet and *editor* to the marketing of dramatic works for literary consumption by the public at large.

A *galería* was a collection of editions of dramatic literature owned by one *editor*, who marketed these works throughout Spain; the term referred to both the collection itself and the firm that owned and administrated dramatic copyrights with full legal and economic powers. The marketing of dramatic literature in Spain as infinitely reproducible *galerías* of material culture distinguishes them from other contemporary European collections (for example, Le magasin théâtral and La France dramatique in France). Spanish dramatic *editores* chose a non-literary metaphor that served to portray their wares as both literature and culture, in contrast to the Bibliothèques or Collections of France and England, which engaged with different cultural projects and, to a greater degree, published novels.[3] The *galería* paradigm transposed the theatrical performance into an alternate space for private readers through which the same gallery of national dramatic treasure could be found in all citizens' homes.

The first dramatic *editor*, Manuel Delgado, selected a dynamic term for his firm that captured the contemporary interest in democratizing art. At the beginning of the nineteenth century (in the 1803 dictionary of the Royal Academy), a *galería* was defined strictly as an architectural term: a 'pieza larga y espaciosa, adornada de muchas ventanas, ò sostenida de columnas, ò pilares que hay en los palacios y casas suntuosas. *Ambulacrum fenestratum*' [long and spacious room, adorned with many windows or held up by columns or pillars, found in palaces or sumptuous houses. A *windowed walkway*].[4] Then, seven years before the first dramatic *galería* was founded, the word retained its structural foundation but acquired a second artistic connotation, as well as a defined purpose. In the 1832 edition of the same Royal Academy dictionary, a *galería* was redefined as a 'pieza larga y espaciosa, adornada de muchas ventanas, ó sostenida de columnas ó pilares que sirve para pasearse ó colocar en ella cuadros, adornos y otras preciosidades' [long and spacious room, adorned with many windows, or held up by columns or pillars, that provides a space in which to walk about or to place paintings, *objets d'art*, and other precious objects].[5] In the second definition, the Spanish Royal Academy describes a *galería* as a space designed for leisure: a luminous room of luxury that invites contemplation. To some degree, this returned to the eighteenth-century definition of the gallery as a space of pleasure: 'La pieza larga y espaciosa, adornada de muchas ventánas, ò sostenida de colúnas ò pilares, que hai en los Palacios, ò Casas magníficas, para tomar el Sol, ù otras diversiones. La etymología de esta voz es mui natural se tomasse del Francés antiguo *Galer*, que valía Holgar' [The large and spacious room, adorned with many windows or supported by columns or pillars, that is found in Palaces or sumptuous Houses for sunbathing or other diversions. The etymology of this word is probably taken from the old French 'Galer,' which meant 'to be at leisure'].[6] But by 1832, the gallery had become a free-standing space, liberated from the sumptuous homes of the wealthy. Its purpose was to provide a space for both pleasure and instruction, in which one can promenade (already present in Latin in the earlier definition) or install paintings and other objects of art.

Delgado's metaphoric brand name was predicated upon a markedly non-theatrical assertion of similarity between the appreciation of art and of dramatic literature, stemming from what was perhaps the most significant cultural ruling of Fernando VII's reign. In response to an Enlightenment-inspired mandate to improve the aesthetic education of the King's subjects, by the royal order of 4 July 1814, the King ceded control of the Buenavista Palace to the Academy of San Fernando in order to establish 'en él una galería de pinturas, grabados, estatuas y ... demás bellezas artísitcas, con la comodidad y decoro correspondiente, así para la enseñanza y aprovechamiento de los discípulos y profesores como para satisfacer la noble curiosidad de naturales y extranjeros y dar a España la gloria que tan justamente merece' [in it a gallery of paintings, engravings, statues ... and other artistic *objets d'art*, with the appropriate comfort and decorum, not only for the education and enjoyment of students and professors but also to satisfy the noble curiosity of Spaniards and foreigners and to give Spain the glory that it so justly deserves].[7] In 1819 the Royal Museum was established as a *galería*, opening the private royal art collections to the Spanish public.[8] The definition of a *galería* as a site for the exhibition of art, acquired between 1803 and 1832, corresponded to the conversion of the private royal art collections into a (limited) public space. The new meaning also reflected the expansion of subjects' access to the symbols of state power and the objects of its culture. José de Madrazo, the court painter, noted that before Fernando VII had begun to collect his paintings in one gallery, all but the most privileged of the Monarch's subjects had been geographically and socially restricted from viewing them. Paintings had existed in the various royal palaces,

> cuya entrada no podia permitirse á toda clase de personas, aunque la bondad de los Soberanos desde muy antiguo se la concediese á los jóvenes

pintores de acreditada conducta y aplicacion, para que los copiasen, igualmente que á los aficionados y estrangeros, y para que los viesen y meditasen; lo cual ciertamente no bastaba para satisfacer la pública curiosidad é instruccion por las distancias de los Sitios Reales, por la altura en que se hallaban colocados los cuadros, y por las malas ó escasas luces de que estos participaban.[9]

[into which entry could not be granted to all classes of people, although the kindness of the Sovereigns had long been conceded to young painters of accredited behaviour and application, also to amateurs and foreigners, so that they could copy them (canvases) and that they might see them and meditate; this certainly did not suffice to satisfy the public's curiosity and (need of) education, given the distance of the Royal Domains, the height at which the paintings were hung, and the bad or scant illumination that they received.]

That is, before the opening of the Royal Museum in Madrid, only a select few had been allowed to behold the paintings. In Madrazo's description, the public's curiosity and the need to educate them coupled to form one motivation for the foundation of the royal art gallery.

The much-celebrated public access to the new royal *galerías* on the Paseo del Prado was restricted to two days per week, and still only to those subjects to whom the Monarch had granted permission.[10] The purpose of this aperture into King Fernando's royal art galleries was to provide a controlled and guided access to the symbols of power and the culture of the state; that is, it was a muted version of the opening of the Louvre, but without its revolutionary tenor. Indeed, unlike in France, this was not a national museum: the pieces were the personal property of Fernando and his heirs. Functionally analogous to the theatrical representation of the nation, the images of the state were likewise inseparable from the person of the Ancien Régime Monarch, who controlled the display and consumption of the pieces in the museum. Thus, originally denoting an exclusively private space in the homes of the elite, in the early nineteenth century the *galería* began to refer to an interstitial environment between the spheres of the public/private and subject/Sovereign: when Fernando's *galerías* opened, individuals could promenade and appreciate art while in a semi-public space controlled by its royal owners. Ultimately, the King's *galería* was a formidable locus of the state's culture and a passageway through which, in theory, anyone could enter to behold Spain's beauty and wealth.

Books were an alternative means to access the visual pleasure and symbols of the royal collections, and their production likewise expanded in this period. The invention of lithography in the nineteenth century permitted delicate and intricate reproductions of an artist's work well beyond the quality and scope available from the expensive woodcuts or metal works in use since the sixteenth century. In 1824, Fernando VII authorized the creation of the Real Establecimiento Litográfico [Royal Lithographic Establishment] by José Madrazo and Ramón Castilla, explicitly to create books with the new technology and widen access to the royal galleries. Between 1826 and 1833, the workshop created a three-volume set with nearly two hundred coloured illustrations of pieces in the royal museums: *Colección lithográphica de cuadros del Rey de España, que se conservan en sus Reales Palacios, Museo, Academia de San Fernando ... y Real Monasterio de El Escorial* [*Lithographic collection of the paintings belonging to the King of Spain, which are held in his Royal Palaces, Museum, Academy of San Fernando ... and Royal Monastery of the Escorial*]. Unlike the provisional privilege to enter the actual royal galleries, these tomes could be purchased (in instalments) and shelved at home, for unlimited private consumption by anyone. The Book promptly became coded as not only a space of visual pleasure, but also a proxy for the semi-public gallery opened by Fernando VII.

Madrazo's luxurious books were enormous (61 x 46 cm) and both useful and beautiful: large enough to imitate truly a canvas when opened and displayed in the home, their structure approximated to the space of an art gallery, with many pictures packed tightly into their pages. These early lithographed books discouraged individual responses in favour of a controlled, collective reception of the images. Echoing Fernando's aim in opening the galleries, Madrazo's books were to expand access to royal galleries and enhance readers' aesthetic education, while also inscribing the subject-readers into the system of the royal symbols of wealth, power, and political and cultural hegemony. Moreover, the lithographs allowed private citizens to adorn their own homes with reproductions of the Monarch's gallery and, in essence, create miniature copies of the palace in their living rooms. Lest the cultural process escape the sphere of royal influence, the textual curators very clearly instructed Fernando VII's subjects how to read and appreciate the pieces that constituted the King's personal collection and the grandeur of his realm.

While only a few of these books were made and their price was somewhat prohibitive for the general population, their impact on the development of dramatic galleries was crucial. Madrazo's books marked a significant step in conceptualizing a book as a proxy for a gallery and a means for further expanding the aesthetic pleasures of a private, palatial gallery to an ever broader public.

When Manuel Delgado created his Galería dramática (within weeks of the 2 May 1839 opening of the Galería de Escultura – a principal wing of the Royal Museum), he crafted a metaphoric association upon a very novel aspect of the term *galería*. First, the architectural concept had moved into the hybrid public-private sphere and had been broadened to house art and its mechanical reproductions. Delgado then extended this meaning to his particular collection of intellectual commodities. Just as Madrazo's books had reproduced the royal galleries in the homes of some of Fernando's non-aristocratic subjects, after the death of Fernando VII, Delgado promoted and indeed capitalized on the enthusiasm to popularize national culture through the medium of the text. Like the monarchy's pictorial art galleries, the *galería* of the *editor* was presented as a showcase of culture available to anyone (with a few cents). However, whereas Fernando's gallery had represented the wealth of the nation, through the person of the Monarch, the *galerías* of the *editores* were an exhibition of property-based power and abundance, as each collection attempted to offer consumers a fuller and more ample selection of titles. The wealth of the variety of dramatic titles in Delgado's collection reflected the essentially luxurious essence of a *galería*, as the latter migrated, in Delgado's formulation and by his promotion, from rich houses (the *casas suntuosas* in the Royal Academy's definition) to the abodes of all Spaniards. For, as a collection of immaterial (intellectual) properties, the *galería* could itself be replicated and purchased an infinite number of times, allowing each consumer to install a *galería* of the national literary culture in his or her own home.

The dramatic *galerías* sought to evoke the ideal space described by the Royal Academy by drawing an analogy between their collections and both the architectural space of a gallery and the visual aesthetic pleasures sheltered within it. First, as a structural design of the imagination, editorial *galerías* provided a proper (both appropriate and personal) edifice in which to explore and encounter texts as art. Delgado's *galería* was not an actual architectural construct (and thus neither geographically nor spatially restricted), but rather a theoretical configuration that served to guide readers in their purchases and was both virtual and portable as well as infinitely reproducible. Moreover, although each title could be bought individually, it was not presented simply as a single book, but rather as part of a larger artistic and cultural whole, organized by Manuel Delgado. Similar to that of a pictorial curator, the responsibility of the dramatic *editor* was to install in his gallery – and offer to the consumer – those works that merited reading or contemplation and would bring profit to himself.

The second association in the analogy between the dramatic collections and art galleries was the equivalence between the types of cultural artifacts housed within them. Contained by the space of the imagined gallery, the editorial collections offered their customers artistic treasures that were metaphorically similar to those in a pictorial *galería* in their visual aspects. Both types of galleries promised a pleasure for the eyes: within the *galerías* of the *editores*, this was to be found both in the highly stylized material arrangement of the text – aesthetically pleasing as an object – and through the visual process of reading. In order to dislodge the work from the established realm of the stage and reposition it within the modern printed edition, printed dramatic poetry became as material and beautiful as a canvas or a sculpture. The layout and typeface of the text gained a new importance, anticipating the elaborate illustrations that would adorn play editions at the end of the century.[11]

The purchasable *galería* that Delgado offered for private consumption in the home was an alternative space to the theatre. Intellectual property had fixed the text for both individual and collective presentations, but whereas the theatre was a public event, immaterial and temporally specific, dramatic literature was private and substantive, and under the reader's control. In Manuel Delgado's *galería*, dramatic texts became material *objets d'art* that a consumer could purchase, own, and peruse at his or her leisure. The *editor* presented the printed page to the consumer as a place to encounter the classics and discover the contemporary luminaries of the Spanish stage, in this way extending the demesne of national culture. A personal art gallery, its individual works of national prestige were accessible in each citizen's home and offered all consumers a glimpse at Spain's best literary art. Delgado and his imitators advertised not only the art gallery's image of prestige but also its popularization, thereby transforming it into an essentially modern entity by eliminating restrictions to it.

The Spanish *galería dramática* was just one of many extra-palatial structures that spatially expanded the realm of privilege to a wider segment of society, and applied the architectural experience of a gallery promenade to a very different context.[12] Throughout Europe in the early nineteenth century, the private, aristocratic gallery was architecturally recreated as a public commercial space: the urban shopping centre, beginning in Paris at the end of the eighteenth century, when passageways between streets were redesigned to redirect pedestrian traffic.[13]

The growth of the arcades as a public space of social interaction (private property designed for public use) was part of the societal reformation from an exclusively aristocratic system of social interaction to a more pluralistic one. After the Revolution in France, they became a meeting place in Paris not only for the notables but for all classes; and, like the Prado galleries in Madrid, they were an example of the opening of exclusive spaces at the end of the Ancien Régime. Discussing their proliferation throughout Western European cities, Geist (quoting Bandmann) notes that the gallery conforms to a 'common tendency of architectural history – a representative genre, which had once been bound to a specific social class is taken over by a rising emancipated class. Following the great French Revolution the bourgeoisie lays claim to the aristocratic gallery.'[14] Margaret MacKeith has noted that galleries 'were extraordinarily successful, taking over the role of the market place as a cultural, social and retail center under glass, contributing an air of novelty and unreality.'[15] The gallery housed all that was central to the modern society and displayed those who chose to situate themselves within it. However, as spaces of the bourgeoisie, the new commercial galleries were in turn reinvented as symbols of their newly acquired cultural authority. Geist explains that 'in its fully developed form, the structure attempts to legitimate its function and hide its orientation toward profit and exploitation by striving to be a[n] artistic gallery.'[16] The dramatic gallery served a similar function for the Spanish dramatic poet – the *editor* and the collection camouflaged the poet's own (initially championed) engagement with capitalism in the literary market, while transposing the labour-free aristocratic spaces of art, theatre and culture onto a commercial sphere.

Dramatic *galerías* had one important difference from the art galleries upon which they were patterned: the absence of an original. Indeed, *galerías* were founded upon the original/reproduction paradox inherent in the Romantic ideology of authorship, for the *editor* served to guarantee the inviolability of the poet's original articulation, and ensured that the uniqueness of the poetic production was faithfully reproduced in each copy. The value of the printed and performed text was predicated upon the existence of an original manuscript – unknown to all but the poet, *editor*, and printer – that was understood to be faithfully reproduced in the *galería* of the *editor*.

In his discussion of the problematic issues of authenticity and originality in reproductions of pictorial art, Walter Benjamin posits the existence of an original *objet d'art* that is both knowable and known, but beyond the immediate reach of the individual. 'The presence of the original is the prerequisite to the concept of authenticity.'[17] In Spanish textual galleries, the original manuscript was as virtual as the property rights it entailed: never displayed, it remained entrusted to the care of the *editor*. Knowledge of the original dramatic poem was obtained solely through the printed editions in the boundless *galerías* – safeguarded and authenticated by the *editor*. Not only was the manuscript unknown, but the original material was ephemeral: unlike the manuscripts reproduced in medieval *scriptoria*, the modern edition (verse and paratext) existed only as type, which, in turn, was a temporary arrangement of letters, numbers, and figures on a press. Nevertheless, the Romantic concept of authenticity was of utmost importance and became the handiwork of the *editor*, created through the multiple reproductions of the temporary type under his supervision. The proliferation of printed editions, owned in each reader's library or personal gallery, visually asserted the stability and value of the unknown original dramatic poem. The paradox of the textual gallery is that the degree of the public's appreciation of an original piece was manufactured through the multiplicity of copies and grew proportionally to the number of reproductions. Without unlimited reprintings, the poet's verse would have been subject to unbridled interpretation and improvisation, as it had been since the Early Modern period. The greater the knowledge of the text among readers, the greater its authenticity and the more immutable or canonical it became.

The *galería* market strategy was based upon the notion that the *editor* was operative through his textual absence. In most cases, it is difficult to ascertain the extent to which an *editor* may have intervened textually between a manuscript and an edition. But Juan Hartzenbusch's editorial work with the texts of Tirso de Molina, Lope de Vega, and other Golden Age dramatists in 1839 illustrates the actual degree of his supposed absence. Hartzenbusch had originally been criticized for proposing new editions of classic texts (for how could one fix the words of Spain's greatest poets without simply creating a *refundición*?).[18] However, he assured readers that as an *editor* he would not change the intended meaning of the venerated Golden Age poets but, rather, erase the traces of previous publishers, improve the paratext, attempt to facilitate reading, and guarantee that the poet's original intent (even when this was distinct from the words found in the seventeenth-century manuscript) was presented to the reader. That is, Hartzenbusch presented himself as textually absent; however, of course, the decision to determine which sections of text were original to Tirso and which were later additions was Hartzenbusch's. His status as a successful playwright granted him the public's trust to not delete incorrectly, and his name as *editor* on the cover of the volumes associated the popularity of his own plays, such as *Los amantes de Teruel*, with the value of his edition of Tirso's plays.

As acclaimed as his work might have been in the nineteenth century, current expectations of the role of an *editor* are vastly different. In terms of methodology, Hartzenbusch explains his editorial approach to be closer to mind-reading than scholarship: 'En todo borrador, como cosa hecha de prisa, yerra la mano, que no escribe siempre todo lo que el pensamiento le dicta' [In every draft, because they are done quickly, the hand errs and does not always write what one's thoughts dictate].[19] Evangelina Rodríguez has discussed Hartzenbusch's problematic editorial philosophy in detail, noting that he is 'a prime example of an editor's intervention in the text of works whose parodic character frequently makes them objects of obvious censorship ... [He] eliminates unashamedly the scatological and carnavalesque vein of Calderón.'[20] As a curator between the poet and the public, Hartzenbusch was as concerned with the favourable reception of Calderón and Tirso by a society distant from the Golden Age as he was with the poet's work.

Omnipresent in the paratext, the *editor* (Hartzenbusch, Delgado, or other figures endowed with the trust of the public and the poet) protected the integrity of the text itself and the perceived perfection of the original poet by preventing the intrusion of any alien voice. Romanticism maintained the proprietary link between the person of the poet and his verses, while *derecho de autor* sanctified the property rights of the owner of the immaterial *work* – of which each copy of Delgado's editions was a faithful manifestation. Therefore, while each consumer of a given dramatic text purchased an original, unique piece of art, it was paradoxically valuable only because it was identical to every other edition of the work.

Contemporary commentators on the *galerías* congratulated the *editores* for the stability, affordability, and reliability (the objectives of all successful modern manufacturers) of their editions: an indication of the general approval of the industrialization of literature. Shortly after the first dramatic galleries were founded, *El entreacto* (always favourable to the *editor* Ignacio Boix) emphasized the value of his contribution, or 'obra,' and its potential to allow more people to buy plays, value dramatic literature, and reward poets. As discussed in chapter 4, Salas y Quiroga praised Delgado's efforts to provide his readers with new literature; here, Boix is likewise commended for creating accessible and appealing editions of dramatic literature, in the collection called Repertorio dramático:[21]

LITERATURA. REPERTORIO DRAMATICO, Ó SEA COLECCION DE LAS MEJORES OBRAS DEL TEATRO MODERNO ESPAÑOL Y ESTRANJERO
Una de las obras de que mas provecho, mas utilidad y mas gloria han de resultar á la literatura española es la titulada *Repertorio Dramático* y que es objeto del presente artículo. En los pocos dias que lleva de vida la ha acogido el público con la mayor benevolencia, apresurandose á comprarla, y ahora á suscribirse segun las nuevas bases que ha establecido su editor el señor BOIX. Mucho tienen que agradecer ciertamente á este no solo la literatura sino tambien las artes de su paises; mucho, porque desvelándose por los progresos de ambas y publicando sus obras, ha de animarlas necesariamente, y ha de contribuir mucho á que no desmayen los artistas y los literatos viendo condenados al olvido sus trabajos, quedando sin publicidad, y privados por consiguiente de lo que mas lisongea al talento; el saber que el público ha de conocer sus producciones, que ha de aplaudirlas, que ha de admirarlas, y que ellas tal vez le han de inmortalizar ... Nosotros no vacilamos en declararnos en favor del *Repertorio Dramático*, porque llena todas las condiciones que en nuestro siglo se exigen de belleza, estraordinaria baratura y mérito literario; garantias suficientes para que pronostiquemos à esta publicacion un éxito grande y merecido, mucho mas cuando sabemos que su Editor piensa seguir perfeccionándola, hasta hacer que compita con otras análogas del estrangero. Tal como es ya hoy dia bien puede compararse con los primeros tiempos del *Magasin Theatral*, y de la *France Dramatique*. El tamaño adoptado en el *Repertorio* es igual al que emplean aquellas; su impresion en nada desmerece tampoco.[22]

[LITERATURE. *REPERTORIO DRAMATICO*, OR COLLECTION OF THE BEST WORKS OF MODERN SPANISH AND FOREIGN THEATRE
One of the most advantageous, useful, and glorious works that has resulted from Spanish literature is the one entitled *Repertorio Dramático* and it is the subject of the present article. In the few days that it has existed, the public has embraced it with the greatest benevolence, hurrying to buy it and to subscribe to it according to the conditions that its editor, Mr Boix, has

established. Certainly, not only literature but also the arts of the country have much to thank him for, because, aware of the progress of both and publishing their works, it will necessarily invigorate them, and will greatly work to ensure that artists and writers don't waste away and see their works condemned to oblivion, lacking a public and consequently deprive them of that which most flatters the writer of talent: the knowledge that the public will know his works, that it will applaud them, that it will be amazed by them and that they might immortalize him ... We don't hesitate to declare ourselves in support of the *Repertorio Dramático*, because it fulfils all of the conditions that our century demands of beauty, extraordinary affordability, and literary merit, sufficient guarantees to allow us to predict a great and deserved success for this publication, even more so as we know that its *Editor* intends to continue perfecting it, to the point that it will compete with similar foreign publications. It is already so good that it can be compared with the first years of the *Magasin Theatral* and the *France Dramatique*. The size that has been adopted by the *Repertorio* is the same that they employ, its printing is no less deserving either.]

The dramatic *editores* aggressively marketed their editions as both reading material and economically accessible replicas of bound books. The format in which they published these plays, *pliego*, was traditionally considered to be of a low quality and culturally inferior to books. In the sixteenth, seventeenth, and eighteenth centuries, the *pliego* was a marginal, commercial means of producing copies of works of sometimes dubious literary quality. María del Mar Fernández explains that 'otras obras literarias son un vehículo de cultura, se compran y venden en función de intereses profesionales concretos, de prestigio cultural de una casa o una biblioteca, pero ninguno de estos condicionamientos se presenta en el caso de los pliegos. La intención del impresor es vender y se pliega a los intereses del público que busca entretenimiento' [other literary works were a vehicle of culture, bought and sold as part of concrete professional interests, or of the cultural prestige of a house or a library, but none of these conditions applied to the case of the *pliegos*. The printer's objective was to sell, and he bowed to the interests of a public in search of entertainment].[23] But, in the nineteenth century, dramatic *editores* employed the same inexpensive format to produce editions of important pieces of dramatic literature that could visually approximate to the cultural status of books.

By opening the *galería*, Manuel Delgado and his fellow *editores* created a novel and utterly modern space for a new readership to discover theatre as literature. The commodity offered for sale was not just the literature but also – and especially – its paratext. Because of the relatively low price of these editions, and their visual appeal, a large number of Spaniards who would not have otherwise read or perhaps even known theatre works purchased and read the creations of the *editores*. As a result, the bourgeoisie continued to attend the principal theatres of the cities (especially Madrid), where they encountered Spanish works orally and via spectacle. In an inversion of the traditional distinction between high and low or written and oral cultures, the *galerías* fostered readership among the general public. Once invited into the leisurely space of the gallery, the new book editions restricted and controlled readers' interactions with a fixed and propertied text, while they freed its interpretation. The copyright purchased by *editores* in order to create the *galerías* now directly impacted the new readers' appreciation of the text.

6 Paratextual Performances in the 'Galerías dramáticas'

The ideological and metaphorical construction of dramatic poetry collections as *galerías* of textual art was visually expressed in the paratextuality of the editions. The material form in which *editores* delivered their literature influenced their new readership legally and sociologically. An examination of the expression of the *galería* metaphor in the paratexts and iconography of these books demonstrates not only that each play text in the collection of the *editor* was presented to the nineteenth-century reader as an *objet d'art* appropriate to a palatial gallery, but also that the space of the *galería* and readers' movement within it were legally restricted according to the economics of liberalism codified in copyright.

Although historians of the book have devised a variety of taxonomies for analysing its materiality, the present discussion of the material play text (the extra-literary aspects of editions themselves) follows the terms established by Gérard Genette in his comprehensive study of a printed work's extra-textual apparatus.[1] 'Paratexte' is his term for the set of signs and signifiers that surround the literary work (fiction, non-fiction, poetry, etc.) reproduced in the *texte* and present it to the reader as a book. Genette partitions the paratext into two complementary but separate spheres: the *épitexte* and the *péritexte*. The first is the accumulation of messages that surround a text, often tools of the media, such as advertisements (not contained in the edition itself) and interviews, or non-public sources like private diaries (10). The second is that which is found materially within the space of the edition: the printed title, author's name, and other elements that modern readers utilize to place the piece in a historical, geographical, and artistic moment. The *péritexte* is subordinate to the text and does not have a significance independent of its service to the literary work.

I will briefly address three aspects of the *épitextes* of nineteenth-century Spanish play texts. The first of these is the concept of the *galería* previously discussed. The images of the *galería* (and, indeed, the word itself) appeared peritextually in the edition. But, as *épitexte*, the concept radiated around each piece and created an imaginary connection among them and a transitory significance that allowed each work to advertise the next. The inclusion of the play within the *galería* granted it a value through context, independent of the quality of the piece itself. That is, readers perceived a certain brand-name literary commonality among all of the pieces in a *galería* collection that both guided their approach to the play at hand as well as influenced their future purchases.

The second epitextual element was the poet's reputation, created and circulated in contemporary newspapers. As discussed above, the practice of divulging the name of the poet at the time of performance, as well as the poet's relationship to the theatrical production of the dramatic poem, evolved over the course of the century. However, by the time of printing (whether or not the poet's name appeared in the *péritexte*), his identity was generally known and, like the degree of prominence of the *galería* in which it was included, attested to the quality and commercial desirability of the piece. Once a public had created an 'autor' in the theatre, readers judged his relative value.

Related to the reputation of the dramatic poet were the previous or subsequent stage performances of the play where the title of authorship was launched or confirmed. In addition to their value as theatrical events and independent works of art, performances also functioned epitextually, adding to the play's overall meaning and marking its quality. The peritextual formula that appeared on the title page of every edition – 'Estrenado con éxito extraordinario en el teatro [X], el [day] de [month], 18[XX]' [Premiered with extraordinary success in the Theatre (X), on the (day) of (month), 18(xx)] – pointed to a primary element of the play's *épitexte* and echoed declarations on Golden Age plays.[2] Those called 'Famosa comedia' [Famous play] listed the royal performances, a practice reinvented as a marker of public, and popular, approval. Although the *editores* of dramatic poetry presented their editions as reading material, not as reflections of the stage, the theatrical versions did serve to code the value of the text, before the reader encountered it in the pages of the edition. Each theatre in Madrid had a status related to the social class of the members of its regular audience, and the venue of the premiere, stated in newspapers and printed on the editions, coded the play accordingly.[3]

The relationship between the printed texts of the *editores* and stage performances was extremely complex. Although the armchairs of middle-class urban readers were the final destination of many play editions, a segment of the play texts' readers were people associated with the stage, for the same editions that individuals purchased for private reading were used as scripts in provincial stage performances by actors, censors, prompters, and directors. Because the *galería* editions were the material source for the distribution of the play for both reading and performance, in their lengthy copyright or ownership statements both activities were addressed equally. For example, the lengthy literary property statement in *Un ángel tutelar*, from 1849, calls the play's performance a 'publicacion en los teatros' [publication in theatres]: a piece could be 'published' (or made public) either in printed or performance form. Actors or impresarios of theatres in provincial cities approached the *galería*-produced editions with a knowledge of their previous successes in Madrid theatres (documented in newspapers with a national readership) that influenced their selections.

The parameters of the *épitexte* extend far beyond those briefly outlined here; however, the inclusion of a play in the *galería*, the poet's reputation, and the success of performances functioned in concert to classify the play as desirable literature and to entice readers to buy it. Many people in nineteenth-century Spain never attended the theatre (for reasons of economics and geography); nonetheless, the performances impacted all readers' encounter with the textual arrangement by the *editor* of the poet's play.

Three aspects of the *péritexte* significantly changed the appeal of nineteenth-century Spanish dramatic literature in the nineteenth century. As a result of legal and technological developments, Spanish dramatic texts underwent a typographical metamorphosis in the 1830s and began to look significantly different from how they had in the previous century: at mid-century, the *editor* expanded the space of the printed text and wrapped the verses with words and images that served to declare his extra-literary presence and legitimate the words within. Examining the edition physically in a manner that replicates the reader's movement through it, the first significant innovation to be encountered is the enclosure of the play within a paper wrapper; the second is the addition, in the mid-1830s, of a title page with a number of invariable elements for every play; and the third is the inclusion of elaborate articulations of property laws. The *galerías* standardized typographical innovations, and the uniformity of the three principal peritextual elements, as well as paper quality, font, and size, visually and emblematically emphasized the property law that stabilized and legitimated the verses printed within.

As discussed above, title pages for single play editions had been printed in the past, but nineteenth-century *editores* reintroduced them as a novelty. No longer the marker of an expensive edition, they were mass-produced to sell a commodity that recycled images from elegant and elite books from the past, but they were modernized for a new readership. After *editores* reintroduced these elements, the nineteenth-century reader's encounter with an edition of dramatic poetry necessarily began with visual and linguistic articulations of modern property law and Romantic originality, and only after two or three pages of the *péritexte* did the reader arrive at the poet's verse. As commodities displayed in the *galería* of the *editor*, these texts were first presented as property before they were assessed as poetry.

Likewise, there had been uniformity in printing practices before the *galerías*, and numbered series of play editions date to the Golden Age. In eighteenth-century copies, the title and name of the poet often figured on the top of the first sheet (like a modern newspaper heading), and the final page indicated the place and conditions of printing. A *péritexte* always codifies the meaning of a text as a cultural artifact within a specific society, and a comparison of the material creation of play texts under royal privilege with those created under liberal property law demonstrates the importance that the two systems placed on the consumption of literature. Independent of the question of textual censorship, the format in which readers encountered literature was determined by its legal classification as privilege or as property. After 1837, dramatic *editores* were no longer conceded privileges but instead purchased *derechos*, and it was these private investors who replaced royal agents in determining how dramatic poetry was to be materially delivered to readers throughout Spain and Spanish America.

After the middle of the nineteenth century, the reader's encounter with the material *péritexte* of a play began with a swath of yellow or green paper that declared the play's ownership and authenticated the 'original' verse printed inside. The information offered on this sheet pertained exclusively to the *galería* and gave no indication of the title or the author of the work to be found within, but it would have been the first material element to appeal to a reader. The repetition of the wrapper around all editions of the *galería* plays restricted the independent significance of the individual piece and instead visually privileged its inclusion in the collection. The uniform presentation confirmed the infinite reproducibility of the plays and suggested that the play reproduced within was indeed the valuable authentic and *original* version, as the standard wrapper metonymically intimated a stability of the text it enclosed.

The outer wrapper was composed of four elements: a frame, the title or name of the *galería*, visual images, and the name of the *editor*, with his home or office address. A typical wrapper from 1842 with a standard layout is reproduced in figure 4. In this example, the entire set of signs on its front cover is contained by a picture frame; this marginal detail subtly realized the *galería* metaphor of the *editor* and coded the play as a visually pleasing work of art, and as a piece worthy of display on a bookshelf in one's home. Manuel Delgado, the owner of the Galería dramática, was solely responsible for the quality and selection of the plays offered in the collection. Indeed, no poets are named, but in the smallest font on the wrapper, the *editor* indicates that the works in the collection were written by 'prominent authors.' Then, emblematically rearticulating the task of the *editor*, these statements are followed by images of the poet's pen and ink, printed books, and the printing press that transformed the former into the latter. In the centre is a lamp – a sign of both learning and marvels that symbolized the dual roles of the *editor* in the realm of books and knowledge. The *editor* is the figure who coordinated all of the agents of literary production: procuring the poet's original manuscript, delivering it to a printer, and distributing books of superior paratextual and textual merit. Like a genie in a magic lamp, the *editor* produced marvels, and as a light of knowledge, he brought learning and 'civilization' to all his consumers. Below, the reader is told where the plays can be purchased in Madrid (on the back cover of the wrapper, the reader can find the provincial branches of the *editor*). The play that was swathed within the wrapper reproduced in figure 4 was *Un amigo en el candelero*, by Gil y Zárate, but, a potential reader or consumer would have been enticed to enter the play only by the signs and symbols of the *galería* and its *editor*.

Without opening the edition, but instead turning to the back cover (or the last of the wrapper's four pages), the reader found a list of booksellers in Madrid and the provinces associated with the *galería*: only these authorized booksellers would stock the plays. (See figure 5 for a list of booksellers authorized to sell the 1840 edition of Larra's *Un desafío*.) Thus, through the inclusion or exclusion of bookstores on the wrappers, the *editores* established a distinction between legitimate commercial sources for their editions and unauthorized pirated copies. The insertion, in every edition, of a list of dealers who could provide and guarantee an authentic edition of the text is evidence of the evolving legal and moral constraints on reading. The information on the back cover of the wrapper mitigated an immediacy between the reader and the play text and instead repositioned him or her as a consumer in the modern market. The classification of the act of reading as licit or illicit was contingent upon whether or not the reader had purchased an authorized copy from a bookseller named on the wrapper.

Dozens (from about one dozen c. 1840 to four dozen c. 1865) of cities and specific bookstores – from Barcelona to Havana – were named on the wrappers as distribution points for (and *de facto* branches of) the Madrid editorial agency, creating an immense network of points of exchange. Again, this organization was relevant for the entire assortment of plays edited by the *galería*, not just for the piece at hand. Systematic circulation further changed the nature of a reader's encounter with the plays. The literary text was no longer a chance discovery, subject to the stock accumulated in a local dealer's store or guided by either luck or perseverance; rather, the acquisition of the works in a *galería* was stabilized by the ubiquity of every play text in all cities throughout the nation. The sense of breadth and plenitude was enormous – not only were texts of dramatic poetry no longer difficult to procure, but also the public was told that a variety of works could be found anywhere. Moreover, not only were the editions visually uniform, but also the intended readers were equal in their anonymity. These editions were created for the market, not for individual patrons. The virtual map of Spain drawn by the huge network of booksellers on the wrappers suggested a cultural homogeneity: the same dramatic texts were read by the public-at-large throughout Spain.

The fiction of a culturally uniform nation was a nineteenth-century invention, integral to a political system based on national sovereignty. The impression of a nation of readers, created by the *galerías*, contributed to the growing belief in a national culture that served a variety of political, social, and economic interests. As Susan Kirkpatrick has explained, 'th[e] myth of an inherent national identity functioned as an imaginary compensation for the loss of the overseas empire and offered an image of national unity that was useful to a weakened absolutist regime; less obviously, perhaps, it also served a bourgeoisie whose vital interests lay in consolidating a national market for its products.'[4] Dramatic *editores* played a vital, if flawed, role in fostering a nationalization of theatre.

The front cover of the wrapper peritextually directed the consumption of each edition of a play by placing it in a specific gallery, while the web of market connections depicted on the back cover of the wrapper illustrated the movement of the gallery throughout Spain. Without opening a single page, the play at hand was positioned within a commercial and geographic context for the reader. Upon opening the wrapper, the reader found another peritextual context. On the *inside* of both the front and back covers were lists of titles owned or administered by the *galería*, typically under the heading 'Catálogo de las obras dramáticas y líricas de la Galería [name]' [Catalogue of the dramatic and lyric works of the [name] Gallery].

The quantity of titles that appeared on the inside covers of the wrappers varied according to the *galería*; however, the lists tended to be extensive, with as many titles as possible squeezed onto the pages, just as paintings were hung in the Royal Museum in the nineteenth century. The titles printed on the wrappers were often an incomplete register of the holdings of the *galería* (full catalogues were published separately), but their intended purpose was simply to provide a sizeable list, not a thorough inventory; indeed, through the sheer magnitude of the number of titles, these pages demonstrated to readers the importance of the *galería* in the realm of dramatic literature. The sea of titles not only illustrated the wealth of the *editor* and his success with poets, but also provided a commercial and literary context into which the reader was to place the work at hand. The play reproduced inside the wrappers was usually not listed in the catalogue that encircled it, but an equivalence between the play at hand and those in the catalogue was suggested through contiguity. This contextual relationship was bilateral: either a previous knowledge of other plays of the *galería* lent meaning to the unknown text inside the wrappers; or, for a reader pleased by the text at hand, the catalogue suggested further reading.

Legally, the *galerías* were founded upon the recognition of a poet's labour and his right to sell the corresponding *derecho*. The wrappers (the metaphoric walls of the architectural space) reflected the curatorial labours of the *editor* after the purchase of the *derecho* and attested to the durability and hence veracity of the original literary property. The information offered in the catalogues was limited; in some *galerías*, plays were organized by number of acts (which dictated the rates of *derechos* to be paid to *editores* for performances), in others by genre, and in most, by title only. But the common editorial guardianship among the plays superseded their heterogeneity in authorship, year and place of publication.

In the catalogue of the Biblioteca dramática (fig. 6), found on the wrapper of *Paraguas y sombrillas* (1848), the *editor*, Vicente Lalama, referred to the plays he owned, not as literary works, but simply as 'properties.' The catalogues on the wrappers of his collection were foremost a proclamation of literary property and announced that the poet had exercised his right to *enajenar* [alienate] the *derecho de autor* [author's right or copyright]. The *enajenación* of a *derecho* first happened when the poet sold or transferred his property right to an *editor*, but the right could be bought and sold an infinite number of times. *Derechos de autor* could circulate like titles of stock or land and, similarly, could appreciate or depreciate in value. For example, later in the century, Alonso Gullón listed recent additions to the immense catalogue of plays held in his Galería Dramática El Teatro in the wrappers of various new dramatic editions. Many of the titles listed were not recent works by new talent but, rather, proven money-making plays first edited years before. In the *Aumento al Catálogo del 1º de ABRIL de 1877*, Gullón announced the recent acquisition of *Don Juan Tenorio*, in three acts, by José Zorrilla. The original sale of the rights to *Don Juan Tenorio* (in 1844) has been used by scholars and others to portray a supposed victimization of nineteenth-century playwrights at the hands of rapacious *editores*, specifically Manuel Delgado.[5] But the April 1st catalogue addition is further evidence of how the nineteenth-century market for dramatic intellectual properties in Spain was much more dynamic than a series of predatory thefts of original *derechos de autor*, which the *editor* would then jealously guard for personal exploitation. *Don Juan Tenorio* only gained an enduring presence in the Spanish repertoire (and traditionally came to be performed on 1 November) several years later, when writers' initial unease toward the industrialization of literature and the public's view of poets as protected from the economic effects of modernization waned.[6] The protagonist of Zorrilla's play has tended to be read as a free spirit who succeeds in thwarting punishment for his misdeeds and adventures, and his ownership by Delgado stretched the plot beyond the stage and into the realities of capitalist society. The larger lesson of *Don Juan Tenorio* was that, in spite of the fantasy in the play, the individual will could be bought, owned, and controlled by others. *Don Juan Tenorio* continued to be a valuable commodity into and beyond the 1870s, and although the Delgado family did own it for much of the century, they were not the only investors to recognize its value, as seen in these wrappers.

The inner pages of the *galería* wrappers influenced contemporary consumers' reading and offer current historians a plethora of information regarding the traffic of dramatic literature as both capital and artistic work in the nineteenth century. In addition to the examples provided above, a close reading of the wrappers demonstrates the power of the *editores* to perpetuate the real existence of a play by maintaining its currency with readers: its inclusion in the catalogue suggested to readers that it was still suitable for purchase. Also, whereas the theatre public of nineteenth-century Madrid had a particularly voracious appetite and only rarely did a play run on one of its stages for longer than one month, new plays were staged outside of the capital years after their Madrid premiere, and the selection of titles displayed and promoted in the *galería* wrappers – presumably of works that the *editores* considered to be profitable – confirms that a wide variety of plays also continued to be popular as dramatic literature, years after their brief run on a Madrid stage.

The wrapper was a complex structure intended to both protect the poet's words from textual pirates and entice the public to enter its space. The wrapper physically contained the text and functioned as a microcosmic architectural gallery; all who desired access to the verse that was held within had to pass through its permeable portal. Using spatial terms, Genette has described the paratext as a '"vestibule" qui offre à tout un chacun la possiblité d'entrer, ou de rebrousser chemin' [vestibule that offers everyone the possibility to enter or to turn back]. It was a space of transition and 'transaction.'[7] This was analogous to the space of a gallery, as projected by the Spanish dramatic *editores* and described by Walter Benjamin: both interior and exterior blended into a site of encounters, inviting the reader (or *flâneur* or consumer) to enter. After passing through the peritextual wrappers of Spanish dramatic texts, the reader was then both inside the gallery and still outside of the literary work: he or she began to assess the quality and possible allure of the material available for consumption, but not to judge its own merits. At this point, the piece to be read was on display in the *galería* (beyond the title page), but its meaning was still only established through association. The door to the individual work had not been opened, and the titular threshold into the interior of the book had not been crossed.

The title page was the second peritextual element re-engineered by the dramatic *editores* of the nineteenth century. This sheet, found inside the wrapper but outside of the text, further codified the meaning of the verses to follow by literally adding another level of linguistic and symbolic signifiers. On facing pages, the reader saw the list of titles available through the gallery and the title page. The latter was strikingly similar to the array of window displays found in a nineteenth-century commercial arcade, or gallery. Each shop was a closed space, but a person promenading through a commercial arcade was surrounded by large display windows, the visual passageways between the arcade and the shops. Johann Geist has explained the rise of window displays at the beginning of the century as related to the space of the commercial gallery. 'The depth of the show window attained an architectural quality and became separate from the shop itself. The presentation of merchandise developed from a mere pile of goods to a collection of displays and finally to window dressings which were the responsibility of a special decorator.' This appendage to and presentation of the quality of the shop developed around 1800.[8] The separate assemblage of meaningful markers of the quality and allure of the items available for consumption within stores was comparable to the rise of title pages on books. These likewise began to be regularly included in every edition of single plays in the early nineteenth century and became part of the architectural structure of a dramatic text inside the *galería*: a special display window to present signs and symbols of the quality of the merchandise offered within. The arrangement of iconography, colours, brand names, and extra-textual references all served the same purpose: to attract the reading consumer.

This display page revealed the title of the individual play and the name of the poet who wrote it; however, these were mediated by a number of other defining elements on the page. The layout of the title sheet permitted a formulaic presentation of information: plays with a title page had an author (usually), title, premiere date, and place of publication. Peritextually, similarities tended to eclipse differences; paradoxically the Romantic plays of the 1830s and '40s, touted as highly original and creative in their texts, were systematically uniform in their *péritextes*. The possible elements in the format of the title page pioneered by Manuel Delgado (such as that in fig. 7) included – moving from top to bottom of the page – the name of the editorial agency, the title of the play, and its genre and number of acts, or market value (this referred to the tiered system of royalties, with more acts drawing in more money). This section was followed by the poet's name and, less often, the translator's name. (Even when there was one, he often remained unacknowledged.) The place and date of the first performance pointed back to the epitextual markers of the play and usually figured centrally on the page. The information above it referred to the poem and the person of the creator, while that which followed referred to the process of transforming the individual manuscript into a book. The second set of symbols on the bottom half of the page included illustrations or the emblem of the collection, the piece's identifying number in the collection, the name of printer, the city of publication, the printer's address, and finally the year of printing. That is, the bottom of the page was reserved for displaying the conditions under which and moment when this intellectual property changed forms and began to circulate as material property to be consumed. Then (if not on the wrapper), the address of the *editor* appeared at the very bottom and completed the frame that was opened with the name of the *galería* on the top of the page. The presence of the *editor* on the title page equaled, when it did not dwarf, that of the play itself. Consider the title page from the second edition of Ventura de la Vega's *El testamento* (fig. 7). Although both the title and the poet's name are prominently displayed (the poet's name in slightly shorter and significantly less bold font), the most striking element of the title page is the initials of Manuel Delgado crowned in laurels – as the *editor* (in a gesture as audacious as that of Napoleon himself) appropriated and crowned himself with the ancient symbol of literary excellence.

After deciphering the title page, and then physically turning the sheet of paper, the reader was presented with the next peritextual element of the edition: the articulation of its ownership, or the *derecho de autor*. Every other aspect of the *galería* paratext rested upon this element, for the productions of the nineteenth-century *editor* would not have existed without the recognition of property codified in the articulation of ownership. It appeared without fail in every edition. Lengthy and often creative declarations of *derecho de autor* testified to the status of the piece in the reader's hands as legally recognized property and dictated the correspondingly appropriate treatment of it to which the reader was bound. *Derecho de autor* was a fundamentally nineteenth-century phenomenon; however, the articulation of the legal status of a printed piece had traditionally been a crucial element of a Spanish text.

During the centuries preceding *derecho de autor*, censors' approbations and royal printing privileges had served to establish the legal status of a printed work and the validity of its physical and intellectual existence within the kingdom.[9] Whereas notations of royal privileges conformed to the place of literature within the governmental structure of an Ancien Régime monarchy, *derecho de autor* directed the movement of literature in a manner that was consistent with, and reflected the laws of, modern economic liberalism.[10]

The length of the articulation of ownership was inversely proportional to the degree to which this property right was generally respected by other *editores*, poets, and theatre impresarios. Among the most lengthy were the series of legal citations included in the editions created mid-century by the Círculo Literario Comercial (see fig. 8). These *editores* inserted a sheet dedicated exclusively to the reproduction of extensive quotes from the *Reglamento del teatro español* (7 Feb. 1849) between the title page and the first lines of the play and thus presented readers with a barricade of legal restrictions on the consumption of the literary work. Although the brief, symbolic, and internationally recognized © could only be the artifact of a remote future, a relatively standard legal articulation of dramatic literary property did eventually evolve later in the nineteenth century. It followed this formula:

> Esta obra es propiedad de su autor, y nadie podrá, sin su permiso, reimprimirla ni representarla en España y sus posesiones de Ultramar, ni en los paises con que haya celebrado ó se celebren en adelante tratados internacionales de propiedad literaria.
> El autor se reserva el derecho de traduccion.
> Los comisionados de las Galerías Dramáticas y Líricas de los *Sres Gullon é Hidalgo*, son los exclusivos encargados del cobro de los derechos de representacion y de la venta de ejemplares.
> Queda hecho el depósito que marca la ley.

> [This work is the property of its author, and no one may, without his permission, reprint it or stage it in Spain or in its overseas territories, nor in countries with whom international treaties of literary property have been signed or will be signed in the future.
> The author reserves the right of translation.
> The agents of the Galerías Dramáticas y Líricas of Mssrs. Gullon and Hidalgo, are exclusively authorized to collect royalties from staging and from the sale of editions.

An edition has been deposited (in the Royal Library) as mandated by law.]

Before the articulation of ownership was standardized in the above formula (c. 1875), it was often a dynamic element of the *péritexte*. For example, the title page of the 1870 lithographic edition of Eduardo Palacio's *La caza del tio* is framed with citations from Spain's literary property laws (fig. 9).[11] Thus, the characterization of the edition as a unique (handmade) object in an art gallery – established earlier in the century – was retained decades later: the property of the play found beyond the title page was only accessible to readers upon passage through the threshold of editorial guardianship presented in the peritextual frame. Moreover, as this edition was a lithograph of the poet's handwriting, the image of a unique 'handmade' *objet d'art* was even more patent. Another creative application of the articulation of *derecho* was its utilization by *editores* (or poets) to present the tone of the play to follow. In an edition from Valencia, printed in 1859, a uniquely peritextual work of literature ensued from the intersection of the verses of the text with the laws that protected them – the verso of the title page offered the following poetic legalese constructed upon an equivalence between poaching and plagiarism:

> Sent del autor propietat
> lo qu'así dins está escrit,
> el dir lo qu'atres han dit
> eu considere escusat.
> Pues ya sap tot gos y gat
> lo qu'aquell reglament resa:
> si vòlen fer esta pesa,
> llisènsia han de demandar,
> Si no se vòlen trovar
> la lley sobre su cabesa.[12]

[As the author is owner of what is written herein, to say what others have said, I will consider unnecessary. Because every dog and cat already knows what the law says: if they (cat and dog) want to do this piece, they must request licence if they don't want to find the law on their heads.]

The cat and dog, predatory animals, metaphorically represent an impresario interested in staging the play. Invoking authors' rights and alluding to the royal orders and the 1847 law of literary property, the poem reminds the reader that poachers poetically place themselves in a position of legal jeopardy and of 'finding' the law on their heads. The predators will themselves become prey – with a play on the word 'trovar' meaning 'to find' in Catalan (and Castilian), and, in Castilian, both 'to write verse' (like a *trovador*) and to imitate a poem but distort its tone or topic. As original as this poetic legalese was, it also pointed to Cervantes's own condemnation of plagiarism. In the Prologue to Part II of *Don Quijote*, the Golden Age author menaced would-be plagiarists (as well as chastised Avellaneda, who had written a 'false' *Quijote* that distorted Cervantes's character) with two jokes that related dogs with plagiarism.

Another poetic fusion of literature and property is found in the 1882 edition of a melodrama originally written in eighteenth-century France. The owner of the copyright of the Spanish translation of Jean Nicolas Bouilly's *L'Abbé de l'Épée* prefaced his edition with a short narrative that not only prohibited unauthorized editions and performances based upon illegal editions but also related a story of the predicaments of the play itself over the course of the nineteenth century. Enrique Arregui suggests a similarity between the integrity of the piece and that of the innocent main character of the *L'Abbé de l'Épée*: a vulnerable being who suffered similar melodramatic tribulations – and presents himself as the hero. Ill-intending theatre companies and editorial pirates had treated the play as an unprotected orphan (*no tenía autor conocido* [had no known author/creator]), and only the careful vigilence of the lawful *editor* could protect the drama from clandestine corruption by evil printers and stage directors.[13] Under the guardianship of Enrique Arregui, only the correct, pure version would be circulated in Spain. As the legally recognized owner, it is the right and responsibility of the *editor* to protect the literary text and his financial investment; yet, the 'autor' of the play referred to by Enrique Arregui in this notice is Juan de Grimaldi, one of the work's translators, and the original author, Jean Nicolas Bouilly, is wholly defrauded of his moral right of attribution over his creation. In a sense, Arregui was protecting a usurper. Indeed, the poet of the original French play was not named anywhere in Arregui's edition, yet he was a playwright of considerable importance. In addition to his success on the Parisian stage, Bouilly's works were known throughout Europe – not least of all through the setting of one of his pieces by Beethoven in the opera *Fidelio*. Moreover, Arregui's claim was highly exaggerated: Grimaldi did not create a play that was then tarnished by later printers – there were several previous Spanish translations of *L'Abbé de l'Épeé* completed well before Grimaldi's version.[14] However, the presentation in the peritextual ownership statement of this play's *derecho* as an abused orphan was a prelude to the plot of the literary melodrama that began on the next page of the edition.

The strong fictional tone of some examples from this mini-genre precludes their wholesale consideration as a reliable documentary source. However, many of the short narratives produced in the articulations of ownership do provide unique chronicles of the history of nineteenth-century theatre. In *El sacristán toreador*, a one-act *sainete* written by Don Ricardo Valero and administered by Eduardo Hidalgo (i.e., the author held the *derecho*, but Hidalgo still performed almost identical editorial functions), there is a particularly illustrative note just above the articulation of ownership:

> NOTA. Principalmente en Andalucía suele representarse este sainete con el título *El Sacristan y el Toro*, lo que recomiendo á los Sres. Corresponsales del Sr. Hidalgo para que no autoricen un abuso con el cual han eludido, hasta la fecha, el pago de la propiedad literaria.[15]

> [Note. Principally in Andalusia this *sainete* is usually staged with the title *El sacristan y el toro*, of which I warn the provincial agents of Sr. Hidalgo, lest they authorize an abuse through which they have lost, until now, revenues from literary property.]

El sacristán toreador has completely vanished from the scene of nineteenth-century theatre studies. However, this play was evidently quite popular (i.e., it was staged repeatedly, as the word 'suele' implies), and sufficient revenue was lost by the illegal title-switching to convince the *editores* to invest in the creation of a new edition with the above note. Additionally, this comment is of literary interest, for the first-person voice (in 'recomiendo' [I recommend]) that speaks here is a rare enunciation of the legendary Romantic 'I.' In this case, it appears outside of the work but inside the edition and thus is not a fictional construction or a narrative pose, but rather the true voice of the historical person of the writer, expressing his relationship with the text and hope for remuneration through royalties. If an authentic authorial 'I' does exist in a nineteenth-century edition of literature, it is to be found here, in the articulation of ownership, within the peritextual space of editorial protection.

Both the content and placement of the *derecho de autor* varied over the course of the century, but the articulation of ownership most often appeared on the verso of the title page. The poet could also employ this space to provide specific directions on characterization or the locus of dramatic action, and thus – from beyond the verses – guide and limit the reader's lawful comprehension of the text and render the piece ever more immutable in the case of performance. For example, in *Las tres jaquecas*, a comedy in Eduardo Hidalgo's Administracion Lírico-Dramática, a note printed just above the articulation of ownership (and below the dramatis personae) invoked the law in order to dictate the portrayal of one of the play's main characters to a provincial public. It stated: 'El papel de la Condesa pertenece de derecho á la actriz contratada de segunda dama. No es una característica. Es una señora de 35 años: jamona, pero bien conservada. Téngase esto en cuenta para el reparto en provincias' [The role of the Countess belongs by right to the actress contracted as second lady. This is not just a detail. She is a thirty-five-year-old woman: aged, but well preserved].[16] More direct was the indication by the Duque de Rivas in 1840: his initial stage direction (above the articulation of ownership) stipulated that 'la decoracion es inmutable' [the set is immutable].[17] Notes such as these were ubiquitous in nineteenth-century dramatic texts, and it is impossible to verify completely the extent to which these authorial directions were followed. Nevertheless, the expression of the author's (supposed) intent regarding the reading or staging of his work could legally transcend the textual limitations of the edition. Copyright attempted to restrict multiple interpretations in publication in both performance and private reading.

Cultural Nationalization

The most far-reaching and ideologically important result of the uniformity and fixing of the text through literary property and the stable *péritexte* was their nationalizing influence upon the various provinces of the nation. Print cultures carried out a task that spectacle-based theatre (even one as important as that of Golden Age Spain) could not. As Benedict Anderson has argued, the birth of a national culture was aided by compiling into print format all that the state decided was relevant, thereby fostering feelings of cultural cohesion.[18] However, in the case of Spain, the Crown outsourced this nationalistic enterprise to the *editores*, who carried it out under the protections afforded by copyright laws.

Intellectual property law turned cultural artifacts into investments, and the editorial agencies of Madrid, concerned with not only plagiarism but also the corruption of their capital, attempted to enforce that, for example, the production of a play staged in Málaga in 1840 was linguistically identical to that staged in Cáceres in 1860, or Vigo in 1885. The by-product of the venture of the *editores* to protect their capital was that the verses of any dramatic work performed on any stage in the nation were, according to the theory of literature as property and the practice of the supremacy of 'speech,' identical in each performance. Because of the emphasis on the textual element of performance, once this property was stable, citizens throughout Spain (although they were aware of the differences in actors' skill, stage sets, etc.) could believe they were attending performances of the same work.[19] That is, the experience of attending the 'same play' could be reproduced many times by Spanish citizens in any city of the nation. In doing so, the public participated in the process of its own cultural homogenization within the new, politically uniform Spain.

The imaginary shared cultural knowledge was disturbed when a text was changed in performance. In an example from mid-century Cadiz, the critic considered the *story* to have been 'maltratada' [abused] when the actors decided to alter the plot of the play:

> En la noche del juéves se representó en [el Teatro del Circo] el drama de don Francisco Martinez de la Rosa: «La conjuracion de Venecia». Sabido es que termina esta produccion con la muerte de Rujiero [*sic*], uno de los cabezas de los rebeldes á la República de San Marcos, y con el triunfo del Consejo de los Diez. Pero los actores, conociendo que de esta suerte no saldria contenta alguna parte del público que concurre al Circo, acordaron que en el mismo instante de ser llevado Rujiero [*sic*] al suplicio, saliesen todos los comparsas gritando !«viva la libertad»! y diesen de cuchilladas á los del Consejo de los Diez: con lo cual los espectadores quedaron muy satisfechos, y la historia estraordinariamente maltratada.[20]

[Last Thursday [the Circo Theatre] staged the drama by Francisco Martinez de la Rosa *La conjuración de Venecia*. Everyone knows that this production ends with the death of Rugiero, one of the leaders of the rebels against the Republic of San Marco, and with the triumph of the Council of Ten. But, the actors, knowing that with this ending no one who attended the Circo Theatre would leave happy, decided that at the moment when Rugiero is taken to the torture chamber, all of the extras would run out yelling 'long live liberty!' and that they would threaten the Council of Ten with knives: with this, the spectators left very satisfied and the story extraordinarily abused.]

The actors' decision to place the desires of the audience before the interior perfection of the text violated the play's stability and challenged the ideology of property upon which nineteenth-century society itself was based. The audience may have been momentarily entertained by the adapted version, but their consumption of it was aesthetically and legally outlawed. When people throughout Spain began to protest changes and believe that the text, or story (fixed as *propiedad literaria*), was the entity represented in the theatre, with other aspects of the stage in service to it, they, in turn, enacted a performance of the ideologies of modern property in the auditorium. During performances, they accepted the work as it was staged (no longer calling out requests to the actors) and then judged it. Once regional audiences relinquished their particular desires, and preferred to consume the same cultural good found throughout the nation, the process of attending the stable play inscribed them into an imagined 'Spanish' culture.

Wadda Ríos-Font has discussed the nationalizing impact of theatre in terms of the way in which the ubiquitous melodramatic plot and its characteristic *mise en scène* contributed to regulating the theatrical experience in the later nineteenth century. During the last decades of the nineteenth century, the melodramatic plot perfected by José Echegaray (Nobel Prize in literature, 1874) set a new role for theatre as a place where the public 'began to look for [melodrama's] reassuring world view,' and it functioned as a 'hegemonic force that appropriated the discourse of progress while simultaneously sustaining conventional ideologies.'[21] This type of theatre dictated taste and guided ideologies, but not as part of any particular nationalist agenda; it similarly impacted the public at large.

The cultural space of the Spanish nation, as revealed on its stages, was partly defined by the protection of dramatic literary property as capital. The Crown did not directly order nationalization of the stage; rather, it decreed laws that turned literature into property and allowed the proprietors to protect their interests: namely, to ensure that each performance was faithful to the protected, 'fixed' text throughout Spain.[22] Capital thereby enabled a shared cultural experience in theatre within the legal boundaries of the nation, even as it partitioned the shared theatrical patrimony of the seventeenth and eighteenth centuries.

The exchange of literary properties as commodities changed theatre from a spectacle to a text-based event and redefined its place in society, from a shared national (royal) patrimony to alienable private property. As a rhetorical thermometer of the degree to which Spain demonstrated its *civilización*, a theatre of private properties was also a marker of the degree to which Spain (theoretically) became a unified cultural space during the reign of Isabel II. By guaranteeing uniformity of the text, copyright legislation provided the possibility for each community of spectators to be presented with a 'nationalized' culture. As the Queen Regent's ministers had suggested in 1837, the scope of Spain's recognition of literary property in its laws would mark it as civilized to its European neighbours. However, the extent to which literary property was respected within its borders reflected the degree to which economic liberalism and the modern state were themselves accepted by (or imposed on) society.

Whereas other elements of the paratext promoted the play's literary, artistic, and financial value (accrued through circulation), the articulation of ownership enumerated the legal restrictions on free circulation of the text in reading and performance. Essentially, it was a list of forbidden means of consumption. As the owner informed readers of his right to control their use of the text, the responsibility to consume it (through reading or performance) in accordance with the law began to lie with them.

It would be historically inaccurate to suggest a clear-cut distinction between the circulation of copyrighted works as printed dramatic literature and professional stage performances: between them were *comedias caseras* and performances by private 'liceos' or theatre circles (or 'acting clubs'), among other ambiguous forms. Legally, these were initially private, non-lucrative events and not subject to the laws of literary property; nevertheless, they were dramatic readings of editions created and owned by the *editores*. The first is mentioned with relative frequency: see for example, Mesonero Romanos's 'El Romanticismo y los Románticos,' and the more lengthy article 'El teatro casero' in *El entreacto*.[23] Acting clubs and home performances were not the result of attempts to circumvent the payment of copyright, but rather specific examples of how the implementation of 'modern' copyright had to be adjusted to meet existing practices and (more generally) how the entire population had to be conditioned to perceive their lives and experiences in terms of private property.

Leonardo Romero Tobar has also discussed 'teatros particulares' and described the custom in aristocratic households (as portrayed by Ramón de la Cruz in *La comedia casera*) in the eighteenth century, noting that by the 1830s, it became common in the homes of both noble and bourgeois families.[24] José Blanco White indicates that performances from plays were taking place in salons in Seville during this same period. Indeed, by the latter part of the eighteenth century, authors began to write specifically for this market: for example, José Concha's *El mas heroico español ... fácil de executar en cualquier casa, para cinco hombres solos* [easy to perform in any home, for five men] (Madrid: Librería de Cerro, 1797); Luciano Francisco Comella's *El casado avergonzado*, written to be 'executada toda por niños' [staged completely by children] (Salamanca: Imprenta de don Francisco de Tóxar, 1790); and Antonio Rezano Imperiali's play *Acrisolar el dolor en el más filial amor*, 'easily performed in private homes, as it is arranged for just seven male parts' (Madrid: Imprenta de García, 1817).[25]

Likewise, the issues of control and censorship pre-dated copyright. In 1632 the *Consejo* of Castille prohibited the staging of 'comedias en las casas particulares sin licencia del Presidente del Consejo' [plays in private homes without a licence from the President of the Castilian Council]. They were again prohibited by royal order on 22 September 1762.[26] In the nineteenth century, there was a great deal of legal concern over whether or not private clubs (or theatres which sold not tickets to a performance but rather the actual seats in an auditorium) could stage a play (or their own version of it) without having to pay the *editor* a *derecho*.[27] In August 1839, *El entreacto* noted that 'se ha suscitado en estos dias la cuestion de si el Liceo artistico y literario es ó no un establecimiento público, y por tanto se halla sujeto ó exento de la censura de los periódicos cuanto en él se hace. Resolver esa cuestion generalmente, será desacertado siempre; porque el Liceo tiene de público y de privado ... De todo esto se deduce que si el Liceo es un establecimiento, cuya existencia es pública, y que tiende á influir en el público de cierta manera, no es ni con mucho una especie de teatro donde *por solo el dinero* se admite á cuantos caben y quieren entrar' [recently the question has been raised of whether or not the artistic and literary 'Liceo' club is or is not a public establishment and therefore subject or not to commentary in the newspapers about what might be done there. It would be foolish to try to resolve this question, as the 'Liceo' is both public and private ... From all this, we can summarize that if the 'Liceo' is an establishment, whose existence is public and which tends to influence the public in a certain way, it is certainly not a theatre where *money is the only* factor that decides who may enter and how many might fit].[28] In their refusal to pay copyright, *El entreacto* saw the 'Liceos' as a space of resistance to capitalism, money, and the commercialization of cultural life.

By 1857, Manuel Pedro Delgado (the son of Manuel Delgado) addressed these groups directly in the copyright statements in each of his play editions, declaring: 'Esta comedia pertenece á la Galeria Dramática, que comprende los teatros moderno, antiguo español y estrangero, y es propiedad de su editor *Don Manuel Pedro Delgado*, quien perseguirá ante la ley, para que se le apliquen las penas que marca la misma, al que sin su permiso la reimprima ó represente en algun teatro del Reino, ó en los Liceos y demás Sociedades sostenidas por suscricion de los Socios, con arreglo á la ley de 10 de Junio de 1847, y decreto Orgánico de teatros de 28 de Julio de 1852' [This comedy belongs to the Galería Dramática, which includes modern, classic Spanish, and foreign theatre, and is the property of its *editor*, *Don Manuel Pedro Delgado*, who will prosecute to the fullest extent of the law anyone who reprints or stages this play without his permission in any theatre in the Kingdom, or in the 'Liceos' and other Acting Clubs organized by subscribing Members, according to the law of 10 June 1847 and the State Decree regarding Theatre of 28 June 1852].[29] As of 1857, Delgado no longer saw acting clubs as between public and private, but as wholly part of the literary marketplace.

Related to the issue of private performances outside of the public theatres was the fact that after copyright, plays were frequently published before they were staged (in contrast to the inverse in previous centuries) and often were not staged in Madrid. Although (according to the title page) it was indeed 'estrenado en el Teatro del Circo de Price en la noche del 18 de Diciembre de 1870,' in the initial 'stage directions' for his play *Camafeo y la porra*, the poet Luis Blanc y Navarro indicates a non-theatrical dramatic space: 'La escena pasa en donde *al lector* le parezca mas conveniente' [The action takes place wherever *the reader* considers most appropriate] (emphasis added). Newspaper articles testify to contemporary tension over the most appropriate medium for the presentation of a dramatic text. In 1849 a writer from Cadiz noted: 'Acaba de publicarse una comedia en un acto titulada «*Las dos bodas descubiertas*», y escrita por el apreciable y laborioso jóven don Juan J. de Arenas, ... su argumento ofrece interés y algunas de sus situaciones deben ser de bastante efecto. Deseamos verle puesta en escena para poder dar con mas acierto nuestro juicio acerca de un género de composiciones hechas mas bien para ser representadas que para ser leidas' [A one-act play by the admirable and hard-working young writer Juan J. de Arenas, titled *The Two Discovered Weddings*, has just been published ... and its interesting plot includes a few situations that promise to produce great effect. We wish to see it staged to better offer our assessment on a genre that is written to be performed rather than to be read].[30]

The lines of literature and property in the nineteenth-century editions of dramatic verse intersected in *derecho de autor* through attempts to produce an authoritative force over the practices of reading and performing. Although the printing of *ediciones furtivas* [pirated copies] transgressed the lines of propertied discourse, the economic nature of the crimes of literature also made it incumbent upon readers to procure a legal copy of a play. Like money, it was illegal not only to make, but to own and read, a counterfeit edition. The laws of literary property were visually asserted through an edition's peritextuality, which in turn established the legitimacy of a reader's interaction with a dramatic poem. The language, layout, and iconography of the *péritexte* offered the reader recognizable symbols of artistic authenticity and testified to the legitimate purchase of the legally consecrated version of a play. In the Romantic age, consumers were ideologically directed to value and desire original works (rather than copies or imitations) for the textual *galerías* installed in their homes. Thus, liberal laws of property, while sanctifying the individual poet's artistic expression, emphasized not only the crimes of publishing but also the crimes of reading, from a desecration of mores in content (reading books on the Index), to violations of form, or the consumption of pirated editions.[31] Even if the printed words of an unauthorized text claimed to match those of the poet's unknowable original manuscript, as pirated property outside of the legally recognized system of commodities, it could not be a legitimate piece of literature.[32] Circulating without an author or owner, it was not an orphan (as Arregui claimed for *La huerfana de Bruselas*), but rather a bastard, without any social or legal source or identity.

As owners of the literary property and creators of the material copies, *editores* created *galerías* and directed the consumption of the texts contained within them. They effectively constructed the sociological meaning of a work by placing it in a specific commercial space and imbuing it with their own authority (the name of the editorial house), while guaranteeing the linguistic purity and economic legitimacy of the copy. Thus, the material format in which the immaterial *derechos de autor* circulated throughout Spain was simultaneously a guarantee of poetic authenticity, an artifact of liberal ideologies of property, and a marketing tool. Paradoxically, Romantic plays were enveloped within the uniform *péritextes* of a commercial institution that visually undermined the individuality of the 'inspired' poet, while his supposed distance from the market made him commercially attractive. Finally, by distinguishing licit from illicit literature according to its economic status, the *péritexte* restricted the viable venues available to a reader for a legitimate interaction with literature in a very real and punishable way.

Conclusion

Like many nineteenth-century ideals (national sovereignty, the nation, 'Spanish' culture, or modernity), the realities of dramatic authorship differed significantly from the philosophies upon which it was theorized. The grand, new 'discovery' of the individual dramatic poet's autonomy was, more realistically, an invention that drew upon a reinterpretation of the past, a revaluation of the role of theatre in Spanish society, contemporary theories of political economy, and specific historical and personal circumstances. Not only is any authorial 'originality' debatable, but also dramatic poets were never free from the market and full 'authority' over the stage could only ever be a fantasy, testing the limits of property and the projection of the individual will. In contrast, dramatic copyright and the legal and economic concepts that codified authorship did engender a profound, real, and lasting transformation of Spanish theatre through the privatization of the text and the subsequent supremacy of speech in performance. The adaptation of cultural practices into the norms of private property distorted relations among the arts of the stage. As theatre bore the marker of modernity, copyright conditioned the reception of dramatic literature by readers and the public. Whether play texts should still be studied as literature or addressed primarily as a springboard for staged interpretations by directors, actors, costumers, and designers must take into account the historically specific process that led to theatre's textualization. This is not simply an academic question, but rather one that concerns all written texts and the place of language in our increasingly visual culture.

After post-structuralism dislodged the illusion of proprietary authorship as an organizing force in discourse, language and writing took its place.[1] But even with the author's departure, this still privileges speech in theatre, in spite of language's necessary dependence on other arts during performance. Poetry was always essential to Spanish theatre; however, textuality did not precede dramatic authorship: stagecraft did. Spanish theatre offers an alternative model to understanding the issues of power and the ownership of discourse, for copyright, authorship, textuality, and the supremacy of language in theatre developed symbiotically. Dramatic proprietary authorship was equally a historically specific illusion, but its difference from lyric or narrative authorship provides an alternative model to post-structuralist understandings of literature after the death of the author.

When members of the public in the Príncipe Theatre asked, '¿Quién es el autor?' and García Gutiérrez then appeared before them to assume the title of dramatic author, they initiated a legal process that reframed previous arguments for intellectual property and culminated in the recognition of a *derecho de autor* for dramatic works in Spain. The liberal ideas of ownership and the Romantic concerns for writing led to the supremacy of the text in performance and, once vested with natural-law property rights, the poet theoretically wrested control over the stage (in *autoría*, or authorship) away from the traditional *autor de comedias*. The theatre created by the 'illiterate' (as Larra qualified them) artists of spectacle, and regulated by the Crown as an event, gave way to a literature-based theory and practice of the stage. However, apart from the immutability of his text, treated as literary capital and protected according to the laws of property, the poet had little direct control over performances after the premiere. The *editor*, who purchased and controlled the literary property, became a crucial figure in the new system of theatre production, as he owned and policed its rights. As a result of literary property, *autoría* (or control of the stage) was in practice transferred from the *autor de comedias* to the *editor*, and only nominally passed through the poet. But, less than seventy years after his birth, the *editor* disappeared, in 1900. The new Sociedad general de autores y escritores [General Society of Authors and Writers] (a trade union for all composers and authors in Spain) obliged the dramatic *editores* to turn over to it the authors' rights that they owned and definitively abolished the nineteenth-century dramatic *editor* from the world of theatre and dramatic literature.[2]

In light of the textualization that provided the foundation for these changes, early nineteenth-century Spanish theatre also provides a useful model for understanding writers' relationship to the rapidly developming literary marketplace. Much of the groundbreaking work by Pierre Bourdieu on the development of the cult of the author, the high/low distinction in literature, and the development of the modern literary field that has framed later studies, covers only the later nineteenth century and focuses primarily on French novels and art. But the basic scenario that he outlines also took place much earlier in Spain. Bourdieu points to the stability of the reign of Napoleon III and the mandate of money, but Mendizábal's Spain, during the instability of the Carlist Civil Wars, was an equally commodities-crazed age, when the ship of state was guided by a blind faith in the market. It only became possible to live as a professional writer for the theatre as a result of its privatization (along with nearly everything else in Spain), but those who refused assimilation to bourgeois art were protected by the *editor*, who facilitated their economic and social positions. Whereas the boom in novels was, to a large degree, a product of the industrialization of print and the development of new formats like the serial in newspapers that took place several decades later, in Spain, the proclamation and display of national sovereignty as well as the implementation of privatization and individual property necessarily took place in the theatre and implicated its writers, as power and representation of the state was wrested from royal hands. These transformations were elemental to nineteenth-century modernity itself, which later set the groundwork for a situation similar to that described by Bourdieu in *The Rules of Art.* Spanish theatre and its transformation after copyright challenge our assumptions about authorship, language, writers in society, and theatre as art in a larger European arena.

Appendix:
AHN Legajo 11387

The documents are transcribed as they appear in manuscript at the Spanish National Historical Archives. The notes in brackets refer to the position of the text on the page or to a change in style or writing instruments. Unless noted, this is black ink. Words crossed out in the original are reproduced with strike-through (e.g., ~~teatro~~); words added to the manuscript later are reproduced in a smaller font. Phrases that were illegible in the document have been approximated and placed in italics. The translations have attempted to include this polyvalence of voice. To aid in readability, some long sentences have been divided into shorter phrases, and a few small stylistic changes have been implemented.

I: Royal Decree of 20 November 1833

Boletín del Comercio. Num 107 Viernes 22 Nov 1833 [n.p.]

Reales Decretos

Se me ha dado cuenta del mal estado en que se encuentran los teatros del reino, y de la conveniencia de mejorar su situacion. Convencida Yo de esta necesidad, y cierta de que es el teatro un elemento de civilizacion, al mismo tiempo que un medio de favorecer muchas industrias, cuya prosperidad está esencialmente enlazada con la del teatro mismo; mando, en nombre de mi cara Hija la REINA Doña ISABEL II, que una comision, compuesta de D. Manuel José Quintana, D. Francisco Martinez de la Rosa y D. Alberto Lista, todos individuos de la academia Española, me proponga lo que estime conveniente sobre los derechos de los escritores dramáticos, sobre [el] establecimiento de escuelas de declamacion, sobre las leyes que infaman la profesion de actor, y sobre la policía de los espectáculos en general, y reuna en un proyecto completo de ley, que me presentará por vuestro conducto, todos los estímulos que puedan darse á un arte que deseo favorecer, y las mejoras de que este ramo del servicio administrativo sea susceptible. Tendréislo entendido, y dispondreis lo necesario á su cumplimiento. – Está rubricado de la Real mano. – En Palacio á 20 de noviembre de 1833. – A D. Javier de Burgos.

Translation:

Bulletin of Commerce. Num. 107, Friday, 22 November 1833, s.p.

Royal Decrees

I have been given an account of the poor state of the theatres of this kingdom and the urgency of improving their condition. I, convinced of this need and certain that the theatre is an element of civilization, at the same time that it is a means of favouring many industries, whose prosperity is essentially intertwined with that of the theatre itself; order, in the name of my dear Daughter, the QUEEN Doña ISABEL II, that a commission, composed of Don Manuel José Quintana, Don Francisco Martínez de la Rosa, and Don Alberto Lista, all members of the Spanish Academy, propose to me appropriate measures regarding copyright for dramatic writers, the establishment of acting schools, laws that defame the actor's profession, and the policing of spectacles, in general. I order that the commission draw up a complete proposal of a law, which will inform me of all of the stimuli that can be given to an art which I desire to favour, and the improvements to which this branch of the administrative service may be susceptible. You are hereby notified and all that is necessary for its completion is at your disposal. – Bearing the rubric of the Royal Hand. – In the Palace on 20 November 1833. – Javier de Burgos.

II: Petition of 4 February 1837

The petition is on two large folios bearing official stamps. There is writing on only one side of each page, and the entire petition was enclosed by the government in a cover with the following identifying title ('Instancia ...').

'Instancia presentada a la reina, firmada por los escritores dramaticos Breton, García Gutiérrez, Hartzenbusch, Ochoa y Gregorio Romero, en la que piden proteccion para los derechos de autor o prop. Lit.'

[Cover] Madrid 1837
[in pencil] 4 Febrero
[ink] Se dirigió hace mas de dos meses á S. M. una representacion firmada por varios escritores dramaticos sobre el uso de la propiedad literaria. Se presento en el Ministerio de la Gubernacion ecsistiendo actualmente en la Seccion de Policia

[in margin] Abril 9/ *1839 Prepare* al despacho sin demora[1]

[Large folio]
[affixed stamp] Sello 4o. 40Ms.
[Preprinted]
Año de 1837
Habilitado publicada la constitucion en 15 de agosto de 1836

[manuscript]

Señora.

Cuando con fecha 20 Noviembre de 1833 se dignó V. M. espedir un decreto creando una Junta para que propusiese lo que estimase conveniente sobre los derechos de los escritores dramaticos, sobre establecimiento de escuelas de declamacion, sobre las leyes que infaman la profesion de autor y sobre la policia de los espectaculos en general; manifestó claramente cuan convencido estaba su Real animo de la decadencia en que se hallan tan interesantes ramos, siendo el teatro como espresa el mismo decreto un elemento su civilizacion, al cual está enlazada la prosperidad de muchas industrias. V.M. quiso que se le propusiese un proyecto de ley completo en él que se reuniesen todos los estímulos que pudieran darse á un arte que deseaba favorecer y las mejoras de que este ramo del servicio administrativo fuese suscetible. Causas que es inu-

[next page]

til determinar han detenido los resultados de tan beneficas intenciones y los trabajos de la Junta no han llegado á producir el efecto que de ellos se esperaba. Aunque la falta de esta ley sea sensible en todos los estremos que abrazaba el citado decreto hay sin embargo algunos en los que la opinion publica á la necesidad han influida favorablemente haciendo en ellos mejoras de consideración; pero uno, él de los derechos de los escritores dramaticos, se halla enteramente desatendido, hallandose estos con la mayor impunidad; cuando por el reglamento de libertad de imprenta vigente debieran considerarse como garantizados. Todas las producciones dramaticas que se representan en algun teatro ó se imprimen y las que aun carecen de alguna de estas dos circunstancias, se ven immediatamente [sic] reproducidas en los demas teatros de la Peninsula sin preceder permiso, ni aun noticia del autor y algunas veces contra su voluntad. Las consecuencias de semejante modo de proceder, se estienden no solo á privar á los autores de su propiedad, quitandoles el justo bueno que de su trabajo de ben esperar, sino tambien son causa de que las obras dramáticas

[next folio, stamp and preprinted heading]

se representen desfiguradas y llenas de mutilaciones, ya por la infidelidad de las copias, que se proporcionan, ya por la ignorancia de los actores y ya enfin por carecer de los oportunos avisos que el autor pudiera comunicar, resultando de todo esto incalculables perjuicios á los literatos que se dedican á escribir para el teatro, y la transgresion de los derechos de propiedad, garantizados por nuestras instituciones y por las de todos los paises civilizados. Por lo que
A V. M. suplicamos se digne espedir un decreto en él que se mande respetar la propiedad literaria en todas sus partes, ordenando para ello que en ningun teatro de la Peninsula se pueda representar ninguna produccion dramatica sin que preceda el consentimiento de su autor y un convenio que asegure á este la recompensa de sus desvelos, sin que el estar ya impresa pueda servir de escusa para contravenir esta disposicion general.
Madrid 4 Febrero de 1837
    Señora
A. L. M. P. de V. M.

[Signed]
Manuel Breton de los Herreros   Gregorio Romero y Larrañaga
Antonio Garcia Gutz
Juan Eugenio Hartzenbusch   Eug° de Ochoa

Translation:

'Petition presented before the Queen, signed by the dramatic writers Breton, García Gutiérrez, Hartzenbusch, Ochoa y Gregorio Romero, in which they request protection for authors' rights or Lit. prop.'

[Cover] Madrid 1837
[in pencil] 4 February
[ink] Over two months ago, a petition signed by various dramatic writers regarding the use of literary property was addressed to Her Majesty. It was presented in the Ministry of Government, currently under the Police Divison.

[in margin] 9 April/ *1839 Prepare* for dispatch without delay

[Large folio]
[affixed stamp] Sello 4o. 40Ms.
[Preprinted]
The Year of 1837
By the Constitution published 15 August 1836

[manuscript]

Madame.

When on 20 November 1833 Your Majesty deigned to decree the creation of a Commission to propose appropriate measures regarding the rights of dramatic writers, the establishment of acting schools, laws that defame the actor's profession, and the policing of spectacles, in general; You clearly manifested your Royal Will to be convinced of the decadence of these crucial branches of state, as the theatre is, according to this same decree, an element of its civilization, with which the prosperity of many industries is intertwined. Your Majesty wished that a complete project of law be proposed to You that would summarize all of the stimuli that could be given to an art which You wished to favour and indicate the most effective means to improve this branch of the administrative service. For reasons that it is

[next page]

unnecessary to enumerate, the results of such benevolent intentions have been halted and the work of the Commission has not produced the effect which was hoped of it. Although the lack of this law is felt in all of the areas which were comprised by the aforementioned decree, there are, nevertheless, some in which the public opinion of their necessity has influenced favourably, producing considerable improvements to them. However, the rights of dramatic writers, are still entirely ignored, these rights suffer the greatest impunity; when, according to the current rules of free press, they ought to be considered as guaranteed. All dramatic productions that have been staged or printed and even those that have not, are immediately reproduced in other theatres in the Peninsula without prior permission, indeed without notifying the author and sometimes against his will. The consequences of this practice result not only in depriving authors of their property, robbing them of the profit that they rightly ought to expect from their labour, but also are the reason why dramatic works

[next folio, stamp and preprinted heading]

are staged disfigured and full of mutilations, either because of errors in the copies that are available, the ignorance of the actors, or the lack of opportune advice that the author might have given them; as a result, the *literati* who dedicate themselves to writing for the theatre have suffered incalculable injury, and the rights of property, guaranteed by our institutions and by those of all civilized countries, have been violated. Therefore,
We beg Your Majesty to deign to decree an order stating that literary property in all its parts be respected, and thereby ordering that in no theatre in the Peninsula may any dramatic production be staged without the previous consent of its author and a contract that assures him a recompense for his labor, and also forbidding that the previous printing of the play serve as an excuse to contravene Your general will.

Madrid, 4 February 1837
   Madame
A. L. M. P. de V. M.

[Signed]

Manuel Breton de los Herreros   Gregorio Romero y Larrañaga
Antonio Garcia Gutz
Juan Eugenio Hartzenbusch   Eug° de Ochoa

III: Draft of Royal Decree from 4 May 1837

Las ~~justas~~ quejas que en esposicion de 4 de febrero último elevaron á la augusta Reina Gobernadora varios literatos de esta Corte sobre la ~~escandalosa~~ violacion del derecho de propiedad literaria en lo relativo á obras dramáticas, han llamado mui particularmente la atencion de S.M. Las leyes 24ª í 25ª, libro 8°, título 16° de la Novísima recopilacion aseguran í protegen esta propiedad en general; pero el espíritu de ignorancia í ~~fanatismo~~ y preocupacion que, ansioso de ahogar todo gérmen de ilustracion í vida para los pueblos no consideraba el teatro sino como una condescencia ~~que era forzoso tener con la relajacion publica, naturalmente~~ necesaria que le era repugnante desdeñó í aun ~~repugno siempre~~ contradijo constantemente la aplicacion de las mencionadas leyes en provecho del arte dramática, elemento de civilizacion, al cual está enlazada la prosperidad de muchas industrias.

   De aqui ha nacido que el ~~natural~~ derecho de propiedad de los escritores dramáticos se halle [~~enteramente~~] todavia desatentido, ~~hallado con impunidad~~ ~~se olvidada en parte~~
Las obras que se representan en algun teatro, ó se imprimen, í aun las que carecen de alguna de estas ~~dos~~ circunstancias, se ven ~~inmediatamente~~ frecuentemente reproducidas en los demas ~~teatros~~ de la Peninsula, sin preceder permiso ni aun noticia de su autor, í á veces contra su voluntad. Este abuso se estiene, no solo á privar á los literatos de su propiedad, ~~quitandoles~~ disminuyendoles el justo ~~lucro que~~ producto de su trabajo ~~deben esperar~~, sino tambien á que sus ~~producciones~~ obras se representen desfiguradas ~~ó llenas de mutilaciones~~ y contrahechas, por la infidelidad de las copias que furtivamente se proporcionan. ~~L[illegible] modo de proceder es una verdadera usurpacion de la propiedad agena.~~

Penetrada, ~~pues~~, S.M. de la necesidad de desterrar este abuso

[next page]

se ha servido resolver que por el Ministerio de mi cargo se forme ~~í presente á la aprobacion de las Córtes~~ un proyecto de lei que declare, deslinde í afiance los derechos respectivos de la propiedad literaria en todos sus accidentes, para presentarlo á la deliberacion de las Cortes.

Pero S.M. que ~~se complace al notar~~ complaciendose con el estraordinario vuelo que la dramática española ha tomado en esta era de libertad, que parece prometer para el reinado de su augusta Hija un nuevo siglo de oro de la poesía nacional, conoce que por lo mismo los perjuicios irrogados á los escritores reclaman mas perentorio remedio, í ~~por tanto~~ á fin de proveerlo se ha servido resolver ademas, provisionalmente, í mientras el citado proyecto de la leí no se discute, ~~se~~ aprueba í sanciona, que las obras dramáticas, como ~~propiedad exclusiva de sus autores~~ toda propiedad, estan bajo la inmediata proteccion de las autoridades; í que teniendo estas producciones, por su especial naturaleza, dos existencias distintas, una por el teatro í otra por la imprenta, ~~ningun autor, director ó empresario de~~ en ningun teatro se podrá en adelante ~~hacer~~ representar una obra dramática, aun cuando ~~estuviere~~ ~~fuere~~ estubiere impresa, o se hubiere representado en otro ú otras, ~~teatros~~, sin permiso de su autor, o dueño o propietario ~~que hubiere adquirido~~.

De real órden lo comunico á V.S. Á fin de que dé la publicidad conveniente á esta resolucion de S.M. í vele sobre su mas exacto cumplimiento. Dios guarde á V. S. Muchos años
Madrid 4 5 de mayo de 1837

Translation:

The ~~just~~ complaints that various writers of this City brought before the august Queen in an exposition this past 4 February, regarding the ~~scandalous~~ violation of literary property law as related to dramatic works, have particularly caught the attention of Her Majesty. The 24th and 25th laws of the 8th Book, 16th Title of the *Novísima recopilacion* assure and protect this property in general; but the spirit of ignorance and ~~fanaticism~~ and preoccupation which, eager to drown any seed of enlightenment and life for the nation, considered the theatre merely as a nec-

Appendix 159

essary indulgence ~~that was obliged to grant for public relaxation, naturally~~ that it found repugnant disdained and even ~~always resisted~~ constantly prevented the application of the aforementioned laws benefiting the dramatic arts, an element of civilization with which the prosperity of many industries is intertwined.

From here it was born that the ~~natural~~ right of property of dramatic writers is found [~~entirely~~] still ignored, ~~suffering the greatest impunity partly forgotten~~
The works that have been staged, or printed, and even those which have not, are ~~immediately~~ frequently reproduced in other ~~theatres~~ in the Peninsula, without prior permission or indeed even without notifying the author, and at times against his will. As a result of this abuse, not only are the *literati* deprived of their property, ~~robbing them~~ diminishing the just ~~profit that~~ product of their labour ~~that they ought to expect~~, but also that their ~~productions~~ works are performed disfigured ~~or full of mutilations~~ and counterfeit, because of the errors in the copies that are furtively distributed. ~~L[illegible] procedure is a true usurpation of another's property.~~

Informed, ~~thus~~, Her Majesty of the need to banish this abuse

[next page]

She has resolved that the Ministry under my charge must formulate ~~and present for approval by Parliament~~ a project of law which declares, delineates, and assures the respective rights of literary property in all its particulars, to present it for deliberation by Parliament.

But Her Majesty who ~~is pleased to note~~ pleased by the extraordinary flight that Spanish drama has taken in this era of liberty, that seems to promise for the reign of her august Daughter a new Golden Age of national poetry, recognizes for the same reason, that the injuries inflicted upon the writers demand a more peremptory remedy, and ~~therefore~~ in order to provide it she has furthermore decided that temporarily, ~~and~~ while the aforementioned project of law is yet to be debated, ~~it shall be approved~~ approves and sanctions that dramatic works, as ~~the exclusive property of its authors~~ with all property, are under the immediate protection of the authorities; and that as these productions, because of their special nature, have two distinct realities, one in the theatre and another in the press, ~~no author, director or owner of~~ it will not be possible henceforth to ~~perform~~ stage a dramatic work in any theatre, even when ~~it were~~ ~~it should be~~ it is in print, or been staged in another or other ~~theatres~~, without permission of its author, or owner ~~who may have acquired it~~.

By royal order I communicate this to Your Lordship so that you may appropriately publicize this resolution of Her Majesty and watch over its exact compliance. May God grant Your Lordship
Many years.
Madrid 4̶ 5 May 1837

Notes

Introduction

1. Although writers' prominence was institutionalized in the nineteenth century and dramatists did write with performance rather than printing in mind during previous centuries, both Lope and Calderón eventually participated in the printing of their plays and voiced concern about unauthorized editions. By the eighteenth century, printed plays constituted a sizeable segment of the book trade, although dramatists were rarely involved in preparing the texts. See Francisco Aguilar Piñal, *Sevilla y el teatro en el siglo XVIII* (Oviedo: Cátedra Feijoo, 1974), and Germán Vega García-Luengos, 'Impresos teatrales sevillanos del siglo XVIII: pautas de un estudio,' in *Trabajos de la Asociación Española de Bibliografía*, vol. 1 (Madrid: Ministerio de Cultura / Biblioteca Nacional, 1993).
2. This relationship, led by the royal advisers the Duke of Lerma and the Count-Duke Olivares, was fully developed by the seventeenth century. However, control was not always as complete as the government wished, as evidenced by its attempts to silence Tirso de Molina in 1625 and its ten-year ban on the printing of plays in Castile.
3. Juan Aguilera Sastre, 'Manuel Bretón de los Herreros y las políticas teatrales de su época,' in *La obra de Manuel Bretón de los Herreros II Jornadas bretonianas (Logroño, 2 al 5 marzo de 1999)*, coord. Miguel Angel Muro (Logroño: Instituto de Estudios Riojanos, 2000), 127.
4. See Susan Kirkpatrick, *Las románticas* (Berkeley: University of California Press, 1989) for a discussion of the double marginalization of Spanish Romantic women writers in the liberal period.
5. *Authors and Owners* (Cambridge: Harvard University Press, 1993), 28.
6. George Armstrong Kelly, *Victims, Authority, and Terror* (Chapel Hill: University of North Carolina Press, 1982), 12.

7 Fernando produced a manifesto to this end in Valencia on 4 May 1814. See Raymond Carr, *Spain, 1808–1939* (Oxford: Clarendon Press, 1966), 118. Not an immediate return to Bourbon-style absolute sovereignty, it allowed for a 'reversion to a traditional monarchy ruling with the historic Cortes and subject to God and the law, a *via media* between imported liberalism and the equally foreign ministerial despotism of the eighteenth century' (Carr 121). However, this never took effect, and the King ruled as an absolutist.
8 *Ley de 5 de Agosto de 1823*. Reproduced in Manuel Dánvila, *La propiedad intelectual*, 2nd ed. (Madrid: Imprenta de la Correspondencia de España, 1882), 62–4.
9 José Antonio Vega Vega, *Derecho de autor* (Madrid: Tecnos, 1990), 56. Also discussed in 'De la propiedad industrial y del real decreto de S.M. de 27 de marzo de 1826 sobre inventos y máquinas,' *Boletin del comercio*, 13 Sept. 1833, n.pag.
10 Martha Woodmansee and Peter Jaszi, 'Introduction,' in *The Construction of Authorship: Textual Appropriation in Law and Literature* (Durham: Duke University Press, 1994), 5.
11 Mariano José de Larra, *Obras de Fígaro*, ed. Carlos Seco Serrano, vol. 1 (Madrid: Atlas, 1960), 123.
12 Ibid., 126.
13 John Elliott, *Spain and Its World* (New Haven: Yale University Press, 1989), 163.
14 Jonathan Brown and John Elliott, *A Palace for a King* (New Haven: Yale University Press, 1980), 32.
15 *Teatro y literatura en la sociedad barroca* (Madrid: Seminarios y Ediciones, 1972), 124–7. Cited by Elliott, 170.
16 Ibid., 167.
17 Louise K. Stein has argued that the rise of opera in Spain during these years was directly tied to its political advantage in the struggle for a high national reputation within Europe. Given that the French minister Mazarin 'intended to dazzle Europe' at the marriage between María Teresa and Louis XIV in 1660, 'Philip's court need not *appear* to the rest of Europe to have succumbed to financial or political debilitation after the treaty, if Spain could match (or even outdo) France in the brilliance and originality of her celebrations.' See *Songs of Mortals, Dialogues of the Gods* (Oxford: Clarendon, 1993), 204–12.
18 The formula of the Queen's name when creating law was 'Doña Isabel II, por la gracia de Dios y la Constitucion de la Monarquía española, Reina de las Españas.' This idea of national sovereignty (by the grace of the con-

stitution, or representative national will) was first articulated in the Cádiz Constitution of 1812.
19 David Gies has discussed the attitude of Fernando VII toward the stage as decidedly different from the stately use by his Habsburg predecessors. Firstly, he was 'a fanatical devotee of the *comedias de magia*.' But also, during the Ominous Decade, highly restrictive censorship compromised the quality of theatre produced during his reign. See *The Theatre in Nineteenth-Century Spain* (Cambridge: Cambridge University Press, 1994),185, 24.
20 Kirkpatrick, *Las románticas*, 40.
21 Ibid., 41.
22 Archivo Histórico Nacional, Legajo 11404.
23 See 'Reglamento de 3 de Septiembre de 1880,' 'Ley de 10 de Enero de 1879,' 'Real orden de 7 de Mayo de 1859,' 'Real decreto organico de 28 de Julio de 1852' (Archivo Histórico Nacional [AHN], Legajo 11405, No. 2–11), 'Real decreto orgánico de 7 de Febrero de 1849' (AHN, Legajo 11404, No. 65), 'Ley de 10 de Junio de 1847,' and 'Real orden de 4 de Marzo de 1844' (AHN, Legajo 11404, No. 31), all concerning Spain; and the 'Convenio de propiedad literaria' between France and Spain (including dramatic works) on 15 November 1853, between England and Spain on 7 July 1857, between Belgium and Spain on 30 April 1859, between Portugal and Spain on 5 August 1860, and between the Low Countries and Spain on 31 December 1862. Other than the three documents whose locations are specified in the Archivo Histórico Nacional, these documents are reproduced in Dánvila, *La propiedad intelectual*.
24 See John Dowling, 'The Madrid Theatre Public in the Eighteenth Century: Transition from the Popular Audience to the Bourgeois,' in *Studies on Voltaire and the Eighteenth Century 265: Transactions of the Seventh International Congress on the Enlightenment* (Oxford: Voltaire Foundation, 1989), 1358–62. Most of the audience was still bourgeois in the mid-nineteenth century.
25 Copyright institutionalized this possibility, but it remained subject to the different degrees of authorial desire to control what happens on the stage. For example, the Duke of Rivas included much more specific stage directions for his *Don Álvaro* (1835) than did Hartzenbusch for his *Los amantes de Teruel* (1837). Even during the Early Modern period, dramatists did attempt to dictate staging: the first edition of Calderón's *Fieras afemina Amor* has an opening stage direction of nearly three pages. My thanks to an anonymous reader for University of Toronto Press for this example.

1 Cultivating Property: *Desamortización* and the Culture of Authors' Rights

1 Rose, *Authors and Owners*, 85.
2 The Estamento de Procuradores, within the first days of sessions (28 August 1834), attempted to create a *Tabla de derechos* (*declaracion de derechos*) for the fundamental rights for all citizens. Among these, 'propiedad' figured prominently, and it was deemed a 'derecho tan respetable que sin él no puede existir vínculo alguno social...' [right so respectable that without it, no social ties could exist] (*El Estatuto Real de 1834 y la constitución de 1837*, ed. Joaquín Tomás Villarroya [Madrid: Fundación Santa María, 1985], 96).
3 Álvaro Flórez Estrada, 'Cuestión social,' from *Curso de economía política*, in *Apuntes para una biblioteca de escritores expañoles contemporáneos en prosa y verso*, ed. Eugenio de Ochoa (Paris: Baudry, 1840), 518–29.
4 Raymond Williams has discussed the historicity of the terms 'work,' 'labor,' 'job,' and a general sense of 'toiling.' See *Keywords: A Vocabulary of Culture and Society* (New York: Oxford University Press, 1976), 282.
5 Michael Iarocci, 'Introduction,' in *Properties of Modernity: Romantic Spain, Modern Europe, and the Legacies of Empire* (Nashville: Vanderbilt University Press, 2006).
6 Flórez Estrada, 'Cuestión social,' 521.
7 Ibid., 527.
8 See Catherine Jagoe, *Ambiguous Angels* (Berkeley: University of California Press, 1994) for a discussion of the *embourgeoisement* of the behaviour of women in the Spanish upper classes after the end of the Ancien Régime. One example of a noble who actively eschewed aristocratic literary pursuits and cast his lot with the liberals was offered by Larra. He described the Count of Campo-Alange's economic and social predisposition for poetry and lauded his choice to instead fight for 'la causa de la libertad' [the cause of liberty] and give up his house and property: 'sus afectos personales, su posición independiente, su mucha hacienda le convidaban al ocio y a la gloria literaria que tan a poca costa hubiera podido adquirir' [his personal belongings, his independent position, and his great property holdings opened the path to leisure and the literary glory that he could have attained at a small price] ('Necrología. Exequias del Conde de Campo-Alange,' in *Artículos*, ed. Enrique Rubio, 12th ed. [Madrid: Cátedra, 1993], 413).
9 A representative example of the standard description of the two poets as a pair of labourers (to be taken as a unit), repeated throughout the century,

can be found in Carlos Guaza y Gómez-Talavera, *Músicos, poetas y actores* (Madrid: Imprenta de F. Maroto, 1884), 147–8: 'Un año despues del triunfo alcanzado por Don Antonio García Gutierrez con *El Trovador*, ofreció otra sorpresa igual la escena española, y otro genio, desconocido tambien y de humilde condición, llamaba á las puertas de la inmortalidad, una de las últimas noches del mes de Enero de 1837. Estrenábase en ella un drama nuevo [*Los amantes de Teruel*], que era obra, segun decian, de un jóven artesano, cuya escesiva modestia, retraimiento y esquivo carácter prometia bien poco sabor á los frutos de su pluma ... el público, entusiasmado, prorumpió, como en el estreno de *El Trovador*, en atronadores aplausos, y pretendió igualmente la presentación del autor en las tablas ...' [One year after the triumph attained by Antonio García Gutiérrez with *El trovador*, the Spanish stage offered up a similar surprise, and another *genio* also unknown and from a humble condition, knocked on the doors of immortality one of the last evenings of the month of January 1837. That night was the premiere of a new play [*Los amantes de Teruel*] by, it was said, a young artisan, whose excessive modesty, timidity, and shy character showed little flavour of the fruits of his pen ... the enthusiastic public broke out – as at the premiere of *El trovador* – in thundering applause and also called for the presentation of the author on the stage ...].

10 See 'Manifiesto de Mendizábal' (14 September 1835), in J. de Burgos, *Anales del reinado de Isabel II*, vol. 2 (Madrid: n.p., 1850), 405; reprinted in Irene Castells and Antonio Moliner, *Crisis del antiguo régimen y revolución liberal en España (1789–1845)* (Barcelona: Ariel, 2000), 147–9.

11 One of the sharpest critiques of Mendizábal's ministry was Larra's 'Dios nos asista' [God help us], republished in *Obras de Fígaro*, vol. 2. (Paris: Baudry, 1848), 44–56. Larra criticizes the fact that Mendizábal won seats from at least seven provinces and presents him to be as much an absolutist as the Carlist government that he claimed to reject. As discussed below, the restrictive electoral law excluded most Spanish men (as well as all non-citizens and all Spanish women) from participating. 'Para que no fuesen las elecciones muy populares bastante amaño era ya la propia ley electoral, en virtud de la cual debian elegir los electores nombrados por los ayuntamientos y los mayores contribuyentes' [Lest the elections become too popular, the electoral law was already rather manipulative and as a result the electors to be elected were those named by the municipalities and the large contributors]. Because of the age and property restrictions, many potential representatives were disqualified, 'así que, unos procuradores no han nacido, otros no tienen renta, ¡qué sé yo!' [so that some of the politi-

cians hadn't been born, others have no income ... I don't know!]. And the resulting accumulation of power in the person of the minister was seen as a perversion of national sovereignty. 'Don Juan Alvarez Mendizabal fué elegido por ejemplo por Barcelona, siendo natural de Cádiz, y no habiendo residido en Cataluña. Decian: «pero no tiene nada suyo en Cataluña, sino los electores» ¿pues eso no es tener? ¿no valen tanto por lo menos los electores como una casa, ó una tapia, ó una cuanta fanegas de pan llevar?' [Juan Álvarez Mendizábal was elected, for example, by Barcelona, having been born in Cadiz and not having resided in Catalunya. They said, 'But in Catalunya he owns nothing but the electors.' Well, isn't that owning something? Aren't electors worth at least as much as a house, or a wall or fields of grain?].

12 He declared: 'Ya solo se reconoce como orígen de todo gobierno las convenciones sociales, y como única causa, como único elemento que puede establecerlos y justificarlos la soberanía del pueblo' [Now we only recognize social conventions as the origin of all government and as the only cause, the only element that can establish and justify them, the sovereignty of the people] (Alfonso García Tejero, *Historia politico-administrativa de Mendizábal* [Madrid: Establecimiento tipografico de J.A. Ortigosa, 1858], 312).

13 Isabel Burdiel, 'The Liberal Revolution, 1808–1843,' in *Spanish History since 1808*, ed. José Alvarez Junco and Adrian Shubert (New York: Oxford University Press, 2000), 30.

14 Ibid., 17.

15 Much later, in a royal order from 2 April 1852, regarding the publication of newspapers, these same requirements were restated in a slightly different form for those who wished to own political or religious newspapers. See José Eugenio de Eguizábal, *Apuntes para una historia de la legislación española sobre imprenta* (Madrid: Imprenta de la Revista de legislación, 1879), 313.

16 Miguel Angel González Muñiz, *Constituciones, Cortes y elecciones españolas: historia y anécdota (1810–1936)* (Madrid: Ediciones Júcar, 1978).

17 Burdiel, 'Liberal Revolution,' 27.

18 See Jesús Cruz, *Gentlemen, Bourgeois, and Revolutionaries: Political Change and Cultural Persistence among the Spanish Dominant Groups, 1750–1850* (New York: Cambridge University Press, 1996) for a discussion of the familial networks of economic authority in Spain during this period and the continuation of established power structures in spite of *Progresista* measures.

19 Burdiel, 'Liberal Revolution,' 17.

20 Antonio Moliner Prada, *Joaquín María López y el partido progresista: 1834–1843* (Alicante: Instituto de Estudios 'Juan Gil-Albert,' 1988), 51.

21 Espronceda, too, penned several attacks on Mendizábal's ministry and policies. Navas Ruiz notes that the article 'El Gobierno y la Bolsa' built upon the ideas of Flórez Estrada. See *El romanticismo español* (Madrid: Cátedra, 1982), 238.
22 Two of the most extensive and provocative articles were Flórez Estrada's 'Sobre el uso que deba hacerse de los bienes nacionales,' written on 28 February 1836 (Madrid, n.p.) in response to the decree that established disentailment on 19 February 1836 (a number of responses to Flórez Estrada's article were in turn printed on 1 and 4 March in the Madrid newspapers) and his pamphlet printed in early March: *Contestacion de Don Alvaro Flórez Estrada á las impugnaciones hechas á su ESCRITO sobre el uso que deba hacerse de los bienes nacionales* (Madrid: Imprenta de D.M. de Burgos, 1836).
23 The impact of *desamortización* on art was noted at the time. Navas Ruiz reports that Espronceda, 'en un trabajo inédito de 1836 critica el despojo del patrimonio artístico derivado de la desamortización' [in an unpublished work from 1836 criticizes the loss of artistic patrimony that has derived from deamortization] (238).
24 Cayetano Rosell, 'Don Antonio García Gutiérrez' in *Autores dramáticos contemporáneos y joyas del teatro español del siglo XIX*, vol. 1 (Madrid: Imprenta de Fortanet, 1881), 86.
25 Antonio Ferrer del Río, *Galería de la literatura española* (Madrid: P. Mellado, 1846), 258.
26 David Saunders, *Authorship and Copyright* (London: Routledge, 1992), 7.
27 The aesthetic value of the piece was appreciated by contemporary reviewers; however, the public did not self-consciously approve the new literary school of Romanticism in which *El trovador* was written. Although scholars of Spanish literature are keen to find one, unlike in France, there was not one single moment of public approbation (or demonstration of displeasure) of the new rules of theatre in Spain. The back cover of the Cátedra edition of *Don Álvaro* (premiered 1835) states: 'El estreno en 1835 de *Don Álvaro* supuso el triunfo definitivo del Romanticismo en el teatro español ...' [The premiere of *Don Álvaro* in 1835 marked the definitive triumph of Romanticism in Spanish theatre ...]. The edition of *El trovador* produced by the same publishing house states on the back cover of the second piece: 'El éxito tumultuoso de *El trovador* ... demostraba la aceptación popular del nuevo teatro romántico, nacional y apasionado' [The stormy success of *El trovador* ... showed the popular approval of the new romantic, national, and passionate theatre]. Within the same series of canonical Spanish works, the moment of the triumph of Romantic theatre cannot be ascertained.

28 For a discussion of the gradual silencing of audiences who began to pay attention to the stage, particularly as concerns musical performances in France, see James H. Johnson, *Listening in Paris: A Cultural History* (Berkeley: University of California Press, 1995). Referring to the chronicles of La Harpe, Johnson notes that the eighteenth-century custom of applauding a member of the royal family at the end of an opera performance began to be replaced in the 1780s. 'At the end of *Tarare* at its premiere it was not a prince in attendance whom the audience demanded to see but Beaumarchais and Salieri, an act, according to press accounts, that "has not been part of the practice of this theater"' (69). Johnson notes that this new behaviour coincided with the twilight of the Ancien Régime monarchy in France. However, the call for Beaumarchais (coincidently, one of the initiators of the legislation of dramatic literary property in France) occurred before any sort of comprehensive restrictive rules on audience behaviour had been published; in Spain, the call for Gutiérrez happened ten years after similar rules had been decreed.

29 Carmen Iranzo, 'Introducción,' in *Los amantes de Teruel*, by Eugenio Hartzenbusch (Madrid: Cátedra, 2004), 33, note 30.

30 1 Feb. 1833, n.pag.

31 This work is, of course, a work of fiction, but Ayguals de Izco uses it to criticize the composition of the claque and its sway over public taste. Claques were standard in nineteenth-century European theatres. See F.W.J. Hemmings, *The Theatre Industry in Nineteenth-Century France* (New York: Cambridge University Press, 1993). Nearly all of the members of the Parnasillo circle were regular attendees of the Príncipe Theatre (in whose café the group met).

32 In their study of European copyright, Martha Woodmansee and Peter Jaszi explain that this same model was employed throughout the Continent in the early nineteenth century to justify intellectual property. Thus Spain was similar to its northern neighbours in the development of literary property at this point in the century, although several decades later, Spain would be unique in drafting the strongest literary property law in Europe. See *Loi espagnole sur la propriété intellectuelle (7 juillet 1877)* (Paris: Imprenta de Gauthier-Villars, n.d.).

33 Guaza, *Músicos, poetas y actores*, 118.

34 Susan Kirkpatrick counsels more than careful attention when reading the articles (including the theatre reviews): 'las actitudes de Larra cambian según las transformaciones de un panorama político complejo, de manera que sus afirmaciones solo pueden adquirir su valor y peso adecuados si se las refiere a *su inmediato contexto histórico* y a la trayectoria general de su

propia evolución' (emphasis added) [Larra's positions change according to developments in a complex political environment, such that the appropriate value and gravity of his statements can only be understood if they are placed in relation to their *immediate historical context* and the general trajectory of his own development] (*Larra: el laberinto inextricable de un romántico liberal* [Madrid: Gredos, 1977], 15).

35 Larra, 'El trovador,' in *Artículos*, 362.
36 Ibid., 368.
37 Discussing the means to improve theatre in a state still under the reign of Fernando VII, Larra wrote: 'Pedimos en primer lugar para los poetas, sin miedo de parecer exigentes, lo que solo ellos no tienen en la sociedad. El derecho de propiedad. 'Repartiéronse mis vestiduras, y sobre mi túnica echaron suertes,' puede exclamar el poeta con mucha razon, si se nos permite mezclar esta expresion sagrada entre nuestras habladurías. En un país en donde las letras han sido casi siempre el recurso del que no ha tenido otro, y donde ha sido tan escasa la gloria que han alcanzado, parece que el premio debiera haber sido mayor; mas por desgracia no han recibido ni premio ni consideracion' [We ask, firstly, for the poets, without fear of seeming demanding, that which only they do not have in society. The right of property. 'They divided up my garments and cast lots upon my vesture,' the poet could very rightly exclaim, if we may be permitted to mix this sacred phrase into our speech. In a country where literature has almost always been the last resort of those who haven't had other means, and where the glory it has attained has been so scarce, it seems that the prize ought to have been greater; but, shamefully, poets have not received either reward or estimation] ('Teatros,' in *Obras de Fígaro* [Paris: Baudry, 1848], 57).
38 Ferrer del Rio, *Galería*, 258.
39 The paradox of liberal commodification of theatre was noted almost immediately: theatre was part of the enactment of liberal ideology, but it could compromise its own importance by being financially motivated and artistically impure (the beginning of the gap between high art and low or commercial art). Four articles in *El entreacto*, published during September and October 1839, addressed these ideas. The fourth article began strongly: 'Arte liberal y especulacion son dos ideas que en este siglo, que á sí propio se llama ilustrado y que la posteridad juzgará Dios sabe como, suelen andar juntas...' [Liberal art and speculation are two ideas that in this century, which calls itself enlightened and God knows how posterity will judge it, tend to go together]. It then returned to the question of the influence of commercial theatre on the culture of Spain. The statement

revealed a migration of economic lexicon and practices from the market to the realm of literature. The author notes that it is art that is 'liberal' (an economic term), not the act of speculation. 'Ni el *Entreacto* es periódico de economia política, ni hay necesidad tampoco de detenerme á demostrar que los espectáculos públicos son una necesidad social: basta recorrer la historia y ver que no nos ofrece el ejemplo de un solo pueblo que no los tenga, mas ó menos cultos segun el estado de su civilizacion, y que á medida que ésta progresa, crecen ellos tambien en importancia' [*El entreacto* is not a newspaper of political economy nor is there need for me to pause to demonstrate that public spectacles are socially necessary: it is sufficient to review history and see that there is not a single society that did not have them, more or less cultured according to their degree of civilization, and that as civilization progresses, the performances, too, grow in importance] (Anon., 'Teatros de Madrid,' 31 Oct. 1839: 243).
40 For example, both Juan Hartzenbusch and Eugenio Ochoa created both anthologies and standard editions of the works of many Golden Age authors.

2 Performative Appeal: From *El trovador* to the Royal Decree

1 'Spanish Romanticism,' in *Romanticism in National Context*, ed. Roy Porter and Mikulas Teich (New York: Cambridge University Press, 1988), 264–5.
2 Navas Ruiz, *El romanticismo español*, 221.
3 José Luis Varela, *Vida y obra literaria de Gregorio Romero Larrañaga* (Madrid: CSIC, 1948), 61.
4 See Carr, *Spain, 1808–1939*, 277, for a discussion of the laissez-faire journal *Economista* from mid-century and its objections to subventions of a national theatre, based on an understanding of art as an industry which, like all others, was expected to be self-sufficient and profitable. Note that these were the same sorts of arguments that had generated literary property in the 1830s.
5 Archivo Histórico Nacional, Legajo 11387.
6 Jean Louis Picoche has surveyed these documents in his introduction to *Los amantes de Teruel* (Paris: Centre de recherches hispaniques, 1970).
7 The exact law is not cited, however, it is likely that the petitioners were referring to the *Reglamento sobre imprenta* published on 4 January 1834. Title 4 deals with the 'propiedad y privilegios de los autores y traductores,' and Article 30 states that authors of original works are granted property rights for ten years and that these rights are transmissible to heirs should the author die within those same ten years. The *Reglamento general para la*

dirección y reforma de teatros from 1807 established a royalty of 8 per cent for plays performed throughout Spain. However, lacking the Romantic ideology to justify this new practice, the law was never put into effect.

8 According to the 1849 'Real Decreto Organico de los Teatros del Reino,' 'este espectáculo es el termómetro de la cultura de los pueblos' [this spectacle is the thermometer of a nation's culture].
9 Reproduced in the Appendix.
10 *Boletín del comercio*, 10 Dec. 1833, n.pag.
11 Stephanie Anne Sieburth, *Inventing High and Low: Literature, Mass Culture, and Uneven Modernity in Spain* (Durham, NC: Duke University Press, 1994), 3–4.
12 David Thatcher Gies, *Theatre and Politics in Nineteenth-Century Spain: Juan de Grimaldi as Impresario and Government Agent* (Cambridge: Cambridge University Press, 1988), 31.
13 Ramón de Mesonero Romanos, *Memorias de un setentón* (Madrid: Oficinas de la Ilustración Española y Americana, 1881), 94. Mesonero dates the inauguration of María Cristina's Conservatorio de Música y Declamación to 1830 and suggests that the tauromachy school was created in imitation of the Queen's idea to foster culture at court. 'Fernando, estimulado por el ejemplo de su esposa, quiso tambien fundar algun establecimiento de instruccion que respondiese á necesidades de otro género, y creó, por aquellos mismos dias ... la *Escuela de Tauromaquia* en Sevilla' [Fernando, stimulated by his wife's example also wanted to found a teaching establishment that would respond to the needs of another genre and created, during that same time, the Tauromachy School in Seville]. Evidently, the two royals had different concepts regarding what spectacle would be most effective for the state.
14 Lope de Vega was, in many ways, a precursor to the practices of the nineteenth-century dramatic marketplace. Not only did he expect compensation for his work and write for the pleasure of the faceless public (the most oft-cited example of that philosophy is found in his *Arte nuevo de hacer comedias*), but also he complained that other writers for the stage took parts of his plays, deformed the original pieces, and incorporated them into their own productions. His condemnation of this practice appears in several of his works (such as *El peregrino* and *La Dorotea*); see Hugo Albert Rennert, *The Spanish Stage in the Time of Lope de Vega* (New York: Hispanic Society of America, 1909) for a discussion of this issue.
15 Seco Serrano dates it to 29 February (*Obras de Fígaro*, ed. Seco Serrano); Pérez Vidal dates it to 1 March (*Fígaro*, ed. Alejandro Pérez Vidal [Barcelona: Crítica, 1997], 769).

16 Mariano José de Larra, 'Teatros,' in *Obras completas de Fígaro*, vol. 2 (Paris: Baudry, 1857), 71.
17 Ibid. Not only did it suffer 'falto de protección' [lack of protection] (71), but the neglect was magnified by that fact that 'en España ... sin duda consideraba la función de los toros como más popular' [in Spain ... the bullfight was considered the most popular event] (72). Later in the article, Larra praises the beneficial outcome of María Cristina's Conservatorio de Música and subtly belittles Fernando's decision to create a tauromachy school rather than patronize other arts.
18 Ibid., 72.
19 Archivo Histórico Nacional, Legajo 11404.
20 The ministers cited the *Novísima recopilación*, Ley XXIV and XXV [tít. XVI, Libro VIII]. The latter codified the 'Real orden de 20 de octubre de 1764,' which had declared that 'los privilegios concedidos a los autores no se extinguiesen por su muerte, sino que pasasen a sus herederos, y que a éstos se les continuase el privilegio mientras lo solicitasen, salvo el caso de que se tratase de Comunidades o Manos Muertas' [the privileges conceded to authors do not expire upon their death, but rather may pass to their heirs, and the privilege will be continued to them as long as they solicit it, except when the heirs are Communities or *mortemain*].
21 See Walter Kendrick, *The Secret Museum: Pornography in Modern Culture* (Berkeley: University of California Press, 1996), especially chapter 1, for a discussion of the etymology of the term 'pornography' and the relationship between art and the prostitute in Western European culture. Mention of 'public' women in arguments for and against the renovation of art was an established rhetorical practice in modern Europe.
22 Jagoe, *Ambiguous Angels*, 19.
23 Carr, *Spain*, 162.
24 'Comision para presentar el proyecto de Ley sobre propiedad literaria,' Archivo Histórico Nacional, Legajo 11404.
25 Bretón de los Herreros was a prolific dramatist and did earn money from his plays, although his official position was at the National Library. He was a vocal theatre critic and remained very committed to the renovation of modern theatre. In spite of his claims, some of Martínez de la Rosa's plays were performed to great critical acclaim; for example, *La viuda de Padilla* (Cadiz, 1812), *Aben Humeya* (Paris, 1830), and *La conjuración de Venecia* (Madrid, 1834). Among the many places in which he described dramatic poetry as his hobby, see 'Advertencia' in *Los celos infundados*, in *Biblioteca de autores españoles*, ed. Carlos Seco Serrano, vol. 148 (Madrid: Atlas, 1962), 295. Also, in the first edition of *La boda y el duelo* (Madrid: Imprenta del

Colegio de Sordo-Mudos, 1839), Martínez de la Rosa claimed: 'Compuse esta comedia algunos años ha, por mero desahogo en una temporada de baños, y sin ánimo de que se representase ...' [I composed this play a few years ago, to relieve myself from stress during the visits to the baths, and without the intention that it be performed].
26 Aguilera Sastre, 'Manuel Bretón,' 118.
27 Archivo Histórico Nacional, Legajo 11404.
28 Ronald Bettig, 'Critical Perspectives on the History and Philosophy of Copyright,' *Critical Studies in Mass Communication* 9 (1992): 131.

3 Authors between Stage and Page

1 Plays had always been read, but not exactly as armchair literature. The printing of plays in Spain dates to at least the late fifteenth century. The oldest surviving editions of single plays, called *sueltas*, date from 1510–20. Collected or single plays began to form a significant part of the book trade, and by 1700 various producers had started their own numbered series. I express my thanks to an anonymous reader for the University of Toronto Press for these dates.
2 Antonin Artaud, *The Theatre and Its Double*, trans. Victor Corti (London: Calder & Boyars, 1970), 68.
3 See, especially, Michel Foucault,'What Is an Author?' in *Language, Counter-Memory, Practice*, trans. Donald F. Bouchard and Sherry Simon (Ithaca, NY: Cornell University Press, 1977), 113–39; and *The Archeology of Knowledge*, trans. A.M. Sheridan Smith (New York: Pantheon Books, 1972).
4 Mariano José de Larra, 'Teatros. ¿Quién es por acá el autor de una comedia? Segundo artículo. El derecho de propiedad' in *Obras completas*, vol. 1, *Artículos*, ed. Luis Iglesias Feijoo (Madrid: Biblioteca Castro, 1996), 211.
5 Seco Serrano dates the first to 26 September 1832 and the second to 10 October 1832.
6 Larra, 'Teatros. ¿Qué cosa es por acá el autor de una comedia?' in Feijoo, ed., *Obras completas*, 198.
7 Ibid., 196.
8 Ibid., 199.
9 Larra presents the system as totalizing but, of course, does not engage with the issues of Caribbean slavery and other forms of unrecognized labour by non-citizens. These articles were written during the reign of Fernando VII and are more optimistic than factual, even in the description of the contractual relationships implicit in private property.

10 Larra, 'Teatros. ¿Quién es por acá el autor de una comedia?' 212.
11 Ibid., 213. It was precisely this linguistic privileging that Artaud confronted. 'If, then the author is the man who arranges the language of speech and the director is his slave, there is merely a question of words. There is a confusion over terms, stemming from the fact that, for us, and according to the sense generally attributed to the word *director*, this man is merely an artisan, an adapter, a kind of translator eternally devoted to making a dramatic work pass from one language into another; this confusion will be possible and the director will be forced to play second fiddle to the author only so long as there is a tacit agreement that the language of words is superior to others ...' (Artaud, 119).
12 A famous poet's name always had commercial value. Both Lope and Calderón's names were attached to plays they did not write. For example, Don Juan de Vera Tassis noted in his edition of Calderón's *Verdadera quinta parte* that 'ay quien assegure, que casi todas quantas se imprimen en Seuilla, para passar à las Indias, las graduan con el nombre de Don Pedro [Calderón] por intereses particulares que se les siguen à los que hazen cambio de los talentos agenos' [someone makes sure that almost everything that is printed in Seville to be sent on to the colonies is graced with the name of don Pedro Calderón, to the benefit of those who play with others' talents] (Pedro Calderón de la Barca, *Verdadera quinta parte de comedias* [Madrid: Francisco Sanz, 1682]). I would like to express my thanks to an anonymous reader for University of Toronto Press for bringing this example to my attention. By the nineteenth century, this practice was illegal, and poets voiced their complaint within the frame of authorship, identity, and property. One such complaint appeared a few months later in the *Boletín del comercio* as a fictional dialogue between a poet and a friend that underscored writers' financial and social motivations for composing for the theatre. The poet relates the fate of his name in provincial theatres:

> Figúrese vmd que en el primer teatro en que se hizo se puso mi nombre añadiéndole el titulo de *celebre* y á la comedia el de *acreditada*.
> – Hombre, ¡qué pronto y á que poca costa se adquiere la celebridad!
> – Cierto; pero los teatros de *fuera* no se paran en barras, y no solamente sacan producto de la comedia; sino que benefician hasta el nombre del autor, atribuyéndole obras que no son suyas. Pero verá vmd lo que sucedió. En vista de los piropos que me habían dado, y del dinero que les produjo mi drama, escribí á los cómicos para que me pagarán mis derechos. ¿Sabe vmd lo que me respondieron? Que era un hombre sin consideracion, un codicioso; que no tenia derecho alguno; que la comedia se habia representado en Madrid, y ya no era

mia; ya estaba en la clase de bienes mostrencos, y á disposicion de
todo el que se le antojase hacer uso de ella; y que me contentára con
la fama que me habian dado, debida, no al mérito de la obra, sino á
lo bien que la habian representado.
- ¿Eso dijeron?
- Sí, señor; y despues de eso, escriba vmd comedias. No, no mas.
Primero que volver á caer en semejante tentacion, traduciré novelas,
que aunque me las paguen á doce reales el pliego de impresion, sé ya
que cuento con algo, y no me espongo á tantos disgustos y desaires.
('Teatros. Desaventuras de un pobrecito autor de comedias' [Theatre.
Misadventures of a poor little dramatic poet], *Buletín del comercio*, 28
June 1833, n.pag.)

[Just imagine that in the first theatre that it was performed they listed
my name, adding to it the title of 'famous' and to the play *worthy*.
- Wow! How quickly and cheaply one can become famous!
- True, but the provincial theatres don't hold back and not only do they
make money on the play but also they benefit even from the name of
the author, attributing to him plays that aren't his. But wait until you
hear what happened. In light of the praise they had given me and the
money that my play had produced for them, I wrote the actors so that
they would pay me my royalties. Do you know how they responded?
That I was inconsiderate, greedy, that I had no rights; that the play
had been staged in Madrid, that it was no longer mine; it was now in
the class of ownerless property, at the disposition of anyone who
wished to make use of it; and that I should simply be pleased with the
fame that they had given me, a result of, not the quality of the work,
but because of how well they had staged it.
- They said this?
- Yes sir! And after all that, go ahead and write plays. No, no more.
Before I fall to that temptation again, I'll translate novels, because
even though they pay twelve *reales* per printed page, I know I can
count on something and I don't put myself at risk of so many disappointments and insults.]

13 Larra, 'Teatros. ¿Quién es por acá el autor de una comedia?' 213. Larra
presented intellectual property as a modern solution to a long-standing
problem. See, for example, the dedication of Calderón's *Quarta parte*
(1672) for comments like 'que le importa a la Republica, que la Comedia
de Iuan ande en nombre de Pedro, ni la de Pedro estè cabal, ò adulterada?' [what does the Republic care if Juan's play goes about as Pedro's

play or if Pedro's play is original or adulterated?]. Indeed, Larra's comments from 1832 almost suggest that he was aware of Calderón's dedication. I am grateful to an anonymous reader for University of Toronto Press for this reference. As Leonardo Romero Tobar has pointed out, Larra's contracts with his publishers reveal his awareness of the importance of his own name and pseudonyms, which he carefully protected and insisted upon using in every article. See 'Larra y los seudonimos transmigratorios,' in *Estudios de literatura española de los siglos XIX y XX: homenaje a Juan María Díez Taboada*, ed. José Carlos Torres Martínez et al. (Madrid: Consejo Superior de Investigaciones Científicas, 1998), 364.

14 See three fascinating articles by Bretón from 1832: 'Crítica teatral: los morcilleros,' in *Obra dispersa, I: El correo literario mercantil*, ed. J.M. Díez Taboada and J.M. Rozas (Logroño: Instituto de Estudios Riojanos, 1965), 449–51, deals harshly with the actors who change their lines during performance (called, and still called, 'blood-sausage vendors'). It was followed one week later by his article 'Teatro: proyecto de estímulo y subsistencia para los autores dramáticos' (in ibid., 451–4), in which he persuasively argues for literary property for dramatic works. His letter to the editor of *Correo literario y mercantil* earlier in the year is an attempt to reclaim control over his name as author and a censure of its misuse by provincial theatre companies.

15 Rennert, *The Spanish Stage*, 175.

16 In his 1668 commentary, Caramuel noted the difference between *autores* and *poetas* in Spanish theatre as one of money: '*Autor de Comedias* apud Hispanos non est qui illas scribit aut recitat, sed qui Comicos alit et singulis solvit convenientia stipendia' (*Rhythmica*, 2nd ed., Campaniae, 1668; quoted by Rennert, 33).

17 Two dictionaries from the early twentieth century illustrate the rapid disappearance of the long-established meaning of a theatrical *autor*. In the *Gran diccionario de la lengua castellana*, by Aniceto de Pagés de Puig (Madrid: Establecimiento tipolitográfico 'Sucesores de Rivadeneyra,' 1902–2?), the fourth definition includes a clear example to describe the antiquated meaning: '4. Autor, ra: En las compañías cómicas de los siglos XVII y XVIII era el que cuidaba del gobierno económico de ellas y de la distribución de caudales, el que hoy se llama <u>empresario</u>. "Autor de comedias" entre los españoles es el que sustenta á los comediantes y les da sus salarios; escritor de comedias es el que las compone y las da á los farsantes. P. JOSÉ DE ALCÁZAR.' The Royal Academy's *Diccionario histórico de la lengua española* (Madrid: Casa editorial Hernando, 1933) changes the fourth definition to 'En las companias comicas, hasta principios del siglo

XIX, el que cuidaba del gobierno economico de ellas y de la distribucion de caudales.'
18 For an early example of this same confusion, see Joseph E. Gillet, 'Caramuel de Lobkowitz and His Commentary (1668) on Lope de Vega's *Arte nuevo de hacer Comedias,*' *Philological Quarterly* 7 (1928): 120–37. Even though Caramuel offers a clear definition, conforming to what the *Autoridades* would confirm fifty years later, Gillet finds the usage of the term 'autor' in the seventeenth century unclear. The definition of an 'autor de comedias' was followed by the definitions of other theatrical agents: '*Escritor de comedias* ille est, qui illas componit, & dat Comicis representadas. *Compañia de Comediantes* est illorum societas, qui sunt ad Comoediam agendam necessarii. Ad quorum etiam numerum spetant personae mutae, quae in obsequiis humilioribus serviunt, & ipsi vocantur *metesillas* quia sellas in theatrum important, &, quando non sunt necessariae, ne forte impediant, extrahunt.' In a note, Gillet muses over the meaning of the term 'autor.' '*Auctor, autor* in the early sixteenth century seems to have meant "author," in the modern sense [here he offers a quote from Torres Naharro]. Later it might also mean "actor" [here he offers an example from Cueva]. Cervantes, in the *Quijote* (I, 48) speaks of "los autores que las componen [las comedias] y los autores que las representan," but in this last passage *representar* may more easily be interpreted as *produce* than Cueva's *recitar.*' Gillet then refers to Lope's use of 'autor' as 'producer' in the *Arte nuevo* yet still has difficulty distinguishing between the characters (132).
19 Jerónimo Herrera Navarro, 'Prólogo,' in *Catálogo de autores teatrales del siglo XVIII* (Madrid: Fundación Universitaria Española, 1993), xvii.
20 In addition to the twelve 'official' licensed companies there were unlicensed acting companies 'de la legua,' which were not allowed to come within a league of large towns. See N.D. Shergold, *A History of the Spanish Stage: From Medieval Times until the End of the Seventeenth Century* (Oxford: Clarendon Press, 1967), 516.
21 See notes by Rudolph Schevill and Adolfo Bonilla in their edition of Miguel de Cervantes, *Comedias y entremeses* (Madrid: Bernardo Rodríguez, 1915), 259; and 'Copia del Reglamento de Teatros dado por la Regencia del Reino en 11 de diciembre de 1812,' Archivo Histórico Nacional, Legajo 11404.
22 'Reglamento sobre las obligaciones del autor y del guardarropa. Año de 1777,' in *Memorias cronológicas sobre el teatro en España* (Vitoria Gasteiz: Diputación Foral de Alava, 1988), 322.
23 Ibid., 322–7.

24 Woodmansee and Jaszi, 'Introduction,' in *The Construction of Authorship*, 3.
25 See Herrera, 'Prólogo,' xi. Specific authors had enjoyed a cult status in the past; in the nineteenth century, authorship as a concept had a novel appeal.
26 A[ntonio] F[errer] del Rio, in *El laberinto*, 16 March 1844, p. 128.
27 '*Los amantes de Teruel*' in *Obras*, ed. Seco Serrano, 295.
28 Michael Iarocci, 'Romantic Prose, Journalism and *costumbrismo*,' in *The Cambridge History of Spanish Literature*, ed. David T. Gies (Cambridge: Cambridge University Press, 2004), 388.
29 Ramón de Mesonero Romanos, *Escenas matritenses*, 4th ed. (Madrid: Boix, 1845), 332.
30 El tercer dato para juzgar del estado de nuestros teatros es el modo con que juzga el público de la representacion. Vease lo que se aplaude, en cada una nótense las bellezas que escapan sin ser advertidas, y gradúese el poco fundamento con que se pide el nombre de un autor, y se le hace salir á las tablas á recibir un lauro que nadie puede apreciar ya, por indiscretamente prodigado. La frecuencia de esto consiste en que muchas veces se toma la voz de unos por la del público; y otras, aunque sea general la peticion, no es efecto del entusiasmo que la obra ha producido, sino de una mera curiosidad de conocer al autor de un drama nuevo. Un pueblo caprichoso y en general no muy ilustrado, un pueblo que tiene casi en desprecio el nombre de *poeta*, un pueblo que no sabe apreciar en todo su valor el gran mérito de un escritor dramático, cuando pide á un autor, es por el placer de satisfacer un antojo: «sal, dice, sal á donde yo te vea, y quiero que salgas por el mero afan de ver que me obedeces, y que pones ahi tu persona en espectáculo.» ('Observaciones sueltas,' *El entreacto*, 13 Oct. 1839, p. 224)
[The third item to judge the state of our theatres is the manner in which the audience judges performances. Look at what it applauds, notice the beauty in each that escapes the public's attention, consider the insignificant basis on which the public calls for the name of an author, and makes him appear on stage to receive laurels so indiscriminately awarded that no one can appreciate them any longer. The frequency with which this happens is a result of the fact that many times the voice of a few is taken for the voice of the public; and other times, although the call for the author is widespread among the public, it is not because they are enthusiastic about the work, but rather motivated by the mere curiosity to know the author of the new play. A capricious – and by and large unenlightened – public, a public that nearly holds the name 'poet' in disdain, a public that does not know how to appreciate the great value of a dramatic writer,

when it calls for an author, it is only to satisfy a whim: 'come, it says, come out where I can see you, and I want you to come out for the mere wish to see that you obey me, and that you put yourself out on display.]
31 *Recuerdos del tiempo viejo* (Madrid: Debate, 2001), 71–9.
32 *El entreacto*, 29 June 1839, 106. Although the writer's name is not given, the dramatic poets Miguel Agustín Príncipe, Juan Eugenio Hartzenbusch, Ventura de la Vega, Patricio de la Escosura, and José Zorrilla were among the regular contributors.

4 *Editores* and Owners

1 This is the subtitle for Part I of the collection of essays *Historia de la edición en España (1836–1936)*, ed. Jésus A. Martínez Martín (Madrid: Marcial Pons, 2001).
2 In his study 'El mercado editorial y los autores: el editor Delgado y los contratos de edición,' in *Escribir en España entre 1840 y 1875*, ed. Marie-Linda Ortega (Madrid: Visor Libros, 2002), 13–33, Jesús Martínez Martín has offered an excellent analysis of the impact of the dramatic *editor* on Spanish literature of the nineteenth century. Other notable exceptions are Rubén Darío, who described them favourably in the essay discussed in this chapter; and Emilio Cotarelo y Mori, 'Editores y galerías de obras dramáticas en Madrid en el siglo XIX,' *Revista de bibliotecas, archivos y museos* 5 (1928): 121–39. See also Francisco Almela y Vives, *El editor don Mariano de Cabrerizo* (Valencia: CSIC, 1949); *The Politics of Editing*, ed. Nicholas Spadaccini and Jenaro Talens (Minneapolis: University of Minnesota Press, 1992); Emilio Delgado López-Cozar and José Antonio Cordón García, *El Libro: creación, producción y consumo en la Granada del siglo XIX* (Granada: Universidad de Granada, 1990); Pura Fernández, 'Datos en torno a la bibliografía y difusión de la literatura popular en el Madrid del siglo XIX: la imprenta manual de Manuel Minuesa,' *Anales del Instituto de Estudios Madrileños* 31 (1992): 225–38; and Leonardo Romero Tobar, *Panorama crítico del romanticismo español* (Madrid: Castalia, 1994), 250–1.
3 Of course, the fixed text that supposedly came to life on the stage was only ever an illusion of centralized culture and authorial presence. See Philip Gaskell, *From Writer to Reader: Studies in Editorial Method* (Oxford: Oxford University Press, 1978). I thank an anonymous reader for University of Toronto Press for this example.
4 Christine S. Haynes, 'Lost Illusions: The Rise of the Book Publisher and the Construction of a Literary Marketplace in Nineteenth-Century France' (Diss., University of Chicago, 2001), 98.

5 Delgado López-Cozar and Cordón García, *El Libro*, 25.
6 Antonio Alcalá Galiano, *Literatura española siglo XIX: de Moratín a Rivas*, trans. Vicente Llorens (Madrid: Alianza Editorial, 1969), 133.
7 Mesonero is describing Madrid during the first decades of the nineteenth century; however, the book trade was built upon a long and complicated past. In the first half of the sixteenth century, it was thriving; by the late seventeenth century (1683–4), Samuel Pepys lamented that in Seville there were 'no books, only sold by the blind [i.e., ephemera, in the street].' See W. Matthews, 'Samuel Pepys and Spain,' *Neophilologus* 20.2 (1935): 120–9. When George Borrow went to Seville in 1839, a local bookseller (who happened to be Greek) claimed he only sold to foreigners, as the Sevillanos only read newspapers or translations of French books. See George Borrow, *The Bible in Spain* (London: J.M. Dent, 1906). I thank an anonymous reader for University of Toronto Press for drawing my attention to these examples.
8 Mesonero Romanos, *Escenas matritenses*, 290.
9 Not all dramatic poets regarded *editores* favourably, although they recognized their necessity. One articulation of that sentiment can be found in the mostly pro-*editor* journal *El entreacto*. The author of this essay does not wish to deal with the market directly; rather, he concludes both that poets should make money and that *editores* should be treated as inferior to, and recognized as dependent upon, poets. He also places the poet's activity somewhere between *ocio* and *negocio*:

> En España, en la época presente, el que hace versos no come, es decir, no come de ellos. De manera que el ser poeta, si no es un vicio que arruina, como el del juego, tampoco es una ocupacion que enriquece como la del sastre ó la del fabricante de fósforos. Utrilla con sus tijeras ha hecho un caudal; y Breton de los Herreros con su pluma no ha podido (yo lo juro) juntar media onza de ahorros para depositarla en la plazuela de las Descalzas. Bardenet con sus *cartones* y *cerillas* achoca buenas onzas: y Zorrilla que ha hecho tantos versos como fósforos el otro, y no menos llenos de fuego, apuesto yo á que se tiene por hombre dichoso el dia que al salir á la calle lleva la seguridad de poder tomar en arriendo una silla del Prado, ó adquirir en el café del Principe el dominio útil de una botella de cerveza.
>
> La prueba de que estos no son casos particulares, sino regla general, está en que aqui la poesia no tiene valor alguno. Los sastres y los fosforistas trabajan en materias de consumo; los poetas son artífices de una cosa que no se gasta. Las personas que en España saben leer algo están en razon de 1>> á 50>>; las que acostumbran á leer (porque hay

muchos que no leen aunque saben) de 1>> á 190; las que gustan de leer versos, de 1>> á 1700; y por último las que los pagan sin aguardar á que se los presten para leerlos, de 1>> á 15000. Ahora bien, calculen vds el valor que tienen los versos en España.

Esta demostracion podria estenderse y llevarse hasta la evidencia. Por ahora solo añadiremos una observacion, y es, que mientras los poetas visiten á los libreros, como ahora sucede, el valor de la poesia está á la baja. En Paris y otras partes, los editores son los que visitan á los poetas, esto es, á los buenos poetas. Mucho nos falta para llegar a este cambio de visitas. (El estudiante, 'La pobreza de los poetas,' *El entreacto*, 3 Oct. 1839, p. 213)

[Today in Spain, he who writes poetry doesn't live, that is, he doesn't live from his poetry. While being a poet is not exactly a vice that will ruin one, like the vice of gambling, it is not an occupation that enriches like that of a tailor or a maker of matches. Utrilla with his scissors has made a fortune; and Bretón de los Herreros with his pen has not been able (I swear it) to gather a half once of savings to deposit in the Descalzas. Bardenet with his *cartones* and *cerillas* has saved a great deal of money; and I would bet that Zorrilla, who has made as many verses as the other has matches, and no less full of fire, would consider himself a lucky man the day that he could go out on the street knowing that he would be able to pay for a seat in the Prado or commandeer a bottle of beer at the Principe café.

The proof that these are not unusual cases, but rather the general rule, can be seen in the fact that here, poetry has no value. Tailors and matchbook makers work in materials for consumption; the poets create something that can't be spent. The number of people in Spain who know how to read a little is something like 1 in 50; those who tend to read (because there are many who don't read even though they know how) is about 1 in 190; those who like to read poetry, 1 in 1,700; and finally, those who will buy poetry without waiting for others to lend it to them to read is about 1 in 15,000. Now, calculate for yourselves the value that poetry has in Spain.

This exposé could continue with further proof. But for now, we'll only add one observation, and it is that as long as poets visit booksellers, as it happens now, poetry will have little value. In Paris and other places, the *editores* are those who visit poets, that is, good poets. We are a long way off from this exchange of visits.]

10 Larra, 'Teatros,' 199.
11 Pierre Bourdieu, *The Rules of Art: Genesis and Structure of the Literary Field,*

trans. Susan Emanuel (Stanford: Stanford University Press, 1995), 141.

12 Victor Carrillo, *L'infra littérature en Espagne aux XIXe et XXe siècles* (Grenoble: Presses Universitaires, 1977), 11; and Haynes, 'Lost Illusions,' 62. Both are writing specifically about *editores* for narrative in France and Spain, but their definitions wholly apply to dramatic literature.

13 In the 'Complemento de la *Galería de la literatura*,' Ferrer del Río actually writes that now that more than just 'well-off' [acomodados] poets write for theatre and it has become a true industry, theatre copyright should be rewritten to 'veda á los libreros y editores la facultad de enseñorearse de las obras de los ingenios ...' [prevent booksellers and *editores* from imperiously seizing poets' works] (*Galería de la literatura española* [Madrid: Tip. de D.F. de P. Mellado, 1846], 306).

14 M.I.,'Un poeta,' *No me olvides*, 30 July 1837, pp. 4–5.

15 Zorrilla, *Recuerdos del tiempo viejo*, 141–55.

16 Rose, *Authors and Owners*, 135.

17 Navas Ruíz, *El romanticismo español*, 51.

18 *No me olvides*, 22 Oct. 1837, p. 8.

19 'Libreros y editores,' in *España contemporánea*, ed. Noel Rivas Bravo (Managua, Nicaragua: Academia Nicaraguense de la Lengua, 1988), 248.

20 Ibid.

21 In a lengthy article ('Plaga de autores dramaticos,' 14 July 1839, s.n.) the editor of *El entreacto* criticized writers with scant literary skill who attempted to write poetry in order to quickly earn money, and certainly plenty of poor literature was written. However, as the *editor* facilitated the creation of new (literary) property in the 1830s and '40s, he also granted to the members of the public the possibility to exercise their power of choice as consumers. According to the philosophy of economic liberalism, as applied to poetry, simple supply and demand would determine the course of literature. As time went on, the dramatic *editor* also began to be a cultural gatekeeper, and, according to *El entreacto*, he solicited the editor of the journal for assistance in selecting dramatic works to publish.

22 Saunders, *Authorship and Copyright*, 10.

23 Marciano Zuritar, 'Historia del Género chico,' in *La Novela Teatral* (Madrid: Editoral Prensa Popular, 1920).

24 G.W.F. Hegel, 'Abstract Right. Section C. The Alienation of Property' (Paragraph 65), in *Elements of the Philosophy of Right*, ed. Allen Wood, trans. H.B. Nisbet (New York: Cambridge University Press, 1991), 95.

25 In 1862, Manuel Dánvila reviewed the various laws decreed in the previous

thirty years regarding the possession of found goods, unclaimed land, buried treasure, and ships without a crew.

26 The contiguity of the commentaries and the ministers' treatment of the content of the two petitions do seem to present the commentaries of the *mesa* as one unified argument. This was an effective rhetorical tactic. Indeed, Picoche has mistakenly dated *all* of the ministers' comments relating to the poets' and Delgado's petitions to 1839, presumably because they were written on the same folios (but dated 1837, as noted in chapter 1, above). See Picoche, 45–6.

27 Archivo Histórico Nacional, Legajo 11404.

28 'Derechos de autor y derechos de dramaturgo en la primera mitad del siglo XIX,' in *Studies in Honor of Gilberto Paolini*, ed. Mercedes Vidal Tibbitts (Newark, DE: Cuesta, 1996), 141–58.

29 For example, in 1839, Delgado attempted to collect payment for the plays that he owned by sending a list of them to provincial theatre companies and censors: 'Lista de las producciones dramaticas que se enagenan para su representacion en el teatro de Burgos para el derecho de propiedad que tienen sus autores confirmada en Real orden de 5 de mayo de 1837' (Archivo Histórico Nacional, Legajo 11931). This is but one instance in which the private property owner and the agents of the Crown worked together to curb uncontrolled dramatic discourse as a theft of property.

30 Censors had always been concerned with adherence to the authorized text by provincial theatre troupes, but not for reasons of intellectual property or private interest. Their primary focus had always been the political and moral elements.

31 Bettig, 'Critical Perspectives,' 131–7.

32 Martínez Martín, 'El mercado editorial y los autores,' 18.

33 See chapter 6 of *Real decreto organico de los teatros del reino y reglamento del teatro español* (Madrid: Imprenta Nacional, 1849).

34 The oxymoron of duplicate original texts was an idea explored by *El entreacto* in 1839, shortly after the second royal order commanding that only one original authentic version could exist (and defining all others as illegal). The situation it described tested the limits of both literary property and the concept of original, authorized poetry, and speculated about the public's confusion if different legal versions of the same work were to exist. The journal assumed that the public would only be satisfied by a performance that perfectly matched their textual copy of the piece.

The narrator of the chronicle describes being in the auditorium of a Madrid theatre to see a performance of *El Campanero de san Pablo, traducido por don Luis Cantejos*. The men sitting around him are reading a text during the performance and become angry as the play progresses:

'¡Pícaros! volvió á repetir con mas calor; ¡engañar asi al público!- Quedéme cortado sin saber que pensar, pero el murmullo seguia; y la representacion seguia su curso; y el sordo seguia leyendo, y mirando el escenario; y yo seguia asustado, y temblando aquellos anuncios de una próxima tormenta. – Entonces advertí que mi sordo leia en un cuaderno amarillo, interpolando su lectura con algunas violentas esclamaciones de ¡pícaros! ¡bribones! – Estaba yo aturdido y absorto. – Pero mi admiracion llegó á su colmo, cuando mi buen hombre cerrando el libro con furor, y esclamando, ¡infames, esto no puede sufrirse! se marchó. – Quedéme con la boca abierta, mirando á aquel ente estraordinario, y me acerqué á otro de mis vecinos, que con otro cuaderno en la mano, igual al del anterior, hacia las mismas esclamaciones.

'¿Quiere V. decirme, caballero, le pregunté, por qué es su enojo?

'¿Qué ha de ser? me respondió... que nos están engañando.

'Santo varon, ¿y se desayuna V. ahora de eso? pues yo hace bastante tiempo que lo tengo olvidado.

'Y tiene V. calma para responder con esa flema? ...

'¿Y qué quiere V.? ¿que me desespere? ¿qué ventaja me resultaria á mí declamar contra los gobernantes?

'¿Qué tienen que ver los gobernantes con los cómicos?

'¡Los cómicos! esclamé yo. Vamos, este hombre delira.

'Sí, señor, los cómicos; los cómicos son los que se están burlando de nosotros. Sino, respóndame V., ¿qué drama se le figura que están representando?

'Está buena la pregunta; *El Campanero de San Pablo*.

'Pues no hay tal, me respondió. Sino vea V.; aqui está el drama, y desengáñese V. por sí mismo. – Cogí efectivamente el cuaderno, busqué la escena en que se hallaban los actores, y ... ¡oh sorpresa! Decian palabras diferentes de las que estaban impresas.

'Lo vé V.? me decia mi vecino. ¿Lo vé V.?

'Sí, señor; esto es una infamia, le contesté yo, y una infamia que no debemos tolerar.'

[...] ¿Y sabes lo que era ...[?] Que el drama que se representaba, era el publicado por don Ignacio Boix; y el que mis adláteres leian, el dado al público por don Manuel Delgado. ('Los dos editores,' *El entreacto*, 1 Aug. 1839, p. 140)

['Thieves!' he repeated more heatedly. 'Fooling the public like this!' – I was taken aback, without knowing what to think, but the mumbling continued and the performance continued and the deaf man continued reading and watching the stage and I continued to be frightened and trembling before those warnings of a coming storm. Then I figured out that the deaf man was reading a yellow notebook, interpolating his reading with violent exclamations of 'Thieves! Rascals!' – I was confused and completely taken in. – But my surprise reached its peak when my good man furiously shut the book and, exclaiming, 'This is vile, I can't take it,' he left. – My jaw dropped as I watched this unusual creature and I went over to another of my neighbours who, with another notebook in hand, the same as the previous gentleman had, was making the same exclamations.

'Could you tell me, sir,' I asked him, 'the reason for your anger?'

'What do you think?' he responded ... 'they are pulling the wool over our eyes.'

'Good heavens, you are just waking up to this now? Why I've already forgotten it.'

'And you are able to remain so relaxed?'

'What do you want me to do about it? Despair? What would I gain by denouncing politicians?'

'What do politicians have to do with actors?

'Actors!' I exclaimed. Well now, this man is delirious.

'Yes sir, actors, it is the actors who are taking us for fools. Otherwise, tell me, what play do you think they are performing?'

'Good question, *Saint Paul's Bellman.*'

'Well, that is not what it is,' he responded. 'Look here, this is the play and see for yourself.' – I took the notebook, looked for the scene where the actors were at and ... to my surprise! They were declaming different words than those that were printed.

'You see?' my neighbour asked me, 'Do you see?'

'Yes sir, this is a disgrace,' I answered him, 'a disgrace that we must not tolerate.'

[...] And do you know what was going on? The play that was performed was the version published by Ignacio Boix, and that which my neighbours were reading was the version published by Manuel Delgado.]

35 Hartzenbusch's *refundición* of his *Los amantes de Teruel* and Gutiérrez's *refundición* of *El trovador* are just two examples of many attempts by poets to reappropriate their plays, perhaps in order to improve, but certainly to resell, the literary property.

36 'Venta y cesion de varias obras dramaticas por la cantidad de seis mil reales otorgada por el Ex˜mo Sr. Dn Manuel Breton de los Herreros à

fabor de Dn Vicente de Lalama. Mayo #6# de 1862,' Archivo Histórico de Protocolos, Madrid.

5 Textual Museums

1 Rubén Darío noted that Delgado's was the first. '[E]n la época romántica se fundaron las «Galerías dramáticas», y creo que el editor Delgado fue el primero que intentó el negocio' (*España contemporánea*, 175). Indeed, Delgado's was the first collection to be called 'galería,' although Ignacio Boix's Repertorio also started within two weeks of the publication of Delgado's *galería* series.
2 Archivo Histórico Nacional, Legajo 11391. Delgado continued to use the older title when addressing the governement. For example, on 16 April 1842 he wrote the political chief of Cadiz as the director of the Comisión de enagenación de propiedades dramáticas on behalf of nineteen principal dramatists (Martínez de la Rosa, Duke of Rivas, Zorrilla et al.) to protest the common 'falsification' of play titles in Cadiz. (He included a list of correct titles to nearly two hundred plays and the copyright royalties he expected the Cadiz censor to guarantee for each) (Archivo Histórico Provincial de Cádiz, Gobierno Civil, 154:30).
3 See Roger Chartier 'Libraries without Walls' (chapter 3), in *The Order of Books* (Stanford: Stanford University Press, 1994), for a discussion of the attempts to create perfect collections.
4 Entry for 'galería,' *Diccionario de la lengua castellana* ..., 4th ed. (Madrid: Viuda de Don Joaquin Ibarra, Impresora de la Real Academia, 1803).
5 Entry for 'galería,' *Diccionario de la lengua castellana por la Academia española*, 7th ed. (Madrid: Imprenta Real, 1832).
6 Entry for 'galería,' *Autoridades* (Madrid, 1734)
7 Mariano de Madrazo, *Historia del Museo del Prado* (Madrid: Bermejo, 1945), 74.
8 The Royal Museum opened to the public on 19 November 1819 (Madrazo, *Historia*, 86).
9 'Prologo' in *Colección lithográphica de los cuadros del Rey de España ...* (Madrid: Establecimiento Litográfico Real, 1826), s/n.
10 Wednesdays and Saturdays (Madrazo, *Historia*, 118).
11 Jesús Rubio Jiménez has studied the illustrated editions of dramatic literature by such *editores* as Manuel Pedro Delgado (Manuel Delgado's son), Renacimiento, and Montaner y Simón, and the Museo Dramático Ilustrado by Vidal, in relation to the art of escenography at the end of the

nineteenth century. See 'Ediciones teatrales modernistas y puestas en escena,' *Revista de Literatura* 53 (1991): 103–50.

Elegant editions were also produced in the early Golden Age period with title pages, decorated borders, or illustrations (see Eduardo Juliá Martínez, *Poetas dramáticos valencianos* [Madrid: Tipografía de la 'Revista de Archivos,' 1929]). However, these were not mass-marketed, were decidedly 'high-art' objects, and pre-dated by several centuries the modern cultural projects that defined the nineteenth-century *galerías*.

12 Johann Friedrich Geist, *Arcades: The History of a Building Type*, trans. Jane O. Newman and John H. Smith (Cambridge: MIT Press, 1983), 54.
13 Walter Benjamin was the first to theorize the importance of the arcade to nineteenth-century society, in 'Fourier, or the Arcades' and 'Paris, Capital of the Nineteenth Century,' in *Reflections* trans. Edmund Jephcott (New York: Harcourt Brace Jovanovich, 1978), 146–62. He also related the hybrid architectural structure to the figure of the *flâneur* (both within and without the space of the city). See 'The Flâneur,' in *Charles Baudelaire: A Lyric Poet in the Era of High Capitalism*, trans. Harry Zohn (New York: Verso, 1997), 35–66. Finally, he attempted to recreate the experience of a *flâneur* in a gallery in the space of a book. See *The Arcades Project*, trans. Howard Eiland and Kevin McLaughlin; prepared on the basis of the German volume edited by Rolf Tiedemann (Cambridge: Belknap Press of Harvard University Press, 1999).
14 Günter Bandmann, 'Die Galleria Vittorio Emanuele II in Mailand,' *Zeitschrift für Kunstgeschichte* 29.2 (1996). Quoted by Geist, 54.
15 Margaret MacKeith, *The History and Conservation of Shopping Arcades* (New York: Mansell, 1986), 15.
16 Geist, *Arcades*, 55.
17 Walter Benjamin, 'The Work of Art in the Age of Mechanical Reproduction,' in *Illuminations*, trans. Harry Zohn (New York: Schoken Books, 1969), 220.
18 Hemos leido en un periódico que el Sr. Hartzenbusch va á publicar una coleccion de comedias del antiguo teatro español, y que se *ocupa en la buena correccion y pureza de lenguage* de dichas comedias. Corregir el lenguage que usaron en sus obras nuestros dramáticos del siglo XVII seria destruirlas, y el señor Hartzenbusch se propone conservarlas: lo que hará el editor de esta coleccion de comedias, será *corregir* los yerros de *las ediciones* antiguas y restituir su *pureza* al *texto*. (*El entreacto*, 21 April 1839, p. 28; original emphasis)
[We have read in a newspaper that Mr Hartzenbusch is going to publish a

collection of plays from our classic theatre and that he will be *concerned with the formal correction and purity of language* in said plays. Changing the language that was used in our dramatic works of the seventeenth century would destroy them, and Mr Hartzenbusch proposes to save them: what the editor of this collection of plays will do is *correct* the flaws of the old *editions* and restore the *text's purity*.]

19 Juan Eugenio Hartzenbusch, 'Prologo del Colector,' in *Comedias escogidas de Fray Gabriel Téllez (El maestro Tirso de Molina)*, vol. 5, Biblioteca de autores españoles (Madrid: M. Rivadeneyra, 1848), vi. Presumably Hartzenbusch was describing his own experience as a writer. Carmen Iranzo has offered a few observations on Hartzenbusch's writing style: 'Muchas de sus obras están plagadas de huecos, contradicciones, cabos sueltos, situaciones sin resolver, libertades históricas, verdaderas legiones de elementos que no aportan nada al argumento' [Many of his works are plagued with gaps, contradictions, loose ends, unresolved situations, moments where he has taken liberty with historical facts, and truly a multitude of elements that in no way further his plots] ('Introducción,' in *Los amantes de Teruel* [Madrid: Cátedra, 1989], 17).

20 'Editing Theatre,' in *The Politics of Editing*, Hispanic Issues, ed. Nicholas Spadaccini and Jenaro Talens (Minneapolis: University of Minnesota Press, 1992), 101.

21 The prospectus of the new collection, and the presentation of the name brand (title) was summarized in 'Telégrafo literario,' *El entreacto*, 7 April 1839:

> REPERTORIO DRAMÁTICO – Con este título va á públicar el editor D. Ignacio Boix, una coleccion de comedias nuevas, originales españolas, y traducidas del francés. La primera, que verá la luz pública á mediados del presente mes, será *el Comico de la legua*, comedia en cinco actos escrita en francés por Mr. Bayard, autor del *Pilluelo de París*; y traducida al castellano por D. Juan del Peral. En la librería de Boix, calle de Carretas, se hallan los prospectos de esta obra.
>
> [REPERTORIO DRAMÁTICO – Under this title, the *editor* Ignacio Boix is going to publish a collection of new plays, both original Spanish and translations from Frnech. The first play, which will be available to the public mid-month, will be *The Provincial Actor*, a play in five acts written in French by Mr Bayard, author of *Pilluelo de Paris*, and translated into Spanish by Juan del Peral. The prospectus for this work is available in the Boix Bookstore, Carretas Street.]

22 Supplement to *El entreacto*, 9 May 1839.

23 María del Mar Fernández Vega, 'Diccionario de pliegos sueltos poéticos catalanes (siglos XV y XVI)' (Diss., Universidad Complutense de Madrid, 2004), 76.

6 Paratextual Performances in the 'Galerías dramáticas'

1 Gérard Genette, *Seuils* (Paris: Éditions du Seuil, 1987).
2 The formula sometimes varied slightly: 'success' could be 'applause' or some other term of approval. However, this peritextual element often blended historical fact with its own formulaic fiction: it did name the place and (usually) stated the correct date of the premiere, but it was printed systematically, even in editions of plays that had only one unsuccessful performance or failed because of poor reviews.
3 Nancy Membrez has explained that until late 1860s, the working class or peasantry 'was conspicous in its absence from what little theatre existed in the capital, instead finding its diversions elsewhere, principally in bullfights and circuses. By the 1850s, Madrid's two main theatres, the Real and the Zarzuela, were patronized exclusively by the aristocracy and by members of the new insurgent middle class ...' (Nancy J. Membrez, 'The Teatro por horas: History, Dynamics and Comprehensive Bibliography of a Madrid Industry, 1867–1922' [Diss., University of California at Santa Barbara, 1987], 109). While theatre attendees in Madrid were *nouveaux riches* and aristocracy, working class *morenos* only began to attend theatres after 1868; until that time, their only access to dramatic productions was at *café-teatros* (Membrez, 117). This marked a return to the kind of audience that had existed before the end of the eighteenth century. (See Dowling, 'The Madrid Theatre Public in the Eighteenth Century: Transition from the Popular Audience to the Bourgeois.')
4 'Spanish Romanticism,' 268.
5 See especially F. Cervera, 'Zorrilla y sus editores,' *Bibliografía Hispánica* 33 (1944): 147–60. Recently, Jesús Martínez Martín has reconsidered their relationship and argued that it was truly amicable. See 'El mercado editorial y los autores.'
6 For a complete study of the dates and locations of performances of *Don Juan Tenorio* after its premiere in 1844, see Hans Mattauch, 'La implantación del rito del *Tenorio* en Madrid,' in *Actas del Congreso sobre José Zorrilla: una nueva lectura. Valladolid, 18–21 de octubre de 1993*, ed. Javier Blasco Pascual, Ricardo de la Fuente Ballesteros, and Alfredo Mateos Paramio (Valladolid: Universidad de Valladolid, 1993), 409–15.
7 Genette, *Seuils*, 8.
8 Geist, *Arcades*, 36.

9. Christian Péligry has studied the process by which Golden Age writers transformed their manuscripts into legally valid printed copies. The privilege (obligatory after 1558) was only granted after the piece received civil and religious approvals and printers or writers paid a fee. Péligry notes that we have no idea what the requirements were to obtain the privilege; it seems to have been done case-by-case. See 'Du manuscrit à l'imprimé: le contrat d'édition dans l'Espagne du siècle d'or,' in *De l'alphabétisation aux circuits du livre en Espagne XVI-XIXe siècles* (Paris: Editions du CNRS, 1987), 335.

10. One example of a play printed before the royal decree of 1837 is Larra's *No más mostrador* (Madrid: Repullés, 1836). On the back cover, in the former locus of the royal privilege, the reader found the following statement: 'Esta comedia es propiedad legítima de su Editor, quien perseguirá ante la ley al que la reimprima' [This play is the legitimate property of its *editor*, who will prosecute before the law anyone who might reprint it]. The proclamation was more hopeful than factual, as literary property for dramatic works had not yet been promulgated. The presentation of the property claim in the traditional position of the privilege subtly illustrated the uncertain status of dramatic poetry: no longer subject to the protection of privilege, but not yet a legally recognized property, it inhabited the peritextual site of the former and enunciated the language of the latter. The definitive relocation of the articulation of ownership to the verso of the title page coincided with the promulgation of the 1837 law.

11. Eduardo de Palacio, *La caza del tio: pieza cómica en un acto orijinal* [sic] *y en verso* (Madrid: Hijos de Cuesta, 1870).

12. Francisco de Paula Rochano, *Els amors d'un Torrentí* (Valencia: Imprenta de El Valenciano, propiedad de V.M. Gamir, 1859).

13. Jean Nicolas Bouilly, *El abate l'Epee y el asesino, o, La huerfana de Bruselas: drama de espectaculo en tres actos arreglado por Juan de Grimaldi*, 3rd ed. (Madrid: Alvarez Hermanos; Enrique Arregui, 1882).

14. Just one example is *El abate de l'Epee, y su discipulo el sordo mudo de nacimiento, conde de Harancour: comedia en cinco actos por Monsieur Bouilly, traducida en castellano por Juan de Estrada y D. Laas-Litzos* (Madrid: B. García, 1803).

15. Ricardo Valero, *El sacristán toreador* (Madrid: M.P. Montoya y Cia, Hidalgo, 1882).

16. Mariano Pina Domínguez, *Las tres jaquecas* (Madrid: Hidago, 1881). There is also a play on words in this comment: 'jamona' sounds like ham, which is cured meat.

17. Angel de Saavedra, *Tanto vales, cuanto tienes* (Madrid: Repullés, 1840).

18 See Benedict Anderson, *Imagined Communities* (New York: Verso, 1991).
19 Intellectual property developed throughout Europe during these same years. According to W.E. Yates, Paris led the way in establishing theatre copyrights and influenced the internationalization of European theatre ('Internationalization of European Theatre: French Influence in Vienna between 1830 and 1860,' *Austrian Studies* 13 [October 2005]: 37–54). In contrast, Spanish translators imported hundreds of French plays for audiences throughout the peninsula during the first half of the century. The public was eager for a French-inspired theatre, but Spanish *editores* and translators did not wish to pay for the rights. In 1853 the French began to request adherence to international copyright agreements between the two countries to stymie uncompensated and, indeed, often un-attributed translations.
20 'Miscelanea,' *La tertulia*, 16 Dec. 1849, p. 8.
21 *Rewriting Melodrama* (Lewisburg, PA: Bucknell University Press, 1997), 12–13.
22 *Editores* were adamant about their right to control provincial performances. As a group, the most important dramatic copyright owners petitioned Queen Isabel II to decree that the seats in the audience designated (by law) to an author for each and every performance of his play be transmissible to *editores* along with the title of ownership. Within months, their petition was addressed, and a new royal order was published to comply with their request (Archivo Histórico Nacional, Legajo 11405, No. 69).
23 16 April 1840, p. 121.
24 Romero Tobar, *Panorama crítico*, 249.
25 José Blanco White, *Cartas de España*, tran. Antonio Garnica (Madrid: Alianza, 1972), 250–1. I would like to thank an anonymous reader for University of Toronto Press for sharing these three examples with me.
26 Armona, *Memorias cronológicas*, 172.
27 See the petitions to Isabel II, Archivo Histórico Nacional, Legajos 11405 and 11404.
28 22 Aug. 1839, p. 164.
29 Quoted from verso of title page in Ventura de la Vega, *Una boda improvisada* (Madrid: Cipriano Lopez, 1857).
30 'Miscelánea,' *La tertulia* (Cadiz), 29 July 1849, p. 7.
31 For a discussion of the concept of crimes of reading, see Anthony Jiulius, 'Art Crimes,' in *Law and Literature*, ed. Michael Freeman and Andrew D.E. Lewis, vol. 2 (Oxford University Press, 1999), 499–532. The classic discussion of the creation of pirated editions as not only the pilfering of profit but also the theft of discourse is by Emmanuel Kant. See *The Science of*

Right, Great Books of the Western World, vol. 42 (Chicago: Encyclopedia Britannica, 1952), 425–6.

32 Before copyright outlawed pirated copies for reasons of property rights, creating or owning an unauthorized version of a book printed by privilege was also a crime. In the early seventeenth century, Alonso Pérez, a bookseller in Madrid (and father of the dramatist Juan Pérez de Montalbán), was prosecuted for illegally reprinting Quevedo's *Buscon*. I thank an anonymous reader for University of Toronto Press for this example. Again, while copyright regulated the relationship between text and reader according to modern law, it was a re-presentation of older practices and recycled as new.

Conclusion

1 See Saunders, *Authorship and Copyright*, 3–5.
2 The only study of the establishment of the Sociedad is the story told by its founder, Sinesio Delgado, in the wildly melodramatic *Mi teatro* (Madrid: SGAE, 1999). (Sinesio Delgado is not related to Manuel Delgado.)

Appendix

1 Although literary property was granted to dramatic works in 1837, centuries of tradition and practice impeded its complete and immediate implementation. In the preparation of its re-promulgation on 9 April 1839 (discussed in chapter 2), the ministers referred to all previous laws related to the topic, and this marginal note is from that later use.

Sources Cited and Consulted

Archives

Archivo Histórico Nacional, Legajos 11391, 11404, 11931, 11387.
Archivo Histórico Provincial de Cádiz, Sección Gobierno Civil. Sig. 154, Exp. 30.

Nineteenth-Century Sources

Apuntes poeticos y medios indispensables para que la empobrecida y desmoralizada España por sus apostatas é hijos negros, vulgo liberales, comuneros, carvonarios y masones, logre recuperar su agonizante vida física y moral. Barcelona: Garriga y Aguasvivas, 1824.

Ayguals de Izco, Wenceslao. *Los pobres de Madrid.* Madrid: Imprenta de Ayguals de Izco Hermanos, 1857.

Balaguer, Victor. *Estudios históricos y políticos.* Madrid: A. de San Martin, 1876.

Bouilly, Jean Nicolas. *El abate l'Epee y el asesino, o, La huerfana de Bruselas: drama de espectaculo en tres actos arreglado por Juan de Grimaldi.* 3rd ed. Madrid: Alvarez Hermanos; Enrique Arregui, 1882.

– *El abate de l'Epee y su discipulo el sordo mudo de nacimiento, conde de Harancour: comedia en cinco actos.* Madrid: B. Garcia, 1803.

Bretón de los Herreros, Manuel. *El editor responsable: comedia en tres actos.* Madrid: Imprenta de Repullés, 1842.

Calderón de la Barca, Pedro. *Verdadera quinta parte de comedias.* Madrid: Francisco Sanz, 1682.

Dánvila y Collado, Manuel. *El libro del propietario.* Valencia: Rius, 1862.

– *La propiedad intelectual.* 2nd ed. Madrid: Imprenta de la Correspondencia de España, 1882.

Diccionario de la lengua castellana, compuesto por la Real Academia Española, reducido á un tomo para su mas fácil uso. 4th ed. Madrid: Viuda de Don Joaquin Ibarra, Impresora de la Real Academia, 1803.

Diccionario de la lengua castellana por la Academia española. 7th ed. Madrid: Imprenta Real, 1832.

Diccionario de la lengua castellana [...] *Tomo quarto. Que contiene las letras G.H.I.J.K.L.M.N.* Madrid: Imprenta de la Real Academia Española, por los herederos de Francisco del Hierro, 1734.

Domínguez, Mariano Pina. *Las tres jaquecas.* Madrid: Hidalgo, 1881.

Eguizábal, José Eugenio de. *Apuntes para una historia de la legislación española sobre imprenta.* Madrid: Imprenta de la Revista de legislación, 1879.

Fernández, Mariano. *Paraguas y sombrillas.* Madrid: Imp. de Lalama, 1848.

Ferrer del Río, Antonio. *Galería de la literatura española.* Madrid: Tip. de D.F. de P. Mellado, 1846.

Flórez Estrada, Álvaro. *Contestacion de Don Alvaro Flórez Estrada á las impugnaciones hechas á su ESCRITO sobre el uso que deba hacerse de los bienes nacionales.* Madrid: Imprenta de D.M. de Burgos, 1836.

– 'Cuestión social.' In *Apuntes para una biblioteca de escritores españoles contemporáneos en prosa y verso.* Ed. Eugenio de Ochoa. Paris: Baudry, 1840. 518–29.

García Tejero, Alfonso. *Historia político-administrativa de Mendizábal.* Madrid: Establecimiento tipografico de J.A. Ortigosa, 1858.

Gil y Zárate, Antonio. *Un amigo en candelero: comedia en cinco actos.* Madrid: Imprenta de Repulles, 1842.

Guaza y Gómez-Talavera, Carlos. *Músicos, poetas y actores.* Madrid: Imprenta de F. Maroto, 1884.

Hartzenbusch, Eugenio. *Apuntes para un catálogo de periódicos madrileños.* Madrid: Sucesores de Rivadeneyra, 1894. Facsimile edition. Madrid: Biblioteca Nacional, 1993.

Larra, Mariano José de. *No más mostrador: comedia original en cinco actos.* Madrid: Imprenta de Repullés, 1836.

– 'Teatros.' In *Obras completas de Fígaro.* Vol. 2. Paris: Baudry, 1857. 71–5.

– *Obras de Fígaro.* Paris: Baudry, 1848.

Loi espagnole sur la propriété intellectuelle (7 juillet 1877). Paris: Imprenta de Gauthier-Villars, n.d.

Madrazo, José de. *Colección lithográphica de los cuadros del Rey de España el señor don Fernando VII.* Madrid: Real Establecimiento Lithográphico, 1826–32.

Martínez de la Rosa, Francisco. *La boda y el duelo.* Madrid: Imprenta del Colegio de Sordo-Mudos, 1839.

Mesonero Romanos, Ramón de. *Escenas matritenses.* 4th ed. Madrid: Boix, 1845.

– *Manual de Madrid.* Madrid: Imprenta de D.M. de Burgos, 1831.

– *Memorias de un setentón: natural y vecino de Madrid*. Madrid: Oficinas de la Ilustración Española y Americana, 1881.
Molina, Tirso de. *Comedias escogidas*. Ed. Juan Eugenio Hartzenbusch. 2nd ed. Madrid: M. Rivadeneyra, 1857.
Novo y Colson, Pedro de, ed. *Autores dramáticos contemporáneos y joyas del teatro español del siglo XIX*. Madrid: Imprenta de Fortanet, 1881.
Núñez, de Arce, Gaspar. *¿Quién es el autor?* Madrid: Imprenta de José Rodriguéz, 1859.
Ochoa, Eugenio de. *Apuntes para una biblioteca de escritores españoles contemporáneos en prosa y verso*. Paris: Baudry, 1840.
Ortiz de la Vega. *Anales de España: desde sus orígenes hasta el tiempo presente*. Madrid: J. Cuesta, 1857–9.
Palacio, Eduardo de. *La caza del tio: pieza cómica en un acto orijinal y en verso*. Madrid: Hijos de Cuesta, 1870.
Pina Dominguez, Mariano. *Las tres jaquecas*. Madrid: [Imprenta de J. Rodríguez], 1881.
Real decreto organico de los teatros del reino y reglamento del teatro español. Madrid: Imprenta Nacional, 1849.
Rochano, Francisco de Paula. *Els amors d'un Torrentí*. Valencia: Imprenta de El Valenciano, 1859.
Rodríguez Rubí, Tomás D. 'Excelencia, importancia y estado presente del teatro.' In *Discursos Leídos ante la Real academia española en la recepción pública*. Respondent: Antonio Ferrer del Rio, 17 June 1860.
Saavedra, Angel de. *Tanto vales, cuanto tienes: comedia en tres actos y en verso*. Madrid: Repullés, 1840.
Valero y Castell, Ricardo. *El sacristán toreador*. Madrid: M.P. Montoya y Cia, 1882.

Nineteenth-Century Periodicals

El alba (Madrid, 1838–9). Index. José Simón Díaz. Madrid: Instituto Nicolás Antonio del CSIC, 1946.
La amenidad; periódico semanal de literatura, modas y teatros (Malaga, 1844–5).
Annales dramatiques. Archives du théâtre. Journal officiel de la Société des auteurs et Compositeurs de l'association des artistes dramatiques. Paris: n.p., 1843.
El artista (Madrid, 1835–6). Introduction. Angel González Garcia and Francisco Calvo Serraller. Madrid: Ediciones Turner, 1981.
Boletín del comercio (Madrid, 1833).
El conservador: revista semanal de politica, ciencias y literatura (Madrid, Sept. 1841–Jan. 1842).

El correo de la moda (Madrid, 1862–4).
La crónica (Madrid, Oct. 1844–Sept. 1845).
Crónica científica y literaria (Madrid, 1817–20).
El entreacto (Madrid, 1839).
Fruto de la prensa periódica (Palma, 1839–40).
Hidalgo, Dionisio. *Boletin bibliografico español y estranjero.* 1–2 (Madrid, 1843–4).
El laberinto (Madrid, 1843–5).
Liceo artistíco y literario (Madrid, 1838). Index. José Simón Díaz. Madrid: Instituto Nicolás Antonio del CSIC, 1947.
El museo universal (Madrid, 1857).
No me olvides (Madrid, 1837–8).
Observatorio pintoresco (Madrid, 1837).
Omnibus literario: o sea reproducción daguerreotipica de todo lo que se publica en todos los periódicos franceses (Madrid, 1844).
Revista literaria de El Español: semanario de literatura, bellas artes y variedades (Madrid, 1846).
Revista semanal pintoresca del avisador Malagueño (Malaga, 1847–52).
Semanario pintoresco español (Madrid, 1836–57).
Los sucesos: semanario ilustrado (Madrid, 1866–8).
La tertulia: periódico semanal de literatura y de artes (Cadiz, April 1849–Dec. 1852; Jan.–Dec. 1854).
El trovador (Barcelona, 1846).
El trovador español (Madrid, 1841).

Modern Sources

Aguilar Piñal, Francisco. *Sevilla y el teatro en el siglo XVIII.* Oviedo: Cátedra Feijoo, 1974.
Aguilera Sastre, Juan. 'Manuel Bretón de los Herreros y las políticas teatrales de su época.' In *La obra de Manuel Bretón de los Herreros II Jornadas bretonianas (Logroño, 2 al 5 de marzo de 1999).* Coord. Miguel Angel Muro, 117–40. Logroño: Instituto de Estudios Riojanos, 2000.
Alcalá Galiano, Antonio. *Literatura española siglo XIX.* Madrid: Alianza, 1969.
Almela y Vives, Francisco. *El editor don Mariano de Cabrerizo.* Valencia: CSIC, 1949.
Álvarez Barrientos, Joaquín. 'El actor español en el siglo XVIII: formación, consideración social y profesionalidad.' *Revista de Literatura* 50 (1988): 445–66.
Anderson, Benedict. *Imagined Communities.* New York: Verso, 1991.
Armona y Murga, José Antonio de. *Memorias cronológicas sobre el teatro en España.*

1785. Vitoria Gasteiz: Diputación Foral de Álava, Servicio de Publicaciones, 1988.
Artaud, Antonin. *The Theatre and Its Double*. Trans. Victor Corti. London: Calder & Boyars, 1970.
Artola, Miguel. *La burguesía revolucionaria*. Madrid: Alianza, 1973.
Benjamin, Walter. *The Arcades Project*. Trans. Howard Eiland and Kevin McLaughlin. Ed. Rolf Tiedemann. Cambridge, MA: Belknap Press of Harvard University Press, 1999.
– *Charles Baudelaire: A Lyric Poet in the Era of High Capitalism*. Trans. Harry Zohn. London and New York: Verso, 1997.
– *Illuminations*. Trans. Harry Zohn. New York: Schoken Books, 1969.
– *Reflections*. Trans. Edmund Jephcott. New York: Harcourt Brace Jovanovich, 1978.
Bettig, Ronald V. 'Critical Perspectives on the History and Philosophy of Copyright.' *Critical Studies in Mass Communication* 9 (1992): 131–55.
Blanco White, José. *Cartas de España*. Tran. Antonio Garnica. Madrid: Alianza, 1972.
Botrel, Jean François. *La diffusion du livre en Espagne*. Madrid: Casa de Velázquez, 1988.
– *Libros, prensa y lectura en la España del siglo XIX*. Madrid: Fundación Germán Sánchez Ruipérez, 1993.
– 'La novela por entrega: unidad de creación y consumo.' In *Creación y público en la literatura española*. Ed. Jean François Botrel and Serge Salaün, 111–55. Madrid: Castalia, 1974.
Bourdieu, Pierre. *The Rules of Art: Genesis and Structure of the Literary Field*. Trans. Susan Emanuel. Stanford: Stanford University Press, 1995.
Bretón de los Herreros, Manuel. 'Crítica teatral: los morcilleros.' In *Obra dispersa, I: El correo literario mercantil*. Ed. J.M. Díez Taboada and J.M. Rozas, 449–51. Logroño: Instituto de Estudios Riojanos, 1965.
– 'Teatro: proyecto de estímulo y subsistencia para los autores dramaticos.' In *Obra dispersa, I: El correo literario mercantil*. Ed. J.M. Díez Taboada and J.M. Rozas, 451–4. Logroño: Instituto de Estudios Riojanos, 1965.
– 'Teatros' (16 July 1832). In *Obra dispersa, I: El correo literario mercantil*. Ed. J.M. Díez Taboada and J.M. Rozas, 272–3. Logroño: Instituto de Estudios Riojanos, 1965.
Brown, Gregory S. 'After the Fall: The Chute of a Play, Droits d'Auteur, and Literary Property in the Old Regime.' *French Historical Studies* 22.4 (1999): 465–91.
Brown, Jonathan, and John Elliott. *A Palace for a King*. New Haven: Yale University Press, 1980.

Burdiel, Isabel. 'The Liberal Revolution, 1808–1843.' In *Spanish History since 1808*. Ed. José Alvarez Junco and Adrian Shubert, 17–32. New York: Oxford University Press, 2000.

Carr, Raymond. *Spain, 1808–1939*. Oxford: Clarendon Press, 1966.

Carrillo, Víctor. *L'infra littérature en Espagne aux XIXe et XXe siècles*. Grenoble: Presses Universitaires, 1977.

Castells, Irene, and Antonio Moliner. *Crisis del antiguo régimen y revolución liberal en España (1789–1845)*. Barcelona: Ariel, 2000.

Cervantes, Miguel de. *Comedias y entremeses*. Ed. Rudolph Schevill and Adolfo Bonilla. Madrid: Bernardo Rodríguez, 1915.

Cervantes Martin, Gregorio. 'Derechos de autor y derechos de dramaturgo en la primera mitad del siglo XIX.' In *Studies in Honor of Gilberto Paolini*. Ed. Mercedes Vidal Tibbits, 141–58. Newark: Juan de la Cuesta, 1996.

Cervera, Francisco. 'Zorrilla y sus editores.' *Bibliografía Hispánica* 3.3 (1944): 147–60.

Chartier, Roger. *The Order of Books*. Stanford: Stanford University Press, 1994.

Coe, Ada M. *Catálogo bibliográfico y crítico de las comedias anunciadas en los periódicos de Madrid desde 1661 hasta 1819*. Baltimore: Johns Hopkins Press, 1935.

Corominas, Joan. *Diccionario crítico etimológico castellano e hispánico*. Madrid: Editorial Gredos, 1980–91.

Cotarelo y Mori, Emilio. *Bibliografía de las controversias sobre la licitud del teatro en España*. Madrid: Est. de la 'Revista de archivos, bibliotecas y museos,' 1904.

– 'Editores y galerías de obras dramáticas en Madrid en el siglo XIX.' *Revista de bibliotecas, archivos y museos* 5 (1928): 121–39.

Cruz, Jesús. *Gentlemen, Bourgeois, and Revolutionaries: Political Change and Cultural Persistence among the Spanish Dominant Groups, 1750–1850*. Cambridge: Cambridge University Press, 1996.

Darío, Rubén. *España contemporánea*. Ed. Noel Rivas Bravo. Managua, Nicaragua: Academia Nicaraguense de la Lengua, 1998.

Delgado, Sinesio. *Mi Teatro*. Madrid: Sociedad General de Autores y Editores en España, 1999.

Delgado López-Cozar, Emilio, and José Antonio Cordón García. *El Libro: creación, producción y consumo en la Granada del siglo XIX*. Granada: Universidad de Granada, 1990.

Diccionario histórico de la lengua española. Madrid: Casa editorial Hernando, 1933.

Dowling, John. 'The Madrid Theatre Public in the Eighteenth Century: Transition from the Popular Audience to the Bourgeois.' In *Studies on Voltaire and the Eighteenth Century 265: Transactions of the Seventh International Congress on the Enlightenment*, 1358–62. Oxford: Voltaire Foundation, 1989.

Eisenstein, Elizabeth L. *The Printing Press as an Agent of Change: Communications and Cultural Transformations in Early Modern Europe.* New York: Cambridge University Press, 1979.
Elliott, John Huxtable. 'Philip IV of Spain, Prisoner of Ceremony.' In *The Courts of Europe: Politics, Patronage and Royalty 1400–1800.* Ed. A.G. Dickens, 169–89. New York: McGraw-Hill, 1977.
– *Spain and Its World, 1500–1700.* New Haven: Yale University Press, 1989.
Escobar, Hipolito. *Historia del libro español.* Madrid: Gredos, 1998.
Escobar, J. 'Romanticismo y revolución.' *Estudios de Historia Social* 36–7 (1986): 345–51.
Fernández, Pura. 'Datos en torno a la bibliografía y difusión de la literatura popular en el Madrid del siglo XIX: la imprenta manual de Manuel Minuesa.' *Anales del Instituto de Estudios Madrileños* 31 (1992): 225–38.
Fernández Vega, María del Mar. 'Diccionario de pliegos sueltos poéticos catalanes (siglos XV y XVI).' Diss., Universidad Complutense de Madrid, 2004.
Fontanella, L. *La imprenta y las letras en la España romántica.* Berne: Lang, 1982.
Foucault, Michel. *The Archaeology of Knowledge.* Trans. A.M. Sheridan Smith. New York: Pantheon Books, 1972.
– 'What Is an Author?' In *Language, Counter-Memory, Practice.* Trans. Donald F. Bouchard and Sherry Simon, 113–39. Ithaca, NY: Cornell University Press, 1977.
Gallagher, Catherine, and Stephen Greenblatt. *Practicing New Historicism.* Chicago: University of Chicago Press, 2000.
García Castañeda, S. *Las ideas literarias en España entre 1840–1850.* Berkeley: University of California Press, 1971.
García Garrosa, María Jesús. 'La Real Cédula de 1783 y el teatro de la Ilustración.' *Bulletin Hispanique* 95.2 (1993): 673–92.
García Gutiérrez, Antonio. *Los hijos del tío Tronera.* Ed. Jean-Louis Picoche. Madrid: Alhambra, 1979.
– *El trovador.* Ed. Carlos Riuz Silva. Madrid: Cátedra, 1994.
Geist, Johann Friedrich. *Arcades: The History of a Building Type.* Cambridge, MA: MIT Press, 1983.
Gellner, Ernest. *Nationalism.* New York: New York University Press, 1997.
Genette, Gérard. *Seuils.* Paris: Editions du Seuil, 1987.
Gies, David Thatcher. 'Glorious Invalid: Spanish Theater in the Nineteenth Century.' *Hispanic Review* 61.2 (1993): 213–45.
– *Theatre and Politics in Nineteenth-Century Spain: Juan de Grimaldi as Impresario and Government Agent.* Cambridge: Cambridge University Press, 1988.
– *The Theatre in Nineteenth-Century Spain.* Cambridge: Cambridge University Press, 1994.

Gillet, Joseph E. 'Caramuel de Lobkowitz and His Commentary (1668) on Lope de Vega's *Arte nuevo de hacer Comedias.*' *Philological Quarterly* 7 (1928): 120–37.
Goldstein, Robert Justin. *Political Censorship of the Arts and the Press in Nineteenth-Century Europe.* New York: St Martin's Press, 1989.
Gómez Aparicio, P. *Historia del periodismo español desde la 'Gaceta de Madrid' hasta el destronamiento de Isabel II.* Madrid: Editora Nacional, 1967.
González Muñíz, Miguel Angel. *Constituciones, Cortes y elecciones españolas: historia y anécdota (1810–1936).* Madrid: Ediciones Júcar, 1978.
Gore, Keith. 'The Playwright in an Institutionalized Theatre: France.' *Theatre Research International* 15 (1990): 150–73.
Granados, Mariano. *Mendizábal: un momento del liberalismo español.* México: [Impresos de Lujo], 1949.
Hartzenbusch, Juan Eugenio. *Los amantes de Teruel.* Ed. Carmen Iranzo. Madrid: Cátedra, 1989.
Haynes, Christine S. 'Lost Illusions: The Rise of the Book Publisher and the Construction of a Literary Marketplace in Nineteenth-Century France.' Diss., University of Chicago, 2001.
Hegel, Georg Wilhelm Friedrich. *Elements of the Philosophy of Right.* Ed. Allen W. Wood. Trans. H.B. Nisbet. Cambridge: Cambridge University Press, 1991.
Hemmings, F[rederick] W[illiam] J[ohn]. *The Theatre Industry in Nineteenth-Century France.* New York: Cambridge University Press, 1993.
Herrera Navarro, Jerónimo. 'Prólogo.' In *Catálogo de autores teatrales del siglo XVIII.* Madrid: Fundación Universitaria Española, 1993.
Hesse, Carla Alison. *Publishing and Cultural Politics in Revolutionary Paris, 1789–1810.* Berkeley: University of California Press, 1991.
Historia de la edición en España (1836–1936). Ed. Jesús A. Martinez Martín. Madrid: Marcial Pons, 2001.
Hobsbawm, Eric, and Terence Ranger. 'Introduction.' In *The Invention of Tradition.* New York: Cambridge University Press, 1992.
Iarocci, Michael. *Properties of Modernity: Romantic Spain, Modern Europe, and the Legacies of Empire.* Nashville: Vanderbilt University Press, 2006.
– 'Romantic Prose, Journalism and *costumbrismo.*' In *The Cambridge History of Spanish Literature.* Ed. David T. Gies. Cambridge: Cambridge University Press, 2004.
Iranzo, Carmen. 'Introducción.' In *Los Amantes de Teruel,* by Juan Eugenio Hartzenbusch. Ed. Carmen Iranzo, 7–78. Madrid: Cátedra, 2004.
Jagoe, Catherine. *Ambiguous Angels: Gender in the Novels of Galdós.* Berkeley: University of California Press, 1994.

Janke, Peter. *Mendizábal y la instauración de la monarquía constitucional en España (1790–1853)*. Madrid: Siglo XXI de España Editores, 1974.
Johnson, James H. *Listening in Paris: A Cultural History*. Berkeley: University of California Press, 1995.
Jovellanos, Gaspar Melchor de. *Memoria sobre los espectáculos públicos*. Gijón: La Voz de Asturias, 1991.
Juliá Martínez, Eduardo. *Poetas dramáticos valencianos*. Madrid: Tipografía de la 'Revista de Archivos,' 1929.
Julius, Anthony.' Art Crimes.' In *Law and Literature*. Ed. Michael Freeman and Andrew D.E. Lewis. Vol. 2, 499–532. Oxford: Oxford University Press, 1999.
Kant, Emmanuel. *The Science of Right*. Great Books of the Western World, vol. 42. Chicago: Encyclopedia Britannica, 1952.
Kelly, George Armstrong. *Victims, Authority, and Terror*. Chapel Hill: University of North Carolina Press, 1982.
Kendrick, Walter M. *The Secret Museum*. Berkeley: University of California Press, 1996.
Kirkpatrick, Susan. 'Constituting the Subject: Race, Gender, and Nation in the Early Nineteenth Century.' In *Culture and the State in Spain*. Ed. Thomas E. Lewis and Francisco J. Sánchez, 225–51. New York: Garland Press, 1999.
– *Larra: el laberinto inextricable de un romántico liberal*. Madrid: Gredos, 1977.
– *Las románticas: Women Writers and Subjectivity in Spain, 1835–1850*. Berkeley: University of California Press, 1989.
– 'Spanish Romanticism.' In *Romanticism in National Context*. Ed. Roy Porter and Mikulas Teich, 260–83. New York: Cambridge University Press, 1988.
Larra, Mariano José de. *Artículos*. Ed. Enrique Rubio. 12th ed. Madrid: Cátedra, 1993.
– *Fígaro: colección de artículos dramáticos, literarios, políticos y de costumbres*. Ed. Alejandro Pérez Vidal. Barcelona: Crítica, 1997.
– *Obras de Fígaro*. Ed. Carlos Seco Serrano. Madrid: Ediciones Atlas, 1960.
– 'Teatros. ¿Qué cosa es por acá el autor de una comedia?' In *Obras completas*. Vol. 1. *Artículos*. Ed. Luis Iglesias Feijoo, 195–9. Madrid: Biblioteca Castro, 1996.
– 'Teatros. ¿Quién es por acá el autor de una comedia?' In *Obras completas*. Vol. 1. *Artículos*. Ed. Luis Iglesias Feijoo, 211–14. Madrid: Biblioteca Castro, 1996.
Lida, Clara E., and Iris M. Zavala. *Liberales y románticos: una emigración española en Inglaterra (1823–34)*. Valencia: Castalia, 1979.
– *La revolución de 1868: historia, pensamiento, literatura*. New York: Las Américas, 1970.

MacKeith, Margaret. *The History and Conservation of Shopping Arcades.* New York: Mansell, 1986.
Madrazo, Mariano de. *Historia del Museo del Prado.* Madrid: Bermejo, 1945.
Mansel, Philip. *The Court of France, 1789–1830.* New York: Cambridge University Press, 1988.
Maravall, José Antonio. *Teatro y literatura en la sociedad barroca.* Madrid: Seminarios y Ediciones, 1972.
Martín, Gregorio C. 'Derechos de autor y derechos de dramaturgo en la primera mitad del siglo XIX.' In *Studies in Honor of Gilberto Paolini.* Ed. Mercedes Vidal Tibbitts, 141–58. Newark, DE: Juan de la Cuesta, 1996.
Martínez Martín, Jesús A. *Lectura y lectores en el Madrid del siglo XIX.* Madrid: Consejo Superior de Investigaciones Científicas, 1991.
– 'El mercado editorial y los autores: el editor Delgado y los contratos de edición.' In *Escribir en España entre 1840 y 1875.* Ed. Marie-Linda Ortega, 13–33. Madrid: Visor Libros, 2002.
Martínez de la Rosa, Francisco. *Los celos infundados.* In *Biblioteca de autores españoles.* Ed. Carlos Seco Serrano. Vol. 148. Madrid: Atlas, 1962.
Mattauch, Hans. 'La implantación del rito del Tenorio en Madrid.' In *Actas del Congreso sobre José Zorrilla: una nueva lectura. Valladolid, 18–21 de octubre de 1993.* Ed. Javier Blasco Pascual, Ricardo de la Fuente Ballesteros, and Alfredo Mateos Paramio, 409–15. Valladolid: Universidad de Valladolid, 1993.
Matthews, W. 'Samuel Pepys and Spain.' *Neophilologus* 20.1 (1935): 120–9.
Membrez, Nancy J. 'The Mass Production of Theater in Nineteenth Century Madrid.' In *The Crisis of Institutionalized Literature in Spain.* Ed. Wlad Godzich and Nicholas Spadaccini, 309–56. Minneapolis: Prisma Institute, 1988.
– 'The Teatro por horas: History, Dynamics and Comprehensive Bibliography of a Madrid Industry, 1867–1922.' Diss., University of California at Santa Barbara, 1987.
Menéndez Pidal, Ramón. *De Cervantes y Lope de Vega.* 3rd ed. Buenos Aires: Espasa Calpe Argentina, 1945.
Mesonero Romanos, Ramón de. *Memorias de un setentón.* Madrid: Publicaciones Españolas, 1961.
Miserachs i Sala, Pau. *Diccionario internacional del derecho de autor.* 2nd ed. Barcelona: Ediciones Fausí, 1988.
Moliner Prada, Antonio. *Joaquín María López y el partido progresista, 1834–1843.* Alicante: Instituto de Estudios 'Juan Gil-Albert,' 1988.
Mollier, Jean Yves. 'L'Edition en Europe avant 1850: Balzac et la proprieté litteraire internationale.' *L'Année Balzacienne* 13 (1992): 157–73.

Moral Roncal, Antonio M. *El reinado de Fernando VII en sus documentos.* Barcelona: Ariel, 1998.
Navas Ruíz, Ricardo. *El romanticismo español.* Madrid: Cátedra, 1982.
Norlund, D.E.C. 'Larra: Theatrical Criticism and Social Revolution, 1833–36.' *Revista Hispánica Moderna* 48.2 (1995): 233–49.
North, Michael. 'Authorship and Autography.' *PMLA* 116.5 (2001): 1377–85.
Olivero, Isabelle. *L'invention de la collection.* Paris: Éditions de l'IMEC, 1999.
Osteen, Mark, and Martha Woodmansee. 'Taking Account of the New Economic Criticism: An Historical Introduction.' In *The New Economic Criticism: Studies at the Intersection of Literature and Economics*, 3–50. London: Routledge, 1999.
Ovilo y Otero, Manuel. *Manual de biografía y de bibliografía de los escritores españoles del siglo XIX.* 1859. New York: G. Olms, 1976.
Pagés de Puig, Aniceto de. *Gran diccionario de la lengua castellana.* Madrid: Establecimiento tipolitográfico 'Sucesores de Rivadeneyra,' 1902–[192?].
Pascual, Pedro. *Escritores y editores en la restauración canovista 1875–1923.* Madrid: Ediciones de la Torre, 1994.
Pavis, Patrice. *Languages of the Stage: Essays in the Semiology of the Theatre.* New York: Performing Arts Journal Publications, 1982.
Péligry, Christian. 'Du manuscrit à l'imprimé: le contrat d'edition dans l'Espagne du siécle d'or.' In *De l'alphabétisation aux circuits du livre en Espagne: XVI–XIXe siècles*, 333–43. Paris: Editions du Centre National de la Recherche Scientifique, 1987.
Pérez Galdós, Benito. *Mendizábal.* Madrid: Alianza/Hernando, 1977.
– 'Observaciones sobre la novela contemporánea en España.' In *Revista de España.* Ed. Laureano Bonet, 105–20. Barcelona: Península, 1990.
Pickett, Terry H. *Inventing Nations: Justifications of Authority in the Modern World.* Westport, CT: Greenwood Press, 1996.
Picoche, Jean Louis. 'Introduction.' In *Los amantes de Teruel*, by Juan Eugenio Hartzenbusch. Paris: Centre de recherches hispaniques, Institut d'études historiques, 1970.
Plaza, Sixto. 'La zarzuela, género olvidado o malentendido.' *Hispania* 73.1 (1990): 22–31.
Ramírez Ángel, Emiliano. *José Zorrilla: biografía anecdótica.* Madrid: Mundo Latino, 1911.
Ravel, Jeffrey S. *The Contested Parterre: Public Theater and French Political Culture, 1680–1791.* Ithaca, NY: Cornell University Press, 1999.
Real Academia Española. *Diccionario de autoridades.* 1732. Madrid: Editorial Gredos, 1979.

Rennert, Hugo Albert. *The Spanish Stage in the Time of Lope de Vega.* New York: Hispanic Society of America, 1909.

Reyna Tapia, J. *The Spanish Romantic Theater.* Washington, DC: University Press of America, 1980.

Ribao Pereira, M. 'Vicisitudes empresariales de los teatros de La Cruz y el Príncipe en el Madrid de la Regencia (1834–40).' *Boletín de la Biblioteca de Menéndez Pelayo* 72 (1998): 141–60.

Ringrose, David R. *Madrid and the Spanish Economy, 1560–1850.* Berkeley: University of California Press, 1983.

– *Spain, Europe and the 'Spanish Miracle,' 1700–1900.* Cambridge: Cambridge University Press, 1996.

Ríos-Font, Wadda. *Rewriting Melodrama.* Lewisburg, PA: Bucknell University Press, 1997.

Rodríguez, Evangelina. 'Editing Theater.' In *The Politics of Editing.* Ed. Nicholas Spadaccini and Jenaro Talens, 95–109. Minneapolis: University of Minnesota Press, 1992.

Rodríguez Moñino, Antonio R. *Historia de los catálogos de librería españoles (1661–1840): estudio bibliográfico.* Madrid: Artes Gráficas Soler, 1966.

Rodríguez Solís, Enrique. *Guía artística: reseña histórica del teatro y la declamación y nociones de poesía y literatura dramática.* Madrid: Establecimiento tipográfico de los hijos de R. Álvarez, 1903.

Rogers, Paul Patrick. *The Spanish Drama Collection in the Oberlin College Library: A Descriptive Catalogue.* Oberlin, OH: Oberlin College, 1940–6.

Romero Tobar, Leonardo. 'Larra y los seudónimos transmigratorios.' In *Estudios de literatura española de los siglos XIX y XX: homenaje a Juan María Díez Taboada.* Ed. José Carlos de Torres Martínez et al., 359–65. Madrid: Consejo Superior de Investigaciones Científicas, 1998.

– 'Noticias sobre empresas teatrales en periódicos del siglo XIX.' *Segismundo* 15–16 (1972): 235–79.

– *Panorama crítico del romanticismo español.* Madrid: Editorial Castalia, 1994.

Root, Hilton L. *The Fountain of Privilege: Political Foundations of Markets in Old Regime France and England.* Berkeley: University of California Press, 1994.

Rose, Mark. *Authors and Owners: The Invention of Copyright.* Cambridge, MA: Harvard University Press, 1993.

Ross, Trevor. 'Copyright and the Invention of Tradition.' *Eighteenth-Century Studies* 26.1 (1992): 1–27.

Rubio Jiménez, J. 'La censura teatral en la época moderada: 1840–1868. Ensayo de aproximación.' *Segismundo* 39–40 (1984): 193–231.

– 'Ediciones teatrales modernistas y puestas en escena.' *Revista de Literatura* 53 (1991): 103–50.

– *El teatro en el siglo XIX.* Madrid: Playor, 1983.
Rueda Hernanz, Germán. *La desamortización de Mendizábal y Espartero en España.* Madrid: Cátedra, 1986.
Ruiz Ramón, Francisco. *Historia del teatro español: desde sus orígenes hasta 1900.* Madrid: Cátedra, 1966.
Saavedra, Angel de. *Don Álvaro.* Ed. Alberto Sánchez. Madrid: Cátedra, 1991.
Sáinz de Robles, Federico Carlos. *El teatro español, historia y antología.* Madrid: M. Aguilar, 1942–3.
Sarrió Rubio, Pilar. 'Sobre los miembros de las compañías teatrales.' *Diálogos Hispánicos de Amsterdam* 8.3 (1989): 853–61.
Saunders, David. *Authorship and Copyright.* London: Routledge, 1992.
Schinasi, Michael. 'Poder estatal en España y política teatral a mediados del siglo pasado.' In *Actas Irvine-92, Asociación Internacional de Hispanistas.* Ed. Juan Villegas, 36–44. Irvine: University of California, 1994.
Schmidt, Michael. 'Loadsamoney: Agents, Authors, Editors.' *Times Literary Supplement* 4445 (1988): 646.
Shaw, Donald L. *The Nineteenth Century.* London: Barnes & Noble, 1972.
Shergold, N.D. *A History of the Spanish Stage: From Medieval Times until the End of the Seventeenth Century.* Oxford: Clarendon Press, 1967.
Shergold, N.D., and J.E. Varey. *Representaciones palaciegas, 1603–1699.* London: Támesis Books, 1982.
Sieburth, Stephanie Anne. *Inventing High and Low: Literature, Mass Culture, and Uneven Modernity in Spain.* Durham, NC: Duke University Press, 1994.
Silver, Philip W. *Ruin and Restitution: Reinterpreting Romanticism in Spain.* Nashville: Vanderbilt University Press, 1997.
Simón Palmer, María del Carmen. 'Construcción y apertura de teatros madrileños en el siglo XIX.' *Segismundo* X (1974): 85–124.
– 'Diversiones populares madrileñas en el siglo XIX.' In *Actas de las jornadas sobre teatro popular en España.* Ed. Joaquín Alvarez Barrientos and Antonio Cea Gutierrez, 185–92. Madrid: CSIC, 1987.
Soufas, C. Christopher, Jr. 'Benavente and the Spanish Discourse on Theater.' *Hispanic Review* 68.2 (2000): 147–59.
Starn, Randolph. *Arts of Power: Three Halls of State in Italy, 1300–1600.* Berkeley: University of California Press, 1992.
Stein, Louise K. *Songs of Mortals, Dialogues of the Gods: Music and Theatre in Seventeenth Century Spain.* Oxford: Clarendon Press, 1993.
Ubersfeld, Anne. *Lire le théâtre.* Paris: Belin, 1996.
– *Lire le théâtre II: l'ecole du spectateur.* Paris: Belin, 1996.
Varela, José Luis. *Vida y obra literaria de Gregorio Romero Larrañaga.* Madrid: CSIC, 1948.

Varey, J.E., and Charles Davis. *Los corrales de comedias y los hospitales de Madrid, 1574–1615*. Madrid: Tamesis, 1997.
Vega García-Luengos, Germán. 'Impresos teatrales sevillanos del siglo XVIII: pautas de un estudio.' In *Trabajos de la Asociación Española de Bibliografía*. Vol. 1, 367–74. Madrid: Ministerio de Cultura/Biblioteca Nacional, 1993.
Vega Vega, José Antonio. *Derecho de autor*. Madrid: Tecnos, 1990.
Veltrusky, Jirí. *Drama as Literature*. Lisse: Peter de Ridder Press, 1977.
Villarroya, Joaquín Tomás, ed. *El Estatuto Real de 1834 y la constitución de 1837*. Madrid: Fundación Santa María, 1985.
Villegas, Juan. *Para un modelo de historia del teatro*. Irvine, CA: Gestos, 1997.
Vindel, Francisco. 'El librero español.' In *Conferencia dada en la Cámara oficial del libro, de Madrid, 17 Marzo 1934*. Madrid: Imprenta Góngora, 1934.
West, James L.W. 'Editorial Theory and the Act of Submission.' *Papers of the Bibliographical Society of America* 83 (1989): 169–85.
Williams, Raymond. *Keywords: A Vocabulary of Culture and Society*. New York: Oxford University Press, 1976.
Woodmansee, Martha. *The Author, Art, and the Market*. New York: Columbia University Press, 1994.
– 'The Genius and the Copyright: Economic and Legal Conditions of the Emergence of the "Author."' *Eighteenth-Century Studies* 17.4 (1984): 425–48.
Woodmansee, Martha, and Peter Jaszi. 'Introduction.' In *The Construction of Authorship: Textual Appropriation in Law and Literature*. Durham, NC: Duke University Press, 1994.
Yates, W.E. 'Internationalization of European Theatre: French Influence in Vienna between 1830 and 1860.' *Austrian Studies* 13 (October 2005): 37–54.
Yelpaala, Kojo. 'Owning the Secret of Life: Biotechnology and Property Rights Revisited.' *McGeorge Law Review* 32.1 (2000): 111–219.
Zavala, Iris M. 'Estudios sobre la España moderna.' *Nueva Revista de Filología Hispánica* 29.1 (1980): 193–204
– 'Románticos y socialistas: prensa española del siglo XIX*. Madrid: Siglo XXI, 1972.
Zerolo, Elías. *Diccionario enciclopédico de la lengua castellana*. 4th ed. Paris: Garnier Hermanos, 1905.
Zorrilla, José. *Recuerdos del tiempo viejo*. Madrid: Debate, 2001.
Zurita, Marciano. *Historia del Género chico*. Madrid: Editoral Prensa Popular, 1920.

Illustration Credits

Archivo Histórico Nacional, Ministerio de Cultura, Spain: Fig. 2, letter from Manuel Delgado (Consejos, Lejago 11.391, exp. 45)

Author's collection: Fig. 1, *El laberinto*

Teatro Español Collection (PQ6217.A2T4 1730), The Bancroft Library, University of California, Berkeley: Fig. 3, censor's approbation, Ventura de la Vega, *La escuela de los periodistas* (v. 25:8); fig. 4, wrapper, Antonio Gil y Zárate, *Un amigo en candelero* (v. 154:14); fig. 5, back cover, Mariano José de Larra, *Un desafío* (v. 76:11); fig. 6, catalogue, Mariano Fernández, *Paraguas y sombrillas* (v. 213:48); fig. 7, title page, Ventura de la Vega, *El testamento* (v. 179:25); fig. 8, copyright statement, Ramón Lias y Rey, *Un ángel tutelar* (v. 60:18); fig. 9, title page, Eduardo de Palacio, *La caza del tío* (v. 209:27)

Index

Abbé de l'Épée, L' (Bouilly), 137–8
Aben Humaya (Martínez de la Rosa), 172n25
absolutism: Bourbon style, 162n7, 165n11; critique of 49, 51–3, 60, 61, 130; end of, 7, 9; principles of, 15
Academy of San Fernando, 113, 115
Acrisolar el dolor en el más filial amor (Rezano), 143
Alcalá Galiano, Antonio, 84, 85, 94
amantes de Teruel, Los (Hartzenbusch): introduction to, 170n6; premiere, 42, 78; *refundición*, 185n35
amigo en el candelero, Un (Gil y Zárate), 128, fig. 4
Ancien Régime: behaviour of women, 164n8, 53, 54; censorship, 85; end of, 118; legacy of, 99; monarch, 46, 114, 135; policy, 7, 14, 26; theatre, 4, 49
Anderson, Benedict, 139
ángel titular, Un (Lías y Rey), 126
Anthony (Dumas), 34
Arenas, Juan J., 143

Armona, José Antonio de, 76, 102
Arregui, Enrique, 137, 145
Artaud, Antonin, 67–8, 174n11
Arte nuevo de hacer comedias (Lope de Vega), 171n14
authorship: alienable, 65, 91, 97; authors as owners, 6, 9, 15, 32; changes to, 17–18; as commodity, 83; as concept, 178n25; cult of, 78; in England, 25; Foucault on, 77; Golden Age, 4, 5; identity, 77–8, 92; individual, 77; legal, 98; lyric and narrative, 148; presence, 179n3; public, 80; recognition of, 16, 31, 42, 68, 81, 82, 100, 134, 147–8; rights, 10, 13, 38, 49, 60, 65, 70, 80, 83, 104, 136; Romantic, 25, 43, 60; theories of, 43; title, 58, 77, 80, 105, 125
autor, 74–6, 99, 106, 125; definition of, 82, 84, 176n17, 177n18; *editor* as, 84
autor de comedias, 6, 48, 74–6, 82, 148, 177n18; poet as, 72
autoría, 148
Avecilla, Pablo, 102
Avellaneda, Alonso Fernández de.

See Fernández de Avellaneda, Alonso
Ayguals de Izco, Wenceslao, 34, 168n31

Bandmann, Günter, 118
Barcelona, 8, 129, 166n11
barón, El (Moratín), 33
Beaumarchais, Pierre Augustin Caron de, 168n28
Beethoven, Ludwig van, 137
Benjamin, Walter, 119, 132, 187n13
Bettig, Ronald, 61, 103
Biblioteca dramática, 131, fig. 6
Bibliothèques (France), 112
bienes mostrencos, 97
Blanc y Navarro, Luis, 144
Blanco White, José, 143
boda y el duelo, La (Martínez de la Rosa), 172n25
Boix, Ignacio, 78, 102, 121, 186n1 188n21
Boletín del comercio, 33, 174n12
bookseller, 18, 32, 75, 83–4, 86, 97, 98, 129, 182n13 192n32
Borrow, George, 180n7
Bouilly, Jean Nicolas, 137
Bourbon dynasty, 12, 46, 52, 60, 61
Bourdieu, Pierre, 88, 149
bourgeoisie, 30, 118, 130; audience, 18, 123, 163n24
Bretón de los Herreros, Manuel, 172n25, 180n9, 185n36; appointment, 55–9; comedies, 73; petition for literary property, 41–5, 47, 50, 62, 98; plays, 104–6; on theatre, 74, 176n14
Buenavista Palace, 113
Burdiel, Isabel, 29, 30
Buscón (Quevedo), 192n32

Cadiz, 7, 140, 186n2; regency, 9, 52, 75
café-teatros, 189n3
Calderón de la Barca, Pedro, 4, 13, 45, 120, 161n1, 163n26, 174n12, 176n13
Camafeo y la porra (Blanc y Navarro), 144
Campanero de san Pablo, El (trans. Cantejos), 183n34
Campo-Alange, Count of, 164n8
Cantejos, Luis, 184n34
Cantos del trovador (Zorrilla), 91
capitalism, 4, 31, 118; and society, 26, 39
Caramuel Lobkowitz, Juan, 176n16, 177n18
Carlism, 30, 37–8, 45, 49, 165n11; war, 62, 149
Carlos María Isidro, Prince (the first Carlist pretender, as Carlos V), 8, 56, 58
Carlos II, King of Spain, 56
Carlos III, King of Spain, 61, 76
Carlos IV, King of Spain, 7, 52
Carrillo, Victor, 88, 182n12
casado avergonzado, El (Comellas), 143
Castilla, Ramón, 115
Catalunya, 166n11
caza del tio, La (Palacio), 136, fig. 9
celos infundados, ó el marido en la chimenea, Los (Martínez de la Rosa), 33, 172n25
Censor de Burgos, fig. 2
Censor de Valladolid, fig. 3
censorship, 15, 18, 47, 85, 126, 127, 135, 143, 163, 183n30; regional, 101, fig. 2, fig. 3; self-imposed, 86, 102

Cervantes, Miguel de, 4, 137, 177n18
Circo Theatre, 140, 144
Círculo Literario Comercial, 135, fig. 8
claque, 33, 35, 168n31
Collections (Great Britain), 112
comedia casera, La (de la Cruz), 143
comedias caseras, 142
comedias de magia, 163n19
Comellas, Luciano Fracisco, 143
comico de la lengua, El (Bayard), 188n21
Comisión de enajenación de propiedades dramáticas, 111, fig. 2
Concha, José, 143
conjuración de Venecia, La (Martínez de la Rosa), 56, 140, 172n25
Conservatorio de Música y Declamación, 47, 171n13, 172n17
Constitution of Cadiz. *See* Constitution of 1812
Constitution of 1812, 7, 10, 30, 40, 52
Constitution of 1836, 7
Constitution of 1837, 42
Contreras, Pedro José de, 14–15
copyright: concentration of, 102; declarations in editions, 109; dramatic, 3, 5, 13, 18, 34, 43, 182n13; dramatic printed editions, 109; early years of, 65, 67; European, 168n32; impact of, 4, 109, 142, 147–9, 163n26; international, 191n19, fig. 3; law, 18, 20, 43, 70, 82, 83, 91, 103, 104, 109, 124, 139, fig. 8; literary, 3; model, 60; for novels, 11; ownership of, 6; protection, 10, 92; as repressive, 101; to restrict interpretations, 139; symbol, 135; utility of, 23, 28, 40
Correo literario y mercantil, 176n13
Cortes, 7, 10, 12, 13, 30, 31, 42, 61, 62, 162n7
Cortes decree of 10 June 1813, 10
costumbrismo, 5
Cotarelo y Mori, Emilio, 179n2
Cruz, Ramón de la, 143
Curso de economía política (Flórez Estrada), 26

Dánvila y Collado, Manuel, 182n25
Darío, Rubén, 94–5, 179n2, 186n1
Decreto-manifiesto en el Puerto de Santa Maria, 10
Delgado, Manuel, 92–100, 102, 106, 112–13, 116–17, 120, 121, 128, 131, 133, 134, 183n29, 186n1, 186n2, fig. 2, fig. 7; petition, 183n26
Delgado, Manuel Pedro, 144, 186n11
Delgado, Sinesio, 192n2
derecho de autor, 134, 135, 139, 148; declarations in editions of, 134, 136; in France, 45; payment of, 143; rates of, 131; right to sell, 130; in Spain, 6, 7, 10, 11, 15, 28, 29, 34, 38, 42, 44, 45, 47–9, 51, 53, 55, 59, 61, 77, 88, 90, 101, 102, 104, 111, 120, 145, 146; theft of, 131
derecho de licencia, 77
desafío, Un (Larra), 129
desamortización, 30, 31, 36, 38, 39, 40, 47, 111, 167nn22–3
diablo mundo, El (Espronceda), 91
didascalia, 19, 109, 139, 144, 163n26
disentailment. See *desamortización*

Don Álvaro o la fuerza del sino (Duque de Rivas): didascalia, 163n26; premiere of, 167n27

Don Juan Tenorio (Zorrilla): enduring presence, 131; lesson of, 132; performances, 189n6; premiere of, 78, 90

Dorotea, La (Lope de Vega), 171n14

dos bodas descubiertas, Las (Arenas), 144

dramatic galleries. *See* 'galerías dramáticas'

dramatic poet, 5, 6, 16, 18, 30, 33, 37, 38, 42, 44, 48, 49, 52, 80, 97, 100, 103, 118, 125, 134; as author, 67, 68, 73, 74, 76–9, 81–3, 102, 104; authority, 81; conditions of, 55, 56, 71, 94; petition for copyright, 99; profession of, 47; rights of, 51, 58, 61, 69, 72; view of *editores*, 88, 91, 180n9

dramatist, 3, 5, 41. *See also* dramatic poet

Dumas, Alexandre, 34

Duque de Rivas. *See* Saavedra y Ramírez de Baquedano, Ángel de

Economista, El, 170n4

ediciones furtivas, 145. *See also* piracy

editor, 8, 18, 20, 65, 77, 83–6, 90, 98 102, 103, 105, 111, 112, 130, 145, 182n13; authorization of performances, 101; as curator, 130 ; definition of, 84, 182n12; editions of, 125, 126, 129; financial returns, 99; French, 88; impact of, 93, 95, 124, 179n2; as modern manufacturers, 120, 122, 123, 127, 133; as property owner, 183n29; relationship with poet, 91; responsibility, 117, 137; rights, 94, 191n19; role of, 91, 92, 97, 118, 119, 128, 139, 148; sale of rights to, 90, 91, 104, 123; task of, 94, 96, 149

editorial house. See *editor*; 'galerías dramáticas'

Elliott, John, 12

Enlightenment, 7, 8, 46, 51, 52, 53

entreacto, El, 8, 80, 81, 120, 142, 143, 169n39, 180n9, 182n21, 183n34

épitexte: definition, 124; of Spanish plays, 125, 126, 134. *See also* 'paratexte'

Escorial. *See* Royal Monastery of the Escorial

Escosura, Patricio, 179n32

escuela de periodistas, La, 101, fig. 3

Escuela de Tauromaquia, 47, 171n13, 172n17

español, El, 36, 50

Espartero, Joaquín Fernández. *See* Fernández Espartero, Joaquín

Espronceda y Delgado, José de, 38, 91, 167n21, 167n23

Estamento de Procuradores, 164n2

Estatuto of 1834, 42

Fernández de Avellaneda, Alonso, 137

Fernández Espartero, Joaquín 39

Fernández Vega, María del Mar, 122

Fernando VII, King of Spain, 7–14, 16, 23, 26, 42, 52, 61, 75, 84, 113–16, 162n7, 163n19, 169n37; school of tauromachy, 47, 171n13, 172n17

Ferrer del Río, Antonio, 31, 32, 182n13

Fidelio (Beethoven), 137

Fieras afemina Amor (Calderón), 163n26
flâneur, 132, 187n13
Flórez Estrada, Álvaro, 26–8, 31, 38, 60, 167nn21–2
Foucault, Michel, 68, 77
France dramatique, La (France), 112, 121
free press, 9, 85

'galerías dramáticas': catalogue of, 130, 131, 132; collections, 18, 19, 95, 111, 117, 123–5, 128, 145; commentators on, 120; definition of, 112, 113, 116; Delgado's, 116, 128, 144; editions, 119, 126; editorial houses, 96; function, 118, 127, 129; Gullón's, 131; Hidalgo's, 139; novelty of, 109, 122; wrapper, 126, 128, 130–4
gallery (art): 116–18, 132, 136; art collections of, 115; definition of, 113–14. *See also* Prado Musuem
García Gutiérrez, Antonio: 23, 28, 40, 42, 56, 78, 91, 104, 165n9; petition for literary property, 41, 44, 45, 47, 49–51, 55, 98; premiere of *El trovador*, 23, 25, 31–8, 59, 65, 148, 168n28; *refundición* of play, 106, 185n35
García Lorca, Federico, 6
Garcilaso de la Vega. *See* Vega, Garcilaso de la
Geist, Johann Friedrich, 118, 133
Genette, Gérard, 124, 132
Gies, David, 163n19
Gil de Zárate, Antonio. *See* Gil y Zárate, Antonio
Gil y Zárate, Antonio, 43, 55–9, 128
Gillet, Joseph E., 177n18

Golden Age: authors, 119, 170n40, 190n9; dramatic texts, 74, 85; editions, 187n11; period, 120; plays, 125, 127; theatre, 4, 13, 45, 61, 62, 139
Gómez de Quevedo y Villegas, Francisco, 59, 192n32
Goya y Lucientes, Francisco José de, 7
Granja, La, 39, 52
Grimaldi, Juan de, 38, 137, 138
Gullón, Alonso, 102, 131, 135

Hapsburg dynasty, 12, 46, 163n19
Hartzenbusch, Juan Eugenio, 28, 42, 51, 55, 56, 103, 179n32; didascalia, 163n26; editorial work, 119, 120, 170n40, 187n18, 188n19; petition for literary property, 41, 44, 45, 50, 98; premiere of play, 78, 165n9; *refundición* of play, 185n35
Havana, 129
Haynes, Christine, 84, 182n12
Hernani (Hugo), 32
Herrera Navarro, Jerónimo, 75
Hidalgo, Eduardo, 102, 135, 138, 139
hijos del tío Tronera, Los (García Gutiérrez), 106
huérfana de Bruselas, La (Azar y Azpe), 145
Hugo, Victor, 32

Iarocci, Michael, 26
Ilustración. See Enlightenment
impresarios, 12, 73, 77, 98–101, 104, 135, 136
individualism, 7, 26, 70; Lockean conception of, 26, 35

214   Index

ingenioso hidalgo don Quijote de La Mancha, El (Cervantes), 137, 177n18
Intellectual Property Law of 5 Aug. 1823, 10
Intellectual Property Law of 10 June 1847, 16, 137, 144, 163n23
Iranzo, Carmen, 33, 188
Isabel II, Queen of Spain, 7, 38, 49, 51–3, 58, 60, 103, 142, 162n18, 191n19

Jagoe, Catherine, 54, 164n8
Jaszi, Peter, 10, 168n32
Johnson, James H., 168n28
José I, King of Spain, 7

Kant, Emmanuel, 191n31
Kirkpatrick, Susan, 14, 41, 129, 168n34

La Harpe, Jean-François de, 168n28
laberinto, El, 78
labour, 25–9, 101; division of, 86, 87; intellectual, 39, 48, 54; of poet, 38, 40, 71, 79, 81, 88, 91, 92, 130; versification as, 100
laissez-faire, 23, 29
Lalama, Vicente, 102, 105, 106, 131
Larra, Mariano José de, 43, 51, 94; articles on authorial identity, 11–13, 23, 31, 35–8, 44, 50, 54–6, 62, 69–71, 73–9, 81, 84, 86, 88, 98, 104, 164n8, 165n11, 168n34, 169n37, 173n9, 175n13, fig. 5; plays, 190n10
Lerma, Duke of (Francisco Gómez de Sandoval y Rojas), 161n2
Liberal Triennium, 9, 10
liberalism: classical, 29; economic, 4, 5, 15, 43, 87, 88, 103, 124, 135, 142, 147, 182n21; ideologies of property, 16; moderate, 60; principles, 15, 25–8, 34, 38, 44, 49, 146, 169n39; suffrage, 30
Liceo of Madrid, 43, 143, 144
Liceu Theatre, 8
lithography, 115, 136, fig. 9
Lope de Vega, Félix, 4, 13, 45, 119, 161n1, 171n14, 174n12, 177n18
Lorca, Federico García. *See* García Lorca, Federico
Louis XIV, King of France, 13, 162n17
Louvre, 114

MacKeith, Margaret, 118
Madrazo, José de, 113–15
Madrid: buildings, 114, 118; editorial agencies, 102, 140; government of, 12, 49; literary scene, 38, 80; Mesonero's description of, 180n7; newspapers, 5, 31; plays sold in, 104, 128, 129, 192; salons, 31; theatre attendees, 189, 132; theatre production, 8; theatre public, 28, 123; theatres, 65, 98, 126, 183n34
magasin théâtral, Le (France), 112, 121
Manual de Madrid (Mesonero), 10
Maravall, Jose Antonio, 12
María Cristina, of Naples, Queen Consort (1829–33) and Regent (1833–40), 7, 8, 13–15, 17, 23, 28, 31, 34, 35, 39, 41, 42, 44–6, 48, 49, 51, 53, 55, 57, 59–62, 98, 99, 101, 103, 104, 142; conservatory, 47, 171n13, 172n17; reformer, 54, 56

María Teresa, of Spain, wife of Louis XIV, 13, 162n17
Martín, Gregorio C., 101
Martínez de la Rosa, Francisco, 33, 38, 43, 55–7, 59, 173n25; plays, 140, 172n25, 186n2
Martínez Martín, Jesús A., 83, 179n2, 189n5
mas heroico español, El (Concha), 143
Mazarin, cardinal, 162n17
Membrez, Nancy J., 189n3
Mendizábal, Juan de Dios Álvarez, 23, 29, 30, 31, 39, 40, 43, 149, 165n11, 166n11
Mesonero Romanos, Ramón de, 10, 43, 79, 85, 86, 88, 94, 97, 102, 142, 171n13, 180n7
Mi teatro (Sinesio Delgado), 192n2
mise en scène, 35, 68, 141
Molina, Tirso de, 4, 13, 119, 120, 161n2
Moliner Prada, Antonio, 30
Moratín, Leandro Fernández de, 33, 56
museum: textual, 109. *See also* Royal Museum; Prado Museum

Napoleon I, Emperor of France, 6, 134
Napoleon III, Emperor of France, 149
Napoleonic occupation, 9
National Library of Spain, 55, 57, 58
nationalism, 59
'natural law.' *See under* property
Navas Ruíz, Ricardo, 34, 91, 167n21, 167n23
neoclassicism, 56
No más mostrador (Larra), 190n10

No me olvides (Salas y Quiroga), 88, 92, 94
Novísima recopilación, 51, 172n20

Ochoa, Eugenio, 35, 43; as editor, 170n40; petition for literary property, 34, 41, 44–5, 50, 62, 98
Olivares, Gaspar de Guzmán Count-Duke, 13, 161n2
Ominous Decade, 163n19
'Oriental and Occidental Theatre' (Artaud), 67

Palacio, Eduardo, 136, fig. 9
Paraguas y sombrillas (Mariano Fernández), 131
'paratexte,' 19, 36, 119, 142; definition, 124; description, 132; of *galería* editions, 109, 120, 123, 128, 134
Paris, 34, 118, 181n9, 191n19
parliament (Spanish). See *Cortes*
Parnasillo circle, 34, 168n31
Paseo del Prado, 114, 180n9
Péligry, Christian, 190n9
Pepys, Samuel, 180n7
peregrino, El (Lope de Vega), 171n14
Pérez, Alonso, 192n32
Pérez de Montalban, Juan, 192n32
Pérez Vidal, Alejandro, 171n15
performance, 4, 11, 18, 19, 40, 65, 67–9, 161n1; as *épitextes*, 125; first, 134; with fixed text, 73, 81, 101, 103, 106, 140, 141; national uniform system of, 103, 109; private, 143, 144; for private readers, 112; unauthorized, 99
péritexte, 124–8, 132–4, 136, 138, 139, 145, 146, 189n2, 190n10. *See also* 'paratexte'

Philip IV, King of Spain, 13
Picoche, Jean Louis, 170n6, 183n26
pilluelo de París, El (Bayard), 188n21
piracy, 44, 129, 132, 137, 145, 191n31, 192n32
pliego, 122
pobres de Madrid, Los, 34
poet. *See* dramatic poet
'poetas dramáticos.' *See* dramatic poet
poetry, 28, 39, 48, 50–2, 55, 58, 94, 119, 129, 148, 190n10; cultivation of, 38; dramatic, 34; lyric: 3, 23, 54, 74
Prado Museum, 19, 109; Galería de Escultura, 116; Prado galleries, 118. *See also* Royal Museum
Príncipe, Miguel Agustín, 179n32
Príncipe Theatre, 33, 168n31; audience at, 41, 42, 65, 69, 76, 148, 180n9; *El Trovador* premiere, 16, 31
printers, 18, 83, 86, 97, 98
Progresistas, 15, 26, 29, 55, 166n18
property: alienation of, 97; cultural, 39–40; holders, 34; ideas as, 103; ideology of, 54; individual, 149; intellectual, 3, 5, 6, 7, 9, 10, 14, 17, 19, 23, 27, 34, 35, 42–4, 46, 51, 61, 109, 117, 134, 168n32; law, 10, 13, 28, 41, 68, 76–8, 83, 102, 103, 105, 127, 136, 140, 168n32; limits of, 147; literary, 9, 10, 12, 13, 15, 16, 25, 26, 30, 32, 39, 47–50, 52, 55, 57, 62, 65, 69, 84, 98, 99, 101, 105, 183n34; literary property in France, 168n28; as merchandise, 111; natural-law model, 35, 39, 48, 60, 68, 90, 148; private, 28, 36, 39, 49, 101; 'propiedad,' 26, 27, 29,
45, 131, 164n2; *propiedades dramáticas*, 96, 106; *propiedad literaria*, 98, 141; recognition of, 134; rights, 38, 44, 72, 135, 170n7; system of, 99; textual, 105; theft of, 99
'propiedad.' *See* property
publisher, 5, 18, 82, 84. See also *editor*
publishing house. See *editor*

Quevedo y Villegas, Francisco Gómez de. *See* Gómez de Quevedo y Villegas, Francisco
Quijote. See *ingenioso hidalgo don Quijote de La Mancha, El*

Real Establecimiento Litográfico, 115
Real Theatre, 189n3
refundición, 106, 119
Reglamento del teatro español, 135
Reglamento de teatros, 12
Reglamento general para la dirección y reforma de teatros, 171n7
Reglamento sobre imprenta (4 Jan. 1834), 23, 170n7
Rennert, Hugo, 74
Repertorio dramático (Boix), 121, 186n1, 188n21
Rezano Imperiali, Antonio, 143
Ríos-Font, Wadda, 141
Rodríguez, Evangelina, 120
Roman Catholic Church, 30; lands, 31, 39
Romanticism, 28, 33, 41, 44, 88, 91, 120, 167n27; concept of authenticity, 119, 127; high, 56; ideology, 43, 49, 82, 171n7; individual, 47; and Liberal movement, 13, 14, 15; literature, 26, 29, 39; magazines,

92; and the nation, 45, 62; period, 47, 88, 95, 102, 111, 145; plays, 23, 32, 42, 133, 146; poets, 86, 88, 90, 91, 93, 94, 97; subjecthood, 49; themes, 106; view of author's work, 71; women writers, 161n
Romea, Julián, 47
Romero, Gregorio, 41, 43, 44, 45, 50
Romero Tobar, Leonardo, 143, 176n13
Rose, Mark, 9, 25, 91
Rosell, Cayetano, 31
Royal Decree: of 1603, 75; of 1826, 10, 23, 84; of 1833, 45–7, 59; of 1849, 103, 171n8; of 1853, 104–5
Royal Library, 136. *See also* National Library
Royal Monastery of the Escorial, 115
Royal Museum, 113–16, 130, 186n8. *See also* Prado Museum
Royal Order: of 1762, 143; of 1814, 113; of 1837, 7, 15–17, 23, 44, 50, 55, 59–62, 80, 90, 92, 98, 100, 103, 190n10; of 1839, 16, 92, 98–102, 111, 183n34; of 1852, 144, 166n15
royalties, 48, 75, 84, 102, 134, 138, 186n2
Rubio Jiménez, Jesús, 186n11
Rueda, Lope de, 74
Rules of Art, The (Bourdieu), 149

Saavedra y Ramírez de Baquedano, Ángel de, 139, 163n26, 186n2
sacristán toreador, El (Valero), 138
Salas y Quiroga, Jacinto de, 88, 92–5, 121
Salic Law, 8
Salieri, Antonio, 168n28
Sastre, Aguilera, 5,
Saunders, David, 32

Second of May, The (Goya), 7
Segunda parte de El zapatero y el rey (Zorrilla), 80
Serrano, Seco, 171n15, 173n5
Sevilla, 143, 171n13, 180n7
Sieburth, Stephanie, 46
Sociedad española de autores dramáticos, 103
Sociedad general de autores y escritores, 148, 192n2
sovereignty, 13, 29, 129, 147, 149
Spanish empire, 8, 109, 130
Spanish Royal Academy, 74, 112, 116
spectacle, 12, 13, 17, 35, 42, 46, 48, 59, 67, 72, 74, 82, 97, 123, 139, 142, 148
stage directions. *See* didascalia
Stein, Louise K., 162n17

Tabla de derechos, 26, 164n2
Tarare (Beaumarchais), 168n28
Teatro del Circo. *See* Circo Theatre
Teatro del Príncipe. *See* Príncipe Theatre
testamento, El (de la Vega), 134, fig. 7
tres jaquecas, Las (Pina), 139
trovador, El (García Gutiérrez): Artal family, 35; audience, 31, 65; Azucena, 34, 35; Leonor, 34; Manrique, 34, 35, 36, 39; premiere of, 16, 17, 25, 31, 32, 34, 39, 42, 44, 50, 51, 62, 91, 165n9, 167n27; *refundición*, 106, 185n35; review of, 36, 38, 54

Valencia, 136
Valero, Ricardo, 138
Valladolid, fig. 3
Vega, Garcilaso de la, 59

Vega, Ventura de la, 101, 179n32, fig. 3, fig. 7
Vera Tassis, Juan de, 174n12
Verdadera quinta parte de comedias (Calderón), 174n12
Verdi, Giuseppe Fortunino Francesco, 32
viuda de Padilla, La (Martínez de la Rosa), 172n25

Williams, Raymond, 46, 164n4

Woodmansee, Martha, 10, 77, 168n32

Yates, W.E., 191n19

Zarzuela Theatre, 189n3
Zorrilla, José, 78, 80, 90–4, 104, 131, 179n32, 180n9, 186n2, fig. 1
Zurita, Marciano, 97

STUDIES IN BOOK and PRINT CULTURE
General Editor: Leslie Howsam

Hazel Bell, *Indexes and Indexing in Fact and Fiction*

Heather Murray, *Come, Bright Improvement!: The Literary Societies of Nineteenth-Century Ontario*

Joseph A. Dane, *Myth of Print Culture: Essays on Evidence, Textuality and Bibliographical Method*

Christopher J. Knight, *Uncommon Readers: Denis Donoghue, Frank Kermode, George Steiner, and the Tradition of the Common Reader*

Eva Hemmungs Wirtén, *No Trespassing: Authorship, Intellectual Property Rights, and the Boundaries of Globalization*

William A. Johnson, *Bookrolls and Scribes in Oxyrhynchus*

Siân Echard and Stephen Partridge, eds, *The Book Unbound: Editing and Reading Medieval Manuscripts and Texts*

Bronwen Wilson, *The World in Venice: Print, the City, and Early Modern Identity*

Peter Stoicheff and Andrew Taylor, eds, *The Future of the Page*

Jennifer Phegley and Janet Badia, eds, *Reading Women: Literary Figures and Cultural Icons from the Victorian Age to the Present*

Elizabeth Sauer, *'Paper-contestations' and Textual Communities in England, 1640–1675*

Nick Mount, *When Canadian Literature Moved to New York*

Jonathan Carlyon, *Andrés González de Barcia and the Creation of the Colonial Spanish American Library*

Leslie Howsam, *Old Books and New Histories: An Orientation to Studies in Book and Print Culture*

Elizabeth Driver, *Culinary Landmarks: A Bibliography of Canadian Cookbooks, 1825–1949*

Deborah McGrady, *Controlling Readers: Guillaume de Machaut and His Late Medieval Audience*

David Finkelstein, *Print Culture and the Blackwood Tradition*

Bart Beaty, *Unpopular Culture: Transforming the European Comic Book in the 1990s*

Benjamin C. Withers, *The Illustrated Old English Hexateuch, Cotton Ms. Claudius B.iv: The Frontier of Seeing and Reading in Anglo-Saxon England*

Mary Ann Gillies, *The Professional Literary Agent in Britain, 1880–1920*

Willa Z. Silverman, *The New Bibliopolis: French Book-Collectors and the Culture of Print, 1880–1914*

Lisa Surwillo, *The Stages of Property: Copyrighting Theatre in Spain*

Dean Irvine, *Editing Modernity: Women and Little-Magazine Cultures in Canada, 1916–1956*

Janet Friskney, *New Canadian Library: The Ross-McClelland Years, 1952–1978*

Janice Cavell, *Arctic Exploration in British Print Culture*

Elspeth Jajdelska, *Silent Reading and the Birth of the Narrator*

www.ingramcontent.com/pod-product-compliance
Lightning Source LLC
Chambersburg PA
CBHW030316080526
44584CB00012B/579